Virtually Anglo-Saxon

UNIVERSITY PRESS OF FLORIDA

Florida A&M University, Tallahassee
Florida Atlantic University, Boca Raton
Florida Gulf Coast University, Ft. Myers
Florida International University, Miami
Florida State University, Tallahassee
University of Central Florida, Orlando
University of Florida, Gainesville
University of North Florida, Jacksonville
University of South Florida, Tampa
University of West Florida, Pensacola

Virtually Anglo-Saxon

Old Media, New Media, and Early Medieval Studies
in the Late Age of Print

Martin K. Foys

University Press of Florida
Gainesville/Tallahassee/Tampa/Boca Raton
Pensacola/Orlando/Miami/Jacksonville/Ft. Myers

12 11 10 09 08 07   6 5 4 3 2 1

Library of Congress Cataloging-in-Publication Data
Foys, Martin K. (Martin Kennedy).
Virtually Anglo-Saxon : old media, new media, and early medieval studies in the
late age of print / Martin K. Foys.
p. cm.
Includes bibliographical references and index.
ISBN-13: 978-0-8130-3039-5 (acid-free paper)
1. Civilization, Anglo-Saxon—Study and teaching. 2. Civilization, Medieval—
Study and teaching. 3. Printing. 4. Visual communication. 5. Digital media.
6. Virtual reality—Philosophy. 7. Virtual reality in higher education. I. Title.
CB216.F69   2007
909.079—dc22   2006028483

The University Press of Florida is the scholarly publishing agency for the State
University System of Florida, comprising Florida A&M University, Florida Atlantic
University, Florida Gulf Coast University, Florida International University, Florida
State University, University of Central Florida, University of Florida, University of
North Florida, University of South Florida, and University of West Florida.

University Press of Florida
15 Northwest 15th Street
Gainesville, FL 32611-2079
http://www.upf.com

For Jennifer

As we experience the new electronic and organic age with ever stronger indications of its main outlines, the preceding mechanical age becomes quite intelligible. Now that the assembly line recedes before the new patterns of information, synchronized by electric tape, the miracles of mass-production assume entire intelligibility. . . . What will be the new configurations of mechanisms and of literacy as these older forms of perception and judgment are interpenetrated by the new electric age?

—Marshall McLuhan

Contents

Figures

Preface and Acknowledgments

As many projects do, *Virtually Anglo-Saxon* arose out of a previous one. In 2001, as I was completing *The Digital Edition of the Bayeux Tapestry*, I realized that the process of translating the medieval textile into digital form had greatly influenced the way in which I now understood the function and the meaning of the work. Until then, short of going to Bayeux, one could study the famous artifact only in print, and the limitations of this medium also limited modes of understanding and interpretation. Thinking about the Tapestry in terms of New Media, as a hypertext (or, rather, a "hypertextile"—a neologism that elicited groans the first time I used it in a conference paper), opened up new critical avenues to explore for medieval expression.

Medieval discourse is not digital in any way, of course, but as New Media theorists like to point out, the medieval and the digital (or the pre-print and the post-print) have much in common that the print medium does not share. Modern print demands physical parameters, fixity, unity, homogeneity, and rigid structures of presentation that in the scholarly realm have now become bulky and imprecise. The lengthy process of formatting this manuscript for publication, following the thirty-odd-page guidelines helpfully provided by University Press of Florida, stands as evidence of how elaborate and at times obstructive the mechanism of print culture has become over the last half millennium. As I write these introductory sentences, I am in the final phase of preparing this manuscript, and now choosing not to include a few last additions and footnotes to various sections because of the difficulty of rearranging the already "fixed" text. With regard to Anglo-Saxon and early medieval studies, the advent of New Media theory and praxis offers alternatives to print that provide a new perspective on the operations, limits, and effects of the older medium, as well as the opportunity to explore what aspects of early medieval expression may have fallen by the wayside in the past five hundred years of study.

Over the five years I worked on *Virtually Anglo-Saxon*, I benefited from the support of many individuals and institutions, without which the project would have never been realized. Research for this book was funded by a Florida State University junior faculty leave, as well as a series of Summer Research Institute and Board of Associates grants from Hood College. I continue to be grateful to Amanda Anderson and the Johns Hopkins University

English Department for my appointment as Fellow-by-Courtesy and the research privileges it includes. Earlier versions of sections in the chapter on the Bayeux Tapestry appeared in *Exemplaria* and *Envoi*, while a section of the chapter on the Cotton *Mappamundi* still appears online in the inaugural issue of Blackwell's *Literature Compass*; they are reproduced here by kind permission of these publications. Additionally, Amy Gorelick and Susan Albury as my editors at UPF have provided clear and steadfast guidance at every step of the publication process.

This book is stronger than it ever could have been for the input, advice, ideas, and/or support of numerous individuals, especially Dan O'Donnell, Peter Robinson, Pat Conner, Allen Frantzen, Will Noel, Kevin Kiernan, Andy Orchard, Simon Keynes, James Cummings, Dot Porter, Jack Niles, David Johnson, Barry Faulk, Mark Cooper, James McNelis, Bob Berkhofer, Chris Fee, Mary Dockray-Miller, Laura Gelfand, Jim Hala, Anne Derbes, Mark Sandona, Scott Pincikowski, Renee Trilling, Jacqueline Stodnick, Yvette Kisor, Chris Henige, Roy Liuzza, Stacy Klein, Michael Lonegro, Jim Caccamo, Asa Mittman, Erica Pittman, Loredana Teresi, Paul Szarmach, Catherine Karkov, and David Way. My work also benefited from invitations from Howard Bloch, Terry Harpold, Mary Swan, Elaine Treharne, Elizabeth Tyler, Wendy Hoofnagle, Richard Burt, Alex Bruce, Linda Neagle, Peter Robinson, Simon Keynes, Catherine Karkov, Karen Jolly, and Sarah Keefer to speak on various aspects of this project, and from the stimulating conversations that ensued. I am especially indebted to Steven Rose for overseeing the photography of the Nunburnholme monument, to Tom Hall and the late Nick Howe for providing unpublished drafts of their own work, to Karen Overbey, Edward Christie, and Richard Burt for reading the manuscript in its entirety and for their invaluable suggestions, and to Elaine Treharne for her expert advice and encouragement as the project neared completion. Whitney Trettien proofread the final version and provided an index we would both want to use. Any errors or flaws that remain are surely only my own. Finally, this work could not have begun or continued without the constant support and patience of my wife, Jennifer, to whom this book is dedicated with all my love.

Introduction

"Nothing like a CD-ROM"

This book begins with a personal anecdote about not writing a book. In September of 2004, I applied for a National Endowment for the Humanities summer stipend to help fund the development of a digital edition of the Cotton *Mappamundi*, a unique Anglo-Saxon map of the world. I soon came to realize that while the NEH application process had for the first time "gone online" that year, its new digital nature remained firmly entrenched in the technologies of print, and still accommodated inked words much more easily than electronic ones. For proposed editions, the NEH Awards Program Guidelines stipulated that "a sample of the original text and your edited/translated version . . . not to exceed one page (4,000 characters, approximately 570 words)" must be provided.[1] The Cotton Map project, though, did not have any pages, and I wondered how to repackage the layout and content of this digital edition into approximately 570 words in a way that did not fundamentally change the nature of that sample. When I e-mailed the NEH to inquire whether the online application process accommodated such newer forms of electronic scholarship, samples of which could be sent electronically on CD-ROM or as color screenshots, I received the following instructions from an NEH senior program officer:

> Martin Foys: Send us two pages via FAX (*do not send us anything like a CD-ROM*) and we will copy them and send them to the panelists who will evaluate your application. The FAX number is provided below.[2]

From this response, I surmised that faxed screenshots counted as pages, and were my only option. What I realized, though, as I assembled, printed, and faxed my two carefully chosen screenshot-pages, was that the readers of my application would be vetting a representation of the digital edition at several removes of media from its original formulation—indeed, what they would see would not be "anything like a CD-ROM." Evaluators would view instead a photocopy of a fax of a laser printout of a screenshot of an area of the digital edition—four levels of degradation from its source. [→16] Beyond the compromised aspects of graphic representation, the photocopy/fax/printout/ screenshot effectively froze the operability of the electronic program on the page, making it difficult if not impossible to convey. In the grant application, digital scholarship still needed to be converted to print (ironically through several forms of electronic and digital technology) for assessment. Had I been writing a book, of course, there would have been no problem; faxes are designed to reproduce words typed on a page, and the functionality of typed words rarely changes through the process of printing and faxing.

Fortunately, things ended well—I received the grant—but this episode also encapsulated for me the new issues that now concern early medieval studies. The increasing prevalence of New Media in scholarship of pre-print cultures makes intelligible (as Marshall McLuhan put it) the relative ability and inability of technological media to reproduce one another, and the complicated relationships that medieval, print, and now digital modes of representation have with each other. For more than half a millennium, print remained the dominant mode of formulating, organizing, and disseminating information, including medieval and other pre-print materials. In the past three decades, as computer technologies have radically transformed the way we handle information, we have entered into what Jay David Bolter terms the "late age of print," and the old foundations of scholarly inquiry, while not cracking, have begun to shift somewhat under the press of digital ones and zeroes.[3]

In the epigraph that opens this book, McLuhan remarks that the ascendancy of alternatives to print in our "new electric age" provides an opportunity to assess the idea and the effect of this precedent technology in ways hitherto unimaginable; with regard to intellectual and perhaps even cognitive development, such changes look to be seismic, akin to how the perception of those two-dimensional shapes in Edwin Abbott's *Flatland* changed when they grasped the third dimension of space.[4] After McLuhan's *Gutenberg Galaxy*, four decades of scholars have furnished a raft of metatypographical studies that have carefully examined, measured, and recorded how print has changed the way we view and reproduce the world.

Meanwhile, though, a comparatively small body of scholarship has considered the effect of print upon medieval studies, and an even smaller set concerns the Anglo-Saxon period. Likewise, medievalists have welcomed with open arms (and often as pioneers in academia) the notion that with digital technology comes software and databases—new tools to aid in traditional forms of study. Yet at the same time, the critical frontier of how New Media theories and methodologies present alternative ways of interpreting early medieval expressions, literary, artistic, or otherwise remains terra incognita—a tantalizing world awaiting further exploration. Accordingly, *Virtually Anglo-Saxon* considers how print technology originally fostered and then shaped scholarly interpretation of Anglo-Saxon texts, objects, and ideas. In tandem, precepts of New Media theory are applied to reinterpret specific objects, texts, and other cultural expressions from both the Anglo-Saxon and post-Conquest periods. Taken as a whole, this study explores the limits print culture has imposed upon the pre-print, and then explores how theoretical aspects of post-print, digital expression provide opportunities to lift those critical limits.

Given its subject, there is, of course, a certain irony that this book is a book, and also, therefore, "nothing like a CD-ROM." Though we might be living in the late age of print, the authority of print remains strong, and signs indicate this age might last for a very, very long time (comparable, in respects, to how natterers have for centuries proclaimed the imminent death of theater). As an academic, and one who has already published a digital edition of a medieval work, I am still drawn by the allure of publishing "the book," by the solid, stolid, and traditional force of the physical object, as opposed to the more fluid but ephemeral stream of digital zeros and ones that flows across your screen but can never be held in your hand. Certainly, from a professional perspective, the book still carries more "weight" for processes like tenure than a Web site does, no matter how good that Web site may be, and my own professional identity is always already formed out of such printed bias.[5] And in ironic lockstep with such authority, most scholarship I reference here happens to have been published in print, not in pixels, no doubt from my anxiety that Web sites might not still be available decades from now. [→194]

This book also doubles, or even triples, the practice of remediation—the complex influence of one representational medium upon another [→6]—as it folds both pre- and post-print forms back into the printed book, while I rely almost exclusively on print scholarship to promote and defend the theses contained herein. Indeed, it might be said that I am as guilty of manufacturing the Anglo-Saxon past out of the printed word as the antiquarians and scholars surveyed in the next chapter. But the argument of this book also uses its medium against itself—books, like all printed material, derive their function and even their authority from their physicality. The pervasiveness of digital culture has grown exponentially in the past few decades, and we are beginning to understand that, like the printing press, New Media can also transform the modern world. The following chapters explore the critical limits and obstructions necessitated by information *qua* atoms, and how digital media, or information *qua* bytes, help illuminate and surmount these limits.

Early medieval culture did not usually employ or favor the representational practices that have dominated the modern age. Each chapter in *Virtually Anglo-Saxon* seeks to move the discussion of how old and new media relate early medieval discourse "around print," from the general and reductive to the historically particular and expansive. This study first panoramically explores the effects of print culture upon Anglo-Saxon studies; subsequent chapters consider particular cases of medieval mixed media, beginning with the written word (Anselm of Canterbury's devotional writings), and then textiles (the Bayeux Tapestry), maps (the Cotton *Mappamundi*), and stone sculpture (the Nunburnholme Cross). As the study moves further afield from the familiar textuality of writing, so does the kind of New Media theory applied: print culture leads to hypertextuality, which links to virtual reality, which in turn develops notions of medieval space, modern perspective, and our technological production of both the medieval past and the scholarly present. But, as Vannevar Bush noted long ago, our minds remain associative in function, not linear,[6] and despite the neat sequence of media and theory laid out just above, as a New Media inquiry, the argument of *Virtually Anglo-Saxon* does not, cannot, really, develop in an orderly and linear fashion. While specific New Media theories tend to anchor one discussion or another, other ideas, elsewhere in the book more fully pronounced, continually crop up. Because of this, and because readers may not choose to read this text in a linear order, a number of "links" (similar to World Wide Web hyperlinks) to germane or explanatory discussions will appear, signified by the → symbol. [→40] These links are only suggestions, and certainly not the only possible ones to be made; they also serve as a reminder of the state of *hypermediacy* that the printed form has reached, and, further, as an easy example of how New Media has already begun to remediate print. [→16] Finally, New Media theories are also beginning to transform the explosion of digital software and applications that scholars continue to design and develop as tools for medieval studies; a (too) brief epilogue considers the practical effect of New Media theory upon the present and future of electronic resources for Anglo-Saxon studies.

As McLuhan observes, "We are today as far into the electric age as the Elizabethans had advanced into the typograph and mechanical age."[7] Through print, early modern scholars of the early medieval world saved much of their subject from destruction, and developed tools and techniques to increase the comprehension and learning of their areas of study by several orders of magnitude. Yet these pioneers, and the scholars who followed them over the next several centuries, also refashioned what they preserved in light of their own ideologies and technologies of representation and reproduction, to the point where technology itself dominated critical ideology and practice. Today, we again live in the process of crossing a major technological threshold. This book arises from this liminal stage of media and scholarship in which all intellectual inquiry need now develop, and is invested with the hope that in some small way it can articulate what is possible in the study of medieval expression when new technology meets, (re)mediates, and revitalizes old, much as when printing press met medieval manuscript more than half a millennium ago.

Print and Post-Print Realities in Anglo-Saxon Studies

The Remediation of Reality

The technology of print was, and for the most part remains, the *sine qua non* of modern scholarship. For the better part of half a millennium, the only possible medium for the researched birth, published life, and citational afterlife of a scholarly discovery, idea, or interpretation has been the printed word. Generations of scholars have lived and died in this typocentric universe, and have had as little reason to question the effect of print as they might to question why we breathe—print was, in effect, the life-giving oxygen of academia. In Anglo-Saxon studies, since Matthew Parker first printed Anglo-Saxon texts in the 1560s, printed editions and scholarship have framed and housed the vast majority of Anglo-Saxonist debate and interpretation. Indeed, the mass production, standardization, and dissemination of rare and often inaccessible manuscripts and objects have provided a vital common ground upon which generations of critics have built scholarly discourses of increasing accuracy and comprehensiveness. Our current and considerable understanding of the Anglo-Saxon world could quite simply not exist without the advantages and advances of the printed word. But until very recently in the history of modern medieval studies, print, while acknowledged as a technological medium, has rarely been regarded as a technological *mediator*. And while print may be the mechanism by which early medieval material might be effectively studied in the modern age, the mediating, or rather *remediating*, power of print culture necessarily reconstructs this material, literally re-producing it as something deeply modern in condition and aspect.

In their recent study on the impact of digital technologies upon modern modes of representation, Jay David Bolter and Richard Grusin develop the notion of remediation, the "formal logic by which new media refashion the prior media forms."[1] Remediation, importantly, is not simply the recycling of other media. Rather, it operates through what Bolter and Grusin term a "double logic"; at the same time that a new media form redefines prior media, the new form itself must develop from the appropriative strategy—in short, as a form remediates, it is also remediated.[2] In the early age of print, this double logic resulted in an intense symbiotic relationship between the medieval and the typographic. Early printers depended heavily on both medieval scribal conventions and manuscript content for their early commercial products, even as the spread of printing in turn inspired the birth and spirited growth of first antiquarianism and then formal medieval studies.[3]

In the past two decades, Elizabeth Eisenstein's groundbreaking work, along with the host of research and commentary that followed in its wake, has firmly established the revolutionary role the printing press played in the profound social, intellectual, scientific, economic, political, and theological shifts that defined the emergence of modern Western culture.[4] Even if, as some critics reasonably contend, print culture cannot be the source of all such social and intellectual change, the technology has had considerable impact on the growth and development of coeval revolutions—perspective, market economics, Newtonian space.[5] Print happened because information in late medieval culture had reached a point of critical mass: contemporary delivery systems were simply not able to serve society's growing needs. In other words, "information overload did not so much originate as culminate with printing."[6] In the first fifty years of the printing press, somewhere between eight and twenty million books were produced—more than the total of a full millennium of scribal production.[7] In turn, print created even *more* information, and allowed for the proliferation of advertising, maps, scientific charts, perspective theory, art, architecture, fashion, and, most important for this study, scholarship, in a way impossible before.

The mass production and dissemination of such information had a pullulating effect on ideas of language and learning in early modern Europe. As the late-sixteenth-century Anglo-Saxon scholar John Foxe observes in his *Actes and Monuments*,

> as printyng of bookes ministred matter of readyng: so readyng brought learnyng: learnyng shewed light, by the brightnes wherof blind ignoraunce was suppressed, errour detected, and finally, Gods glory, with the truth of hys worde, aduaunced.[8]

Foxe places print at the head of the ontological trail, not as a platonically corrupt form of God's word, but as an error-detecting (and, by implication, correcting) gateway to that Word, banishing lower, more ignorant forms. Foxe's assessment of print also dramatically remediates the long-standing medieval and Neoplatonic belief in Augustinian sign theory, where writing moves further from the perfection of divine *Verbum*. For Foxe, the new medium of print instead moves closer to such perfection, and becomes the basis, not the representation, of the reality of "Gods worde" and, by extension, the created world. [→49]

In Foxe's world, the new dominance of print "imposed a structure and organization on a 'natural' language system, and educated the eye so that it could better compare and organize ideas."[9] The restructuring effect of print coincided with the cultural ascendancy of its major attributes throughout Europe: homogenization, repeatability, quantification, mensuration, concatenation, and linearity. As Walter Ong has demonstrated, writing restructures consciousness, and the printing revolution amplified this process exponentially.[10] Ong also reminds us that both writing and printing are technologies that gradually have become integrated into modern life to the point that they appear to function organically in their representational roles, as "intelligence is relentlessly reflexive, so that even the external tools that it uses to implement its working become 'internalized,' that is, part of its own reflexive process."[11]

Foxe's quotation further reminds us that early modern society often viewed print as a more accurate and precise mechanism to *reproduce* reality. Along with the word, the typographic image—though eventually subsumed under what Michael Camille calls the "philological iconoclasm" of print culture—also played a key role, ironically, in this reality of print.[12] The uniform repeatability of printed images, in conjunction with the rise of single-point perspective, had incalculable effects upon science and scholarship, but also signaled a wholesale shift in the way the world was viewed.[13] [→167] As Eisenstein has shown, medieval illustrations (and early woodcuts copied from them) illustrated text, but sixteenth-century printed images began to be thought to illustrate nature. That is, in the viewer's eyes the images approached reality, which led to the assumption that the printed version was a faithful copy of the real, as opposed to the artificed representation of it.[14] Or, as McLuhan declares, if "the entire Middle Ages had regarded Nature as a Book to be scanned for the *vestigia dei*," the typographic man "took the lesson of print to be that we could now literally get Nature out in a new and improved edition."[15]

In other words, the representational function of print, coupled with a new magnitude of dissemination by mass production, its cognitive interiorization, and the early modern ideology that man can create as well as contemplate the world, ultimately resulted in the *production* of reality.[16] In "editions" of reality the natural world is remediated by the all-pervasive presence of print technology: "what is 'natural' is what is manufactured; what is 'real' is what is artificial."[17] Thus, in Bolter and Grusin's terms, one of the primary effects of technological remediation is a movement toward "transparent immediacy," where composite cultural expressions in print integrate representations of reality, and simultaneously perform cultural work that renders the remediation inseparable from the reality represented.[18] [→46]

ANGLO-SAXONISM: HISTORY AND EFFECT

The earliest modern scholars of Anglo-Saxon England promoted such transparency; the printed editions they produced in turn produced and then remediated the reality of the Anglo-Saxon period, and their own Elizabethan age. Print's remediation of the medieval happened in tandem with the invention of the printing press, not only in the pseudepigraphous incunabula's formal emulation of medieval manuscripts, but in the content of the printed product as well. In the first two centuries of print production, in the estimate of one study, more than 90 percent of the printed material was medieval in origin or content.[19]

Anglo-Saxon material, however, did not enjoy such immediate attention. Though Bede's *Historia* was one of the first historical works to appear in print, in 1475, few other Anglo-Latin texts and no Old English texts were printed in the century after Gutenberg, as almost no Anglo-Saxon material was known to late medieval readers.[20] But in the rise of antiquarianism-cum-scholarship that rapidly followed the standardization and widespread dissemination of medieval material, John Leland, Robert Talbot, and Robert Recorde, and then John Foxe, Matthew Parker, Laurence Nowell, John Joscelyn, and the rest of the late-sixteenth-century "Parker circle" focused on collecting and then printing editions and commentaries of Anglo-Saxon texts. As Allen Frantzen, Richard Clement, Peter Lucas, and others have shown, the printed publications of Matthew Parker and his contemporaries were shaped by political and theological bias and desire, most specifically with regard to proving a historical basis for many of the practices of the nascent Anglican Church.[21] To support their claims, early Anglo-Saxon antiquarians argued that print enabled the transparent recovery and restoration of a "unified and integral" version of the Anglo-Saxon past in harmonious continuity with the Elizabethan present—a historical past through which their labors, in John Foxe's words, became "full and perfect," and "a Pristine state of olde conformitie."[22] Similarly, William

L'Isle in the preface to his 1623 edition of Ælfric's *Saxon Treatise Concerning the Old and New Testament* pointed to the importance of studying Old English, so that

> we may be able to declare vnto all men, whom it concernes, the true meaning of their titles, charters, priuiledges, territories and precincts, comparing with the nature of each thing, the name thereof so fitted, as the one to this day plainly points out the other.[23]

In their literary and political efforts, L'Isle, Foxe, Parker, and others took full advantage of print technology to realize what they took to be an "ostensibly transparent contact with the past."[24] The invention of Anglo-Saxon type fonts that emulated Old English script furthered the faith that technology brought an immediacy to the past's representation; in 1574 Parker proclaimed that reading printed works such as his edition of Asser's *Life of Alfred* (with his specially designed typeface) would "restore for you the memory of the ancient language, our former mother tongue."[25] But the material effect of print also subtly manipulated its presentation of Anglo-Saxon expression, as early modern typography's ability to subliminally authenticate an ancient text gradually became replaced by the authority of the distinctively modern-looking edition.[26]

While the earliest printed editions of Anglo-Saxon texts focused on the authorizing visual impact of the manuscripts they (re)produced, the tools developed to do so were soon applied to different ends. Because of their perceived power to confer authenticity, within eight years of their creation the Old English fonts designed by Parker were being employed ahistorically to print Latin texts.[27] Even the particulars of font size and layout came to subjectively dictate meaning: Parker would use different point sizes in accordance with his conception of the authority of his texts, while the use of such devices as italics, pointing, and alternating fonts all orchestrated a specific mode of interpretation.[28] Indeed, as Peter Lucas has shown, the very ownership of Anglo-Saxon types and matrices itself became highly politicized, as access to the historical and custom typefaces in the sixteenth century was tightly controlled, and led, in at least one instance, to deceptive schemes to borrow a set of types in order to illegally recast them.[29]

Ultimately, even as it worked to preserve, recover, and restore the past, the political and practical realities of early Anglo-Saxonist printing produced an antiquity as artificial as it was real, and anticipated the much more severe manipulation of text and layout to come in later modern scholarship.[30] The efforts of these sixteenth-century pioneers, however, differ from later scholarly work in their liminal connections back to medieval textualities. Leland, Talbot, and Recorde, among the earliest of Old English antiquarians, did not have their work printed at all, but rather only transcribed texts, thereby continuing the *compilatio* of manuscript culture. In their work, the Parker circle liberally annotated the manuscripts they studied and prepared for print, and freely collated variants, using bits and pieces of one Anglo-Saxon text to supplement and "complete" another.[31] William L'Isle took this practice even further, deliberately manipulating passages of Middle English texts to appear like Old English in order to print fuller versions in the older language.[32] Incomplete texts also could be considered scrap—Matthew Parker destroyed a fragment of one unique Old English homily, using it as binding because he did not have the complete text.[33]

Such methodologies jar the sensibility of modern medievalists, who now painstakingly work to recover single letters of Old English from damaged texts. One can almost feel the horror in V. H. Galbraith's mid-twentieth-century account of Parker's treatment of one medieval manuscript:

> [Parker] defaced the manuscript by writing over the margins, crossing out words in ink, inserting headings, enclosing passages in brackets, interlining passages for insertion, keying up the manuscript to pages of the printed version—in a word, treating it like copy for a printer.[34]

Parker *was* treating the manuscript like copy for a printer, and his actions in part reflect the belief that the medium more accurately articulated a textual reality only partially realized in medieval manuscripts. But many of Parker's alterations to the manuscript—marginalia, deletions, insertions, interlineations—also reflect standard practices of medieval scriptoria, where, without the economic facility of print, written products were treated as ongoing, collaborative documents. [→197] Parker and his contemporaries worked in a mode as close to their Anglo-Saxon scribal predecessors as to twentieth-century literary critics, if not closer. Today's scholars (much like Galbraith) operate in a world almost wholly typographic in orientation. Manuscripts are no longer physically revised, of course—that would be academic apostasy. But rewriting and manipulation still occur through the essential remediation of printed editions and scholarship. Parker and his circle, printing in what could be called "the late age of manuscript," did much the same, of course, but with a material practice much closer to the dynamics of medieval scribal culture.[35]

Edward Christie maintains that if in "Anglo-Saxon writing the letter saves the past from oblivion . . . in the Early Modern typographical remediation of Old English documents, the letter is represented as a material encryption of the past."[36] The divide of this double logic of the past's preservation and encryption only continued as aspects of modern scholarship developed in accord with print culture's growing emphasis on science, systemization, indexing, and linguistic analysis. In the seventeenth century, the establishment of university studies of Anglo-Saxon at Cambridge and Oxford coincided with the printing of the first major editions of Old English texts.[37] The end of this century and the beginning of the next saw the production of the first "great tools" for Anglo-Saxon study: publications like William Somner's *Dictionarium Saxonico-Latino-Anglicum* (1659, with an edition of Ælfric's *Grammar*) and George Hickes's *Thesaurus* (1705, with Humphrey Wanley's catalogue of Anglo-Saxon manuscripts).[38] These tools in turn set the stage for the development of the New Philology (now Old Philology) in the nineteenth century, solidifying the belief that the rational precision of modern scholarship, fueled by Herculean publications of editions, indices, concordances, dictionaries, and the like could realize a more complete picture of Anglo-Saxon language, literature, and culture than ever before possible.[39]

While retaining a *summa*-like faith in the historical transparency of their work, successive generations of Anglo-Saxonists produced printed treatments that gradually leached away more and more medieval aspects of the expressions they represented. Innovations in typography "introduced a precise and ordered structure where previously, with manuscripts, flexibility and sinuous variation had been a necessity," abrading the basic assumptions of what constituted a medieval text.[40] As print became more standardized and precise, medieval script, layout, and ornamentation became more difficult to reproduce.[41] By the time roman type was adopted as the standard for printing in the eighteenth century, the presentation of medieval texts had grown quite distanced from the form of the original material it sought to more accurately reproduce.[42]

Notwithstanding, widespread access to printed editions led to a sense of critical empowerment. In his analysis of George Hickes's stylistic examinations of Old English poetry—arguably one the earliest examples of modern Anglo-Saxon literary criticism—Seth Lerer articulates the new power of print scholarship:

> It is as if, perhaps, Hickes is flipping through his books: here a bit from Rawlison's edition of Boethius, there a page from Thwaites's *Judith*, and now and then a selection from Junius's Caedmonian biblical poetry.[43]

What Lerer describes is possible, of course, only with print; it is a process worlds away from Parker's transitional stage of Anglo-Saxon study, but distinctly familiar to a modern scholar. Hickes, to be sure, did massive manuscript study as well, without which his accomplishment would have been impossible. But his analysis differs from medieval accretion—the conceptual scale of the overview and analysis presented depends in many ways not on manuscript study but on the sheer number of resources made more accessible by print.[44] Lerer's depiction of Hickes's scholarly process also describes the movement from the baldly political agenda of the earliest Anglo-Saxonists to a critical, academic agenda. Parker worked to put manuscripts in print. Hickes worked from manuscripts in print, and with Humphrey Wanley created in his *Thesaurus* a print resource for Anglo-Saxon study unrivaled until the mid-twentieth-century catalogues of N. R. Ker.[45]

After critical empowerment, however, comes critical entitlement, and by the nineteenth century Anglo-Saxonists began to take for granted that the breadth and depth of the data and learning now at their disposal, along with the technology to reproduce it, enabled modern academics to produce a medieval text superior to a medieval redaction. J. M. Kemble, in an oft-quoted passage from the introduction to his 1833 edition of *Beowulf*, proclaims,

> A modern edition, made by a person really conversant with the language he illustrates, will in all probability be much more like the original than the manuscript copy, which, even in the earliest times, was made by an ignorant or indolent transciber.[46]

Kemble's declaration marks a tectonic shift in the critical view of modern print versus medieval manuscript. For Parker and company, manuscripts served as the immediate source of the medieval text to be assembled and presented. Three centuries later, the modern scholar had supplanted medieval scribe as producer of the text. Certainly modern attitudes have more recently tempered Kemble's bias, but its spirit still remains in much of the scholarly work of the past century.[47]

Printed editions of medieval material now serve as the basis for the majority of scholarship produced; more than half of the accepted emendations to the text of *Beowulf*, for instance, derive from the work of editors who never saw the manuscript.[48] Such typographic dominance sets the stage for the next phase in the remediation of the medieval by the modern. Fred C. Robinson has theorized that "the development of printing with movable type brought into being the modern literary concept of 'the text,'" while Jerome McGann has argued that "when we use books to study books, or hard-copy texts to analyse other hard-copy texts, the scale of the tools seriously limits the possible results."[49] The contradiction found between these two statements—the technology that enables literary study also disables it—summarizes the current critical (in both senses) dilemma of much of contemporary Anglo-Saxon scholarship. In the past century, the dynamic of print scholarship has continued the remediating paradox begun in the sixteenth century. Printed editions and the kind of literary criticism they facilitate have allowed the continued growth of Anglo-Saxon studies, and preserved and disseminated practically the entire corpus of Anglo-Saxon artistic, historical, legal, and theological expression to successive generations of scholars and students. At the same time, the limitations of print culture have created rather bulky and imprecise simulacra of actual medieval discourse.[50] But the pervasiveness of print's convenience and (at times) necessity, coupled with its inherited (and now interiorized) ideology of precision, accuracy, and epistemological superiority, has in turn created a discourse accepted as more real than artificed, maintaining the centuries-old (but increasingly more fragile) illusion of transparent immediacy to the Anglo-Saxon past.

In Jean Baudrillard's terminology, the dominance of print in representation of early medieval discourse now approaches the *hyperreal*, where the sign of the real approaches the real itself, where the copy precedes the original and ultimately obscures it, and where reality is not reproduced but in fact produced by the signifying medium.[51] [→117–18] Today, the bulk of study and scholarship of Anglo-Saxon England still occurs through print; a priori, print produces for most modern readers the reality of Anglo-Saxon England. Inevitably, print becomes the foundation of the study of manuscript itself; Kevin Kiernan, to cite one particularly cogent example, has demonstrated how the printed edition of a twelfth-century manuscript of Boethius's *Consolatio* ended up serving as the basis for readings of a tenth-century manuscript that substantially differed in its formal structure.[52]

Vannevar Bush, in his prescient 1945 essay "As We May Think," understood that modern scholarship needed to move beyond print: "Professionally our methods of transmitting and reviewing the results of research are generations old and by now are totally inadequate for their purpose."[53] As Anglo-Saxon studies progressed during the four-hundred-odd years since Matthew Parker, layer upon layer of academic discourse has accreted, leaving the most recent generation of scholars to stretch the referential capacity of the printed page to the point of unwieldiness. A footnote from Lerer concerning his presentation of Hickes's quotations of the Old English *Exodus* reveals the complicated status of early modern *and* contemporary treatments of such texts, as well as the multiplying layers of editorial traditions that must now be navigated:

> Hickes prints Old English in half lines in a single column, each line beginning with a capital letter and ending with a period (or a colon). For purposes of space, I have realigned these half lines into full lines corresponding to the lineation of modern editions. But I have kept Hickes's spellings, even when they differ from modern editions (on Hickes's, or his printer's, lapses of transcription, see the appendix). The standard, modern text of *Exodus* (and other Old English poems) can be found in George Philip Krapp and Elliott Van Kirk Dobbie, eds., *The Anglo-Saxon Poetic Records*, 6 vols. (New York: Columbia University Press, 1931–53), vol. 1, pp. 103–4, lines 447–51. Hereafter, where available, references to this modern edition will be given by volume, page, and line numbers in brackets, following the *Thesaurus* page reference. All translations from the Old English are my own.[54]

Understandably, the majority of those reading Lerer's essay are unlikely to check actual sources referenced: Hickes, Lerer's appendix, and Krapp and Dobbie. The printed text of *Exodus* alluded to here, however, is not the original Old English, nor is it Hickes's, or Krapp and Dobbie's. Lerer, has, in effect, created a new, multivalent text out of all of these, one that collapses a now dense diachronic textual genealogy into a momentary network, frozen on the page. This surrogate is constructed out of the necessities and limitations of printing conventions and the homogenizing need for standardization of type and citation reference. It is then authenticated (and accepted as "real") by the reader's own interiorized notion of the primacy of print. Lerer's footnote also emphasizes the precision and accuracy of more modern textualities by indicating the flawed nature of Hickes's own early modern edition, though these elements are of spatial necessity relegated to an appendix, itself literally at a distance from the corresponding text. All of this considerable apparatus exists in order to accurately reproduce four lines of Old English poetry. Notably, no reference to the immediate manuscript context of the Old English poetry is provided—the printed edition "naturally" suffices. Or, in Neil Kleinman's words, the technology of print has "imposed a structure and organization on a 'natural' language system, and educated the eye so that it could better compare and organize ideas ... an emphasis on form over content: *The structure (i.e., the design) of information is exaggerated while content becomes secondary.*"[55]

Lerer's footnote provides evidence for McLuhan's claim that print is moving from a "hot" medium, where the limit of routinization and determinism is established, to a "supercool" medium, where this limit is passed, "bombarding readers with such a plethora of codings that conventional interpretation collapses."[56] As early as the mid-1920s, Walter Benjamin already considered that the printed book had passed its scholarly prime, writing,

> the book is already, as the present mode of scholarly production demonstrates, an outdated mediation between two different filing systems. For everything that matters is to be found in the card box of the researcher who wrote it, and the scholar studying it assimilates it into his own card index.[57]

The point-to-point mediations between scholarly filing systems are, in Deleuzian terms, striated meaning, and stand in sharp contrast to the smoother space of medieval meaning. [→179] The current, systematic complexity of print scholarship's elaborate referential systems has also become the scion of Benjamin's dissatisfaction. Designed to support the hyperreality of print more than anything else, notes such as Lerer's indicate that we do indeed live in the late age of print, and that we are more rapidly approaching the "supercool" end of typographic conventions. In Bolter and Grusin's terms, scholars can no longer operate under even the presumptive illusion of transparent immediacy. Instead, print scholarship has arrived at the tipping point of *hypermediacy*, whose logic "acknowledges multiple acts of representation and makes them visible," as the interface of representation becomes foregrounded, and the content represented recedes to the background.[58]

In the past few decades, the problems with the hypermediacy of print scholarship in medieval studies have become more and more apparent, as a number of scholars have increasingly critiqued the dominant mode of their own scholarship, acknowledging that meaning occurs not only through the linguistic code of words but also through the "bibliographic code" of layout, illustration, type, and other formal elements of print.[59] Some of the earliest qualms expressed concerned the intrusive, and possibly distorting, effect of modern punctuation on the editing of Old English texts. To most readers of modern English, the operation of the complex system of punctuation now employed in writing has largely disappeared—we rely on capitalization, commas, semicolons, periods, and the like in the subconscious mode; only rarely, when puzzling out a particularly difficult, usually hypotactic, sentence, do we consciously consider the presence of punctuation.

Medieval applications of *punctus, punctus elevatus, punctus versus*, and their brethren rarely align with modern notions of punctuation, which arose in part from typographic necessity in the Renaissance when early modern humanists needed to systematize the printed editions of ancient and medieval texts for scholars. Such systemization then gradually developed over three hundred years of Old English editing until the medieval text now enters fully dressed in modern grammar and punctuation.[60] In the late age of print, however, modern methods of punctuation have "arrived at near perfection paradoxically just at the time when these editorial methods have become obsolete."[61] In printed editions of Old English literature, as critics first argued in the 1970s and 1980s, the prescriptive punctuation now employed often fundamentally misrepresents the grammar, syntax, and meaning of the medieval material so treated.[62] Bruce Mitchell, for instance, condemns the continued use of standard systems of modern punctuation by students and scholars, contending it betrays much of the medieval sense of Old English: "We are in a sense being forced into unnecessary dogmatism by our use of modern grammatical punctuation, which produces Modern English sentences instead of Old English verse paragraphs, verse paragraphs which . . . defy strict grammatical analysis."[63] However, Mitchell's ultimate solution, to add even more characters of punctuation such as arrows, double commas, parentheses, and other symbols to indicate the cruces and subtleties of Old English literature that standard typographic conventions cannot, in essence amplifies the hypermediacy of Old English editing even as it attempts to more precisely represent its subject, and further highlights the "super cool" dilemma of modern print in relation to Anglo-Saxon studies.[64]

Such debates over the difficulties of editing Old English, usefully distilled by Paul Szarmach into issues of nonintervention versus conjectural emendation, rage on today, exacerbated by the increasingly pronounced limitations of print.[65] Modern punctuation and standardized spellings continue to make Old English literature more readily available to the modern reader, but such practices and their differentials of quality also continue to increase the gap between the representing and represented media. Meanwhile, the steady evolution of the technology of printing has moved the very iteration of print away from its original form and meaning. As one printer who worked through most of the twentieth century noted, late-twentieth-century technological advances in publishing no longer produced a page of type, but rather "a picture of a page of type"—moving the typographic technology even further from the bodily labor of the scribal practice it remediates.[66] The digital advances in word processing and publication increase the gap even further.

During this time of technological change, Anglo-Saxonists and other medievalists have also begun to return to the manuscript, and to consider more rigorously the isolating and limiting effect that the printed edition has upon the material it ostensibly reproduces. Fred Robinson, for instance, has argued that modern Anglo-Saxon literary criticism ignores the manuscript context of its subject, and that "if a text is detached from its codicological environment (as texts normally are in our modern editions), we risk losing that part of its meaning."[67] Likewise, Michael Camille's formulation of "philological iconoclasm" makes the case that the logocentric exigency of print "erases not only the marks of pictorial making from the [medieval] page but also any signs of material labor that are not pertinent to disembodied textual meaning."[68] Further, the ready utility of the printed edition ensures that, paradoxically, the original material and paleographic form of the medieval text studied often now comes last in line in the critical and educational process, if it is consulted at all.[69] Robinson, in the end, concludes that even the increasing presence of photographic facsimiles, arguably a remedy to the remediation of printed editions, inserts yet another level of representation between scholar and subject, and "can lead us to lose touch with the physical reality upon which our field is largely founded."[70] Most recently, metacriticism of medieval studies has moved past practical considerations and into the realm of the theoretical. In his call for the end of the critical edition, Murray McGillivray reestablishes the primacy of the medieval text, contending that the process of the modern critical edition inevitably must reject some manuscript readings and witnesses— as "to fail to reject *any* manuscript reading would be to be *un*critical"—and therefore must efface some aspects of the reality of medieval textuality in the modern representation.[71]

Even the dual bulwarks of modern medieval literary studies, the strategies of best-text and base-manuscript stemmatics, ultimately arose from limitations of print.[72] From the beginning, the production of printed editions has been governed by the desire to present a single, primary and unified text; arguably, such a desire developed because it was difficult, more or less, to configure a critical edition otherwise in print.[73] The reality of medieval manuscript culture is that rarely, if ever, did a uniform, authoritative version of a text exist; even the Bible, the ultimate Word, remained irregular and unstable throughout most of the Middle Ages.[74] However, as McGillivray indicates, the desires of both stemmatic and "best-text" studies create an ontological crisis that limits access to the medieval by positing an original, ideal text, an unreal version that in turn rationalizes the technical mandate of centering some text while marginalizing other text to the edge, gutter, or appendix. But in the eyes of recent critics, printing less is not more; less is actually less. The modern printed edition is a perfect paradigm of remediation and the *hyperreal*, a conflation of medieval manuscript variants in a "best text" that replaces both the technological medium and the textuality of the medieval with that of the modern.

In the past two decades, the culmination of such self-examination among Anglo-Saxonists has led to a growing understanding that centuries of printed redactions of medieval discourse have, in the end, produced material with distinctly un-medieval qualities. Editorial methods of culling medieval texts approach the works in ways no medieval reader would; the vast scale of proliferation and reception made possible by print produces a textual mentality no Anglo-Saxon scribe, author, or reader would ever experience.[75] [→190] In all criticism, all that remains is the degree to which the modern is permitted to remediate its cultural predecessor. At best, our work can still seek a clarified vision of the medieval through the filter of modern media and thought; in the worst cases, we promote "a speculative reconstruction [that] has the effect of obscuring the medieval texts themselves."[76] Transparency, the *eidos* of all scholarship, cannot be assumed to spring automatically from technological innovation, and the opacity of our own media is what the current generation of Anglo-Saxonists must acknowledge and obviate. Otherwise we void the notion that material expressions from the past have escaped the destruction of time, as the technological modes of scholarship deflect or distort aspects of the cultural work and meaning it seeks to preserve and replicate.

TWO CASE STUDIES: ROOD CROSSES AND POINTING FINGERS

In his critique of the modern punctuation of Old English writing, Bruce Mitchell observes:

> We would rightly laugh at any scholar who decided that Bede's *Historia* is a television documentary, that *Beowulf* is a film script, or that *Apollonius of Tyre* was intended for radio presentation. Is it any less ridiculous for a modern scholar to pretend that OE texts are suited by modern punctuation?[77]

The brief historical and critical survey of the effect of print upon Anglo-Saxon writing presented above extends Mitchell's question, and ponders how well the medium of print as a whole suits the early medieval form, function, and cultural meaning of Anglo-Saxon discourse. The examinations of *The Dream of the Rood* and Bede's *De computo vel loquela digitorum* below illustrate the power of print to produce *and* remediate Anglo-Saxon meaning, and show how the function of print also continues a process of remediation that stretches back into pre-print systems of signification.

In the late age of print, Anglo-Saxon texts, art, or other cultural expressions reach us through the accrued layers of technology and scholarship. This modern process builds upon earlier layers of pre-print mediation and remediation as well. Early medieval discourse undergoes technological mediation from the moment it is first recorded, whether on vellum, stone, or any other medium. When it is copied or otherwise reproduced in the medieval period, it continues to be mediated, or remediated if the technological mode of representation changes. The successive and interconnected stages of remediation in print and then modern scholarship merely continue the reconstruction and redefinition of the earlier expression begun in its pre-print existence.

Treatments of the Old English poem *The Dream of the Rood* (ca. 960–80), found in the Vercelli manuscript, reveal much about pre-print and print stages of remediation for Anglo-Saxon literature. Martin Irvine has commented that this poem functions as a particularly complex "network of discourses and codes learned from prior systems of representation."[78] Though Irvine's analysis ultimately remains rooted wholly in the textual realm of Latin and Germanic rhetoric, grammar, and literature, his view that the meaning of the poem functions axiomatically, as opposed to simply linearly in progression, provides a useful starting point for considering how this Old English poem actually exists on and outside the page, and how the printed edition is only one of the more recent, if most influential, layers of remediation. *The Dream of the Rood* does exist within a complicated discursive network—it shares text with an eighth-century sculpture, the Ruthwell Cross, and also with a lesser-known tenth-century silver reliquary, the Brussels Cross.[79] But in modern considerations, the typographic conventions used to represent this network of cultural objects also redefine the three expressions within it by a textuality fundamentally alien to Anglo-Saxon expression.

Michael Swanton's critical edition of *The Dream of the Rood* is a case in point. Swanton does work hard to connect the Old English poem to one of its material analogues, the eighth-century Ruthwell Cross. In addition to a thorough treatment of the poetic text, the edition dedicates substantial space to the cross (some thirty pages), discusses the connections between the sculpture and poem, collates the earlier and now fragmentary runic text of the stone sculpture against the poem in facing-page layout (see figure 1), and prints two images of Ruthwell that include all of the runic text.[80] The overall effect of such presentation *textualizes* the stone cross. [→103] The typographic limitations of the printed edition remediate the stone cross to printed text and image (two pages each) hierarchically presented in the service of the poetic text. Such an effect is not, of course, planned, but rather an inevitable outcome of the technological and cultural parameters of the print medium.

The physical constraints of print, along with its tendency to privilege the word over the image, also influence critical perception and presentation of the relationship between Anglo-Saxon cross and Old English poem. Accepting the usual date of Ruthwell as early eighth century, and the congruence of the Ruthwell runic poem to the monument's visual material, the runes of Ruthwell predate the Vercelli manuscript's late-tenth-century text of *The Dream of the Rood* by more than two hundred years.[81] Studying the interconnections between the Ruthwell and Vercelli texts, Swanton contests the notion that the earlier version could have been composed for the monument, basing his argument on the fragmentary and defective quality of the runic text, which stands in contrast to the full and finished detail found in the later poem.[82] Swanton notes also that the Ruthwell artist in his iconographical representation of Scripture operates as "an habitual quoter," concluding that "no doubt he chose appropriate parts from a singularly pertinent and masterly poem to fill the margins of the more universal motifs along the sides of the shaft."[83] Through the practical focus of this edition, the later Old English poem *The Dream of the Rood* becomes by default this "singularly pertinent and masterly poem." In effect, the tenth-century poem has become the critical source for the eighth-century inscription, and the Ruthwell runes, originally designed for the margins of an iconographic monument, now serve the margins of the modern textual edition. To apply Swanton's very first mention of these runes in the modern edition, they have become "the lesser text of *The Dream of the Rood*."[84] [→13]

As George Landow—building on the work of McLuhan, Eisenstein, Bolter, and others—observes, since modern scholarship occurs by and through print technology, it traditionally mandates and emphasizes the very qualities of the medium that produces it, namely, linearity, fixity, and unity.[85] In the past century, critical treatments of *The Dream of the Rood* (working largely from printed editions) further extend print's remediating effect upon the poem,

TEXTS

RUTHWELL TEXT

I

[+ Ondḡerede hine God almehttig,	39
þa he walde on galḡu gistiḡa,	40
[m]odig f[ore allæ] men.	41
[B]ūḡ[a ic ni dorstæ . . . .]	42

II

[Ahōf] ic riicnæ Kyniŋc,	44
heafunæs Hlafard, hælda ic ni dorstæ.	45
Bismæradu uŋket men ba ætḡad[re]; ic [wæs] mĳþ biōdæ	48
[b]istēmi[d],	
bigoten of . . . .]	49

beswyled mid swātes gange,   Hwilum mid since
    gegyrwed.
Hwæðre ic þær licgende   lange hwile
beheóld hreówcearig   Hælendes treów,   25
oððæt ic gehyrde   þæt hit hleoðrode.
Ongan þā word sprecan   wudu sēlesta:
" Þæt wæs geāra iū,   (ic þæt gȳta geman),
þæt ic wæs āheāwen   holtes on ende,
āstyred of stefne mīnum.   Genāman mē ðǣr   30
    strange feóndas,
geworhton him þǣr tō wæfersȳne,   hēton mē
    heora wergas hebban.
Bǣron mē ðǣr beornas on eaxlum,   oððæt hie
    mē on beorg āsetton,
gefæstnodon mē þǣr feóndas genōge.   Geseah ic
    þā Frēan mancynnes
efstan elne mycle   þæt hē mē wolde on gestigan.
Þǣr ic þā ne dorste   ofer Dryhtnes word   35
būgan oððe berstan,   þā ic bifian geseah
eorðan scēatas.   Ealle ic mihte
feóndas gefyllan,   hwæðre ic fæste stōd.
Ongyrede hine þā geong hæleð,   (þæt wæs God
    ælmihtig),
strang ond stīðmōd;   gestāh hē on gealgan   40
    hēanne,
mōdig on manigra gesyhðe,   þā hē wolde mancyn
    lȳsan.
Bifode ic þā mē se beorn ymbclypte;   ne dorste
    ic hwæðre būgan tō eorðan,
feallan tō foldan scēatum.   Ac ic sceolde fæste
    standan.
Rōd wæs ic āræred.   Āhōf ic riicne Cyning,   45
heofona Hlāford;   hyldan mē ne dorste.

Figure 1. Sample page of *The Dream of the Rood*. By permission of Exeter University Press.

adding a number of interpretative layers, each rooted in the qualities identified by Landow, and obscuring aspects of the *original* remediation of Anglo-Saxon writing upon its own content.

The Dream of the Rood remains, next to *Beowulf,* one of the best-known Anglo-Saxon poems, in no small part because of its opening, a twenty-seven-line presentation of the cross to the dreamer couched in vivid, kaleidoscopic, and then prosopopoeic terms:

> Hwæt, ic swefna cyst   secgan wylle,
> hwæt me gemætte   to midre nihte,
> syðþan reordberend   reste wunedon.
> Þuhte me þæt ic gesawe   syllicre treow
> 5 on lyft lædan,   leohte bewunden,
> beama beorhtost.   Eall þæt beacen wæs
> begoten mid golde;   gimmas stodon
> fægere æt foldan sceatum,   swylce þær fife wæron
> uppe on þæm eaxlegespanne.   Beheoldon þær engel Dryhtnes ealle
> 10 fægere þurh forðgesceaft;   ne wæs þær huru fracodes gealga,
> ac hine þær beheoldon   halige gastas,
> men ofer moldan   and eall þeos mære gesceaft.
> Syllic wæs se sigebeam,   ic synnum fah,
> forwunded mid wommum.   Geseah ic wuldres treow
> 15 wædum geweorðod   wynnum scinan,
> gegyred mid golde;   gimmas hæfdon
> bewrigen weorðlice   Wealdendes treow.
> Hwæðre ic þurh þæt gold   ongytan meahte
> earmra ærgewin,   þæt hit ærest ongan
> 20 swætan on þa swiðran healfe.   Eall ic wæs mid sorgum gedrefed
> forht ic wæs for þære fægran gesyhðe   geseah ic þæt fuse beacen
> wendan wædum and bleom;   hwilum hit wæs mid wætan bestemed,
> beswyled mid swates gange,   hwilum mid since gegyrwed.
> Hwæðre ic þær licgende   lange hwile
> 25 beheold hreowcearig   Hælendes treow,
> oððæt ic gehyrde   þæt hit hleoðrode
> ongan þa word sprecan   wudu selesta

[Hark—I wish to recount the best of dreams—what met me in the middle of the night, when the speech-bearers dwelled in sleep. It seemed to me that I saw a most wondrous tree raised in the air, wound around with light, the brightest of trees. That beacon was all covered with gold; beautiful gems stood at the corners of the earth; there were five such upon the shoulder-span. All, glorious by eternal decree, beheld there the angel of the Lord; nor was it there a gallows of the wicked, but holy spirits, men across the world, and all this great creation there beheld him. Wondrous was this victory-beam; I was stained by sins, wounded by evil doing. I saw the tree of wonder honored with raiment, shining with joy, adorned with gold; gems had worthily covered the Ruler's tree. Yet through that gold I could perceive the old strife of the wicked ones; by that had it first begun to bleed on the right side. I was all afflicted with sorrow; I was frightened by that unusual sight, and I saw that eager beacon move through garments and hue—sometimes it was soaked with wetness, drenched with the flowing of blood; sometimes with treasure adorned. Yet I was lying there, troubled, a long while, seeing the Savior's tree, until I heard what it spoke; the best of trees began then to utter words.][86]

The vision presents a cross of mutable quality and scale—one bathed in light, adorned with gold, studded with gems stretching to the ends of the earth, luminous with emotion (*wynnum*), bleeding with Christ's wound, moving through (*wendan*) color and adornment while (*hwilum*) soaking wet, and drenched in blood, and also while (*hwilum*) adorned with ornament.

Since A. S. Cook's 1905 assessment that in this work the poet "presents sharp contrasts, yet with unity of effect; with glooms and splendours fashioned into a masterly chiaroscuro," critics invariably have commented on the complexity of the dream vision presented, yet at the same time attempted to resolve interpretative difficulties within the text by locating it within contexts of unity, order, or sequential progression.[87] In a small but representative sample from the last four decades of commentary, John C. Pope comments that here "complexities of meaning and emotion are conveyed, order is maintained, and a significant progression is unfolded"; Bernard Huppé depicts a structural movement from the inanimate to the functional to the metaphoric; Michael Swanton, among others, reads the sequence of the cross's appearance as referring to two other sequences: the seasonal cycle of the liturgy and the subsequent liturgical processionals that would then carry a cross; Carol Braun Pasternack, in a rigorous syntactical analysis, argues that the topical, stylistic, formal disjunction of such scenes in the end also supports "a formal unity" of "the idea of the cross, presented according to several different perspectives";

while David Johnson aligns the shifting nature of the cross with the movement of the dreamer from sin to eschatological revelation.[88]

Such readings remain valuable for modern readers as ways to organize and assess this decidedly unmodern material and, in some cases, to connect the vision to other early medieval practices and perspectives that may have informed the composition and reception of the poem. But most such readings also imply, a priori, that this opening vision follows an ordered sequence, and that the order of the visual details in the text matches the order of the dreamer's vision as he experienced it. If anything, though, the poem presents a vision of a cross that palpably resists the notion of the ordered, the sequential, and even the knowable, even as it relates the experience through the syntactical progression of language.

The vision takes place while the speech-bearers (*reordberend*) sleep. The use of the kenning *reordberend* to represent the dreamer's community emphasizes, as Irvine notes, "the signifying sounds which unite minds in communication," that is, language.[89] Of course, the *reordberend* are also all asleep, a detail that signals that while language is present, it is also paradoxically absent from the visionary experience. Further, Pasternack reminds us, the representation here actually emphasizes not language but vision: verb after verb in this passage denotes some aspect of sight, not speech.[90] Until the cross speaks in line 28, and thereby effectively begins to *translate* the nature of the vision into language for the dreamer, the poem does not represent a sequence of events, but rather the presentational simultaneity of a vision impossible to render accurately in words. As Thomas Hall argues, the poem's opening vision is instead "dynamic and transformative"; it "redefines itself even as the dreamer is describing it, and the difficult and contradictory images that comprise it attest to the dreamer's inability to communicate the richness of his vision."[91]

Hall challenges the notion that we need to read the vision inside a sequence or progression, and instead relates the descriptive language of the episode to medieval theories of prophetic seeing, and such theories' recognition of the breakdown of language as it attempts to represent the ineffable. [→45] The performance of language, of course, operates sequentially in time and, in the case of written language, in space. Hall, however, considers the opening vision an attempt to represent "homospatial thinking," wherein discrete ideas operate not in sequence but in simultaneity.[92] In other words, the vision of the dreamer describes an instantaneous collocation of objects and sensory perceptions, and it is the syntactic demands of language that render, to use

Susanne Langer's terminology, the presentational moment of the visual into linear form.[93] [→97]

Indeed, the manner in which time and space intersect in this vision supports its interpretation through notions of simultaneity instead of sequence. As the dreamer first gazes upon the cross raised above him, the rood does not change over time but rather over space: *Hwæðre ic þurh þæt gold ongytan meahte earmra ærgewin* [Yet *through* that gold I could perceive the old strife of the wicked ones]. In other words, the vision functions through a homospatial depth, as opposed to temporal shifts.[94] The continuation of the cross's description, framed through the verb *wendan* and the *hwilum . . . hwilum* [while . . . while] construction, then, does not occur as a sequence but rather as an ongoing, winding series of concurrent "whiles," alternating only in their textual representation.

Inside the Anglo-Saxon context of the poem, the opening "sequence" of *The Dream of the Rood* imposes the discursive qualities of the medium of writing upon the theophanic vision. In effect, the mechanism of writing intermedially translates the experience as it recounts it. By analogy, modern scholars, in interpretations of this episode driven by senses of unity, sequence, segment, and progress, further the process of translation through a remediation in print, re-rendering the recursive Old English vision through the assumption that the order of the text fulfills the *ordo* of meaning. In part, such dianoetic readings understandably pick up on the syntactic operation of the Old English language and writing. But critical approaches of modern scholarship, enacted through the formal conventions of print, also transform the Old English poetic text, just as the Old English text, driven by the formal conventions of poetic language and then literacy, originally transformed the notion of the ineffable moment of divine revelation.

If *The Dream of the Rood* demonstrates the effect of media upon the representation and interpretation of the divine, the first chapter of Bede's computistical treatise *De temporum ratione* (On the reckoning of time) reveals through successive technologies the gradual conversion of a human function to a mechanical one.[95] *De computo vel loquela digitorum* (Of calculating or speaking with the fingers) details the classical system of numerical representation from one to ten thousand using various positions of fingers on both hands. An additional, elaborate system for continuing counting and calculation of figures up to one million is also described, using not only the hands but the entire body—a late addition unknown in Roman times.[96] Significantly, Bede's description of this physical system is entirely textual; though some later manuscripts of *De temporum ratione* do include an illustration, nothing in Bede's text indicates that he did so originally.

De computo vel loquela digitorum essentially adapts the system that had been used throughout the Greco-Roman period.[97] Bede's description of number formation from 1 to 29 details the basic premise of the system's operation:

> Cum ergo dicis unum, minimum in laeva digitum inflectens, in medium palmae artum infiges. Cum dicis duo, secundum a minimo flexum, ibidem impones. Cum dicis tria, tertium similiter adflectes. Cum dicis quattuor, itidem minimum levabis. Cum dicis quinque, secundum a minimo similiter eriges. Cum dicis sex, tertium nihilominus elevabis, medio dumtaxat solo, qui medicus appellatur, in medium palmae fixo. Cum dicis septem, minimum solum, caeteris interim levatis, super palmae radicem pones. Iuxta quem cum dicis octo, medicum. Cum dicis nouem, impudicem e regione compones. Cum dicis decem, unguem indicis in medio figes artu pollicis. Cum dicis viginti, summitatem pollicis inter medios indicis et impudicis artus immittes.

> [So when you say "one," bend the little finger of the left hand and fix it on the middle of the palm. When you say "two," bend the second from the smallest finger and fix it on the same place. When you say "three," bend the third one in the same way. When you say "four," lift up the little finger again. When you say "five," lift up the second from the smallest in the same way. When you say "six," you lift up the third finger, while only the finger in between, which is called *medicus*, is fixed in the middle of the palm. When you say "seven," place the little finger only (the others being meanwhile raised), on the base of the palm. When you say "eight," put the *medicus* beside it. When you say "nine," add the middle finger. When you say "ten," touch the nail of the index finger to the middle joint of the thumb. When you say "twenty," you insert the tip of the thumb between the middle joints of the index and middle fingers.][98]

In this method, the last three fingers of the left hand form the numbers 1 to 9, to which may be added the place number in tens by configuring the thumb and first finger. Similarly, hundreds are made and/or added on the right hand the way tens are made on the left, while thousands use the right hand to form the same configuration of ones from the left hand. Tens and hundreds of thousands can be indicated by placing the arms in various positions on the body—

for instance, "Porro decem millia cum dicis, laevam medio pectoris supinam appones, digitis tantum ad collum erectis" [when you say "ten thousand," you place your left hand flat on the middle of your chest].[99]

Faith Wallis has demonstrated that the system Bede describes can indeed be used to perform calculations of some complexity.[100] And while systems of finger and body counting may be found throughout preliterate societies, most Western readers would now find the description of this arithmetical system difficult to grasp without serious contemplation and concentration, for a number of reasons.[101] Most obviously, the physicality of *De computo vel loquela digitorum* precludes the sequential and textual aspects of arithmetic assumed by most modern people. When we use our fingers in arithmetical operations, we usually do so only in a simple, linear sequence, to count a small quantity. Hand calculation plays only the smallest part, if any, in most modern arithmetic, as most of our ability to calculate has successively developed through a series of technologies, beginning with Arabic writing and culminating (for now) with microchip processing.[102] At the time of Bede's writing, however, the written notation of Roman numerals did not facilitate written calculations.[103] Bede certainly regarded this system of finger calculation as vital to his work; he chose to begin his master treatise on the computation of time with it. At the same time, the system he describes must have been deeply interiorized to have been of any real use to him, for outside of the basic mechanics, he gives little detail about application and use of the system.

Bede's representation of *De computo vel loquela digitorum* also reveals the ongoing process of technological mediation, as well as the fundamentally different way that the Anglo-Saxon subject combined technology, body, and language to "do math." For Bede, the activity of arithmetic was a physical one, a functional extension of the body that contrasts with modern notions of calculation much in the same way oral speech differs from writing.[104] Bede, in fact, connects organic notions of language and this kind of arithmetic in his rubric—*computo vel loquela digitorum* (the calculating *or* speaking of the fingers)—indicating how close a relation he sees between computation and speaking in this system. Further, Bede's description of the process integrates voice and body, as Bede couches the formation of each number in figures of orality: "Cum dicis duo, secundum a minimo flexum, ibidem impones" [when you *say* "two," bend the second from the smallest finger and fix it on the same place].[105] Bede later connects calculation to language in a second way, explaining that using the fingers to represent numbers can also be used as "a sort of manual language" [Potest autem et de ipso quem praenotavi computo quaedam manualis loquela], where words can be spelled out, and therefore silently and secretly communicate meaning at a distance, fooling the uninitiated "as if by magic" [imperitos quosque quasi divinando deludens].[106]

Despite such relations of natural language and the body to the process of calculation, Bede also mediates this process through his writing of it. Writing the "speaking of fingers" increases the distance of readers (modern or medieval) from the early medieval practice, as it inserts a technological filter between the "natural" process and its representation. Bede also uses textual authority to impress upon his students the importance of learning how to finger calculate, and in the process shows how the praxis of writing has been heavily interiorized, and how permeable the line between the natural and the technological has become. Bede, no doubt addressing the resistance of students to learning or practicing calculation, explains that "one ought not to despise or treat lightly that rule with which almost all the exegetes of Holy Scripture have shown themselves well acquainted, no less than they are with the shapes of letters [literarum figuras]."[107] For Bede, then, the elemental importance of the shapes of numerical signification made by fingers corresponds to the "literarum figuras" made through the technology of writing. Continuing the association of the physical with the textual, Bede then cites a specific example from Jerome, where the exegete uses the finger positions for thirty, sixty, and one hundred as allegories of sexual experience.[108] In the same way that the very writing of theophany in *The Dream of the Rood* was always-already textualized, and therefore altered, the experience, Bede's recording of *De computo vel loquela digitorum* translates the signification of the physical expression, and likewise remediates it through the interiorized technology of writing.

Notably, I did not first come across this system in written form—not in one of the 240 manuscripts in which Bede's *De temporum ratione* survives, nor in a printed edition of one of these manuscripts, nor through a reference to one of them in a critical treatment of Bede, nor from anything concerned with medieval studies at all, for that matter. In fact, my initial encounter with this system did not include a single word from Bede's original account. I first saw a representation of *De computo vel loquela digitorum* as an image, in a reproduction of a 1727 German engraving entitled *Der Alten Finger-Rechnung*, or "The Old Finger Counting" (see figure 2), from Jacob Leupold's *Theatrum arithmetico-geometricum*, in Eisenstein's study of print culture; though Eisenstein did not note it, the engraving bore a caption from Leupold attributing the system to Bede.[109] Leupold, a mechanical engineer noted for his study of machinery, became involved in the development of a calculating machine,

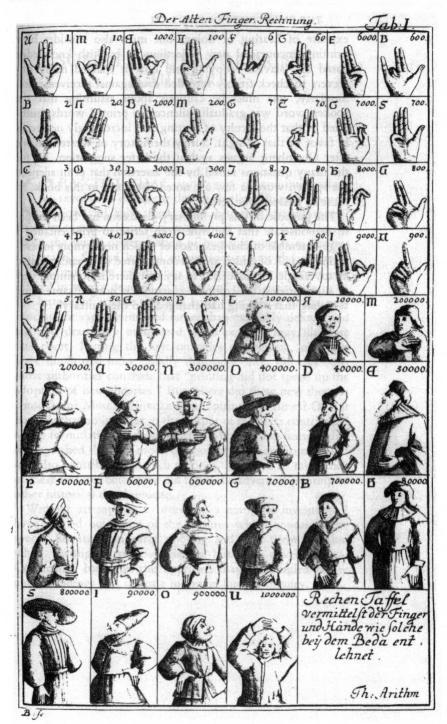

Figure 2. Jacob Leupold's *Der Alten Finger-Rechnung*, from *Theatrum arithmetico-geometricum* (1727), tab. I.

designing the plans for one but never building it. He published an illustration of Bede's counting system as the first in a series of tables representing the history of calculation. The eighth table in this series, an illustration of Gottfried Wilhelm Leibniz's seventeenth-century design for a calculator (see figure 3), contextually frames Leupold's use of Bede as an indicator of both the historical foundation and the technological progress of the mechanics of calculation.[110]

Eisenstein notes that even though printed arithmetic books, charts, and tables had superseded medieval systems of calculation such as Bede's, "these ancient arts were codified and given a long lease on life in printed form."[111] But while Leupold's printing of *Der Alten Finger-Rechnung* does preserve Bede's system, the most immediate context of its reproduction revises its meaning to the point of distortion. Aspects of the engraving reveal a substantial drift from Bede's text, as the images no longer conform to Bede's instructions. Leupold's engravings for 60, 70, and 80 confuse the positions of thumb and index finger; more drastically, the engraving repeats the 400 position for 500, and reverses the representation of numbers in the hundreds and thousands, swapping 100 and 1000, 200 and 2000, and so forth.[112] These mistakes indicate that Leupold, though attributing the visual chart to Bede, either did not have access to Bede's actual text, worked from a corrupt graphic redaction of the system, or both. The errors also suggest that, though elaborate systems of finger calculation continued to be employed throughout the Middle Ages, by the dawn of the mechanical age in the eighteenth century the system was no longer used, or possibly even understood, by those who reproduced it in print.[113]

Far from accurately preserving and disseminating an early medieval system of thought and practice, then, print here serves to codify inaccuracy and signal a fundamental displacement of the system's original function. Leupold's printing of Bede's system curatorially situates it as the primitive antithesis to Leibniz's and his own complex engineering schemes for mechanical calculation. For Bede, one started with finger calculation because it was the foundation of all subsequent computistical work. For Leupold, Bede's system also comes first, but not because it is foundational—rather, because *Der Alten Finger-Rechnung* provides historical contrast to modern technology and innovation. Far from simply preserving Bede's system, Leupold's printing charts its transformation from an integral practice to a historical curiosity.

In the early and then late ages of print, the reproduction of *De computo vel loquela digitorum* furthered the process of technological conversion begun in Anglo-Saxon England by Bede's written description, recording several suc-

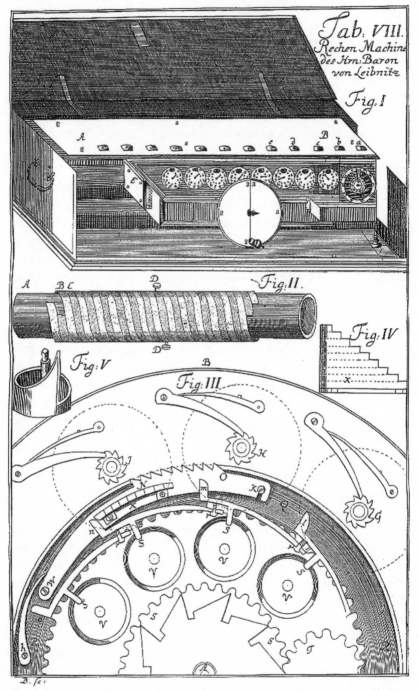

Figure 3. Jacob Leupold's *Rechen Machine des Hrn. Baron von Leibnitz*, from *Theatrum arithmetico-geometricum* (1727), tab. VIII.

cessive stages of mediation and remediation. In medieval manuscripts, Bede's textual description of finger calculation was often illustrated by drawings, which then served as the basis for early modern engravings of the system, one of which, no doubt, Leupold used as his source.[114] In the eighteenth century, Leupold in turn printed a modern engraving of a medieval visualization of an Anglo-Saxon written account of a classical system of finger reckoning, all in support of his own quest to develop a mechanical calculator. In the late twentieth century, Eisenstein would reprint Leupold's engraving in her study of print culture to make a (somewhat misleading) point about the preservative effect of print on pre-print practices. Such modern typographic events fashion new versions of Bede's (now absent) text that have little, if anything, to do with Anglo-Saxon form, content, and purpose.

The process by which media technology affects and alters Anglo-Saxon discourse is long and idiosyncratic. *The Dream of the Rood* survives in one manuscript, with "fragments" of the same poem occurring on one stone cross and on one silver reliquary. In the medieval period, *De temporum ratione* was Bede's most popular work, surviving in some 240 manuscripts in one form or another; the work, especially the chapter on finger calculation, continued to be popular during the early age of print.[115] Bede's text may therefore be counted as one of the most popular in the Middle Ages, while *The Dream of the Rood* remained mostly, if not completely, unknown after the Norman Conquest. In contemporary medieval studies, however, the situation has reversed: *The Dream of the Rood* has achieved canonical status, is included in standard literary anthologies, and receives regular critical attention, while Bede's text remains, on the whole, relatively obscure and rarely discussed in academic criticism—or anywhere else, for that matter.

What happened to these two Anglo-Saxon texts, both writings rooted in the intersection of Anglo-Saxon body, voice, and mind? One could argue that, as evidenced by Leupold's mechanical bias, Bede's system of finger reckoning became obsolete, superseded by technologies of Arabic numeration, then printed mathematical tables, and finally mechanical calculators, finally falling completely out of cultural currency. But is the Old English language and poetic expression of *The Dream of the Rood* any less obsolete? The question of cultural survival of these two examples of Anglo-Saxon expression depends to some degree on their congruency with the print medium. As a written expression, *The Dream of the Rood* can be translated into printed form, and continuously updated—albeit with its content and meaning revised, and supported, and even concealed by an increasingly bulky apparatus—through successive layers of print culture. [→15] By contrast, when one prints, or in Bede's case even sets down in writing, the ancient system of finger reckoning, this meaning is not necessarily *translated* but rather *converted* into something wholly other than its original, nontextual form. While printed versions of *The Dream of the Rood* remediate and change the textuality of the Old English poem, they maintain the illusion that the function of this poem continues. But textual redactions of *De computo vel loquela digitorum* do not enact such "functional remediation," and therefore instead foreground the notion of the work's increasing irrelevance with every remove of medium. *The Dream of the Rood* continues to flourish, relatively speaking, precisely because its textual qualities allow functional remediation, sustained through the illusion of printed preservation.

LEVEL FOUR INFORMATION AND ANGLO-SAXON STUDIES

Writing about Bede's *De computo vel loquela digitorum* on my iBook computer, I remediate his system one more time as I convert his *loquela digitorum* to digital zeros and ones. There is a certain technological irony to this: my iBook and Bede's system do the same thing—execute algorithms—but they now stand just about as far removed from each other on the functional and historical registers as possible.[116] The ancient method of finger computation was outmoded by the early modern age because its technology—or, rather, its lack thereof—was ill suited to handle the continuing growth of society's informational needs. Such needs also spurred the revolutionary development of the printing press, and, as detailed above, all of its attendant social, technological, and intellectual transformations. The printing press heralded the movement into the third level of civilization and information management (the first two being the development of language and then the development of writing).[117] In the past few decades, modern society has entered into a fourth level of information management, occasioned by the explosion of digital technology, and is in the process of undergoing similar cultural transformations.[118] As the print culture influenced the rise and subsequent character of Anglo-Saxon studies, so will this new culture of technology "thoroughly rewrite the writing space" and fundamentally change not only the tools by which we study the Anglo-Saxon period but the very epistemology of such studies.[119]

The advent of New Media then, places the discipline on the threshold of a new stage of academic apperception. The fluidity of digital technology promises fresh modes of representation and study that can provide very real alternatives to the medium of print, and perhaps recover aspects of the Anglo-

Saxon world that have remained unaccounted for in print.[120] Of course, such technological thresholds are where the double logic of remediation functions most forcefully. Even as digital media begin to effect all sorts of discursive change, these media and the initiatives they engender likewise are influenced by the prior character of print in their development. Unfortunately, much digital work in academic scholarship has yet to grasp that new media should not simply extend the power of print.[121] [→192] Indeed, so many of the electronic initiatives and their metacriticism in medieval studies have focused on the very aspects that print privileged—standardization, logocentrism, linear analysis—that Peter Robinson has recently argued that "almost without exception, no scholarly electronic edition has presented material . . . in a manner significantly different from that which could have been managed in print."[122] But this is no longer because there is no other way to study the past. In his critique Robinson insists: "For long, we have been used to seeing data in list form: lists of variants, lists of manuscripts: essentially, in a single linear dimension," and calls for editing of medieval manuscripts to take place "in a third digital dimension."[123]

Robinson's spatial metaphor for the expansion of critical paradigms recalls the earlier discussion of Seth Lerer and George Hickes, and that the printed form of medieval scholarship has compressed and/or elided layers of interpretation that have accrued through both the medieval and modern periods.[124] The representational flexibility of digital media, freed from the physical limitations of the page and able now to "link up" information in virtually limitless and simultaneous ways, in tandem with its ever developing modes of encoding, processing, and producing all kinds of data, means that additional digital dimensions need not be limited to a third.

In Anglo-Saxon studies, where practical applications of electronic media have flourished, most critical commentary on New Media has remained restrained either to descriptions of these applications and their practical utility or to discussions of the impact of technology on editorial method.[125] Such work, while valuable, may also work to, as Nicholas Howe puts it, "reassert traditional working practices against new theoretical developments."[126] But alongside the practical applications of digital technology, emergent theories have begun to document and explain how New Media now creates textualities across a range of media that operate in ways unimaginable a few decades ago. These new alternatives to print also suggest a series of homologies between the post-print and the pre-print. Early New Media commentators were quick to point out that digital media and medieval discourse have in common a number of traits that print does not share. McLuhan contrasted the cultural functions of "medieval plurality and modern homogeneity," remarking that on the cusp of the computer age "we live on the frontier between five centuries of mechanism and the new electronics, between the homogeneous and the simultaneous"; Walter Ong deemed post-typographic electronic expression a "secondary orality" that in many ways harkens back to premodern models of communication, while Jay David Bolter more explicitly claims that, in contrast to the printed book, "only in the medieval codex were words and pictures as unified as they are on the computer screen."[127] [→58] More recently, an increasing number of critics have refined such functional analogies, further developing how pre- and post-print worlds connect through analogies of their respective operation.[128]

Importantly, before the particular discussions of New Media theory and early medieval expression in the following chapters, it must be stressed that digital media are not silver bullets and do not offer any sure way to precisely and accurately recover the "essence" of medieval expression any more than the technology of print does. The digital is anything but "real" in its formulation of medieval texts and objects. The virtuality of the screen, for instance, can move the post-print viewer even further away from the bodily involvement and the (in some ways) sensory aspects of medieval manuscripts.[129] If anything, the "virtual" quality of the digital is doubly so; as Edward Christie maintains in his analysis of the *Electronic Beowulf*, the compelling visual transparency with which New Media can present an Anglo-Saxon artifact must not be confused or conflated with historical transparency. Digital technology creates an even more potent version of hyperreality than print, and it becomes easy to convince oneself that an exquisitely rendered digital edition can be "more authentic than the original."[130] To do so is to fall in behind a long line of Anglo-Saxonists who believed that modern technical innovation had the capability to "out-medieval" the medieval source.

But given that print has conditioned the past half millennium of scholarship, the moment is ripe to explore the fresh critical perspectives New Media theory may yield in regard to Anglo-Saxon texts and objects from the period. Until now, what little theoretical consideration of the medieval-digital nexus there has been has largely dealt with later medieval discourse. As an early stage of medieval culture, the Anglo-Saxon period itself embodied a time of great cultural development and transformation. Likewise, scholars have come to realize that long past 1066, England experienced what could be termed "the late age of Anglo-Saxon," as the transition to an Anglo-Norman culture was not sudden, but quite gradual.[131] As we shall see in the next chapter, Anselm, writing at Canterbury in the twilight of the Anglo-Saxon age, experimented with a new textuality that pushed the boundaries of writing in ways reminiscent of how digital texts now push against the boundaries of print. In all of the following chapters, the experimental nature of the pre-print texts and multimedia from Anglo-Saxon England teaches us that we still have much to learn about the intersection of technology and culture, and how each helps produce the other.

Anselm's Hypertext

Because the subject of this printed book is the coming of the electronic book, I have found it particularly difficult to organize my text in an appropriate manner—appropriate, that is, to the printed page. In my mind the argument kept trying to cast itself intertextually or "hypertextually." Electronic text falls naturally into discrete units—paragraphs or sections that stand in multiple relation to one another. An electronic text is a network rather than the straight line suggested by the pages of a printed book, and the network should be available for reading in a variety of orders. . . . Indeed, a many-voiced text that is large enough to contain and admit its own contradictions may be the only convincing form of writing in the electronic medium.

—Jay David Bolter

At the opening of his influential 1991 book *Writing Space: The Computer, Hypertext, and the History of Writing,* Jay David Bolter remarks upon a writer's block only recently possible. Though Bolter's subsequent arguments present the case for electronic text's evolution from and eventual usurpation of the "late age of print," he chooses, given the dominance of print, to publish his work on paper and not in pixels. [→195] The resulting liminal discourse remains rooted in traditional textuality and yet resistant to it as it considers the new frontier of digital writing. While Bolter's own subject, he admits, cannot (yet) supplant print, the project of describing the operation of electronic texts in print does remediate the process and product of this traditional and powerful media. [→6] And Bolter pushes the formal boundaries of this remediation by offering readers an "electronic shadow" of his commercial publication: a diskette, available from the publisher, in which "the rules of print are ignored. The argument falls into short paragraphs, [and] the reader is given a choice of paths to follow."[1]

Nine hundred years before such thoughts on electronic texts were possible, the theologian Anselm, first at Bec and then at Canterbury, composed a series of short devotional texts collectively now known as *Orationes sive Meditationes* (Prayers and Meditations, hereafter *OsM*).[2] In the preface to the *OsM*, Anselm includes instructions for reading that suggest that, like Bolter, he struggled with a perceived gap between the content of his writings and the linear and continuous process through which the written word is received:

> Orationes sive meditationes quae subscriptae sunt, quoniam ad excitandam legentis mentem ad dei amorem vel timorem, seu ad suimet discussionem editae sunt, non sunt legendae in tumultu, sed in quiete, nec cursim et velociter, sed paulatim cum intenta et morosa meditatione. Nec debet intendere lector ut quamlibet earum totam perlegat, sed quantum sentit sibi deo adiuvante valere ad accendendum affectum orandi, vel quantum illum delectat. Nec necesse habet aliquam semper a principio incipere, sed ubi magis illi placuerit. Ad hoc enim ipsum paragraphis sunt distinctae per partes, ut ubi elegerit incipiat aut destinat, ne prolixitas aut frequens eiusdem loci repetitio generet fastidium, sed potius aliquem inde colligat lector propter quod factae sunt pietatis affectum.

> [The prayers and meditations written below, since they are intended to excite the reader's mind to the love or fear of God and are uttered in conversation with him, are not to be read where there is noise but in quiet, nor superficially and at speed but slowly, with intense and profound meditation. Nor ought the reader intend to read any of them all the way through, but only as much as, with God's help, will do to kindle a longing for prayer, or as much as is satisfying. Nor need anyone always begin at the beginning but wherever suits best. For this reason, the prayers are subdivided into paragraphs, so that one may begin or end where one chooses, in case too many words or frequent repetition of the same section should lead to boredom. Let the reader take from them what they were meant to provide, the warmth of devotion.][3]

The ideological premises behind Bolter's and Anselm's instructions could not be more different, of course. Bolter writes of a digital revolution, while Anselm constructs a textual springboard for divine prayer and conversation. And unlike Bolter's work, Anselm's devotions do not actively critique the logocentric environment of manuscript culture in which they are produced, nor do they acknowledge, or even apprehend, that an alternative technological medium might replace writing as the textual mode. Yet these prefaces present some specific and important homologies between post-print hypertext at the end of the second millennium and pre-print devotional innovation at the end of the first. The surface attributes of Anselm's outlined reading strategy—the de-emphasis on beginnings and endings, the empowerment of the reader to dictate the course of the narrative experience, and formal arrangement of the writing into discrete units only loosely affiliated with each other—are also key aspects of hypertextuality.

Hypertext, first defined by Theodore Nelson in the 1960s, does not consist of a set sequence of text, as in print, but of a network of textual blocks, or *lexia*, realized electronically and connected through a theoretically limitless number of pathways by means of addressed links.[4] Conceivably, hypertext can also be a function of hypermedia, that is, text fluidly linked to other verbal or nonverbal media, such as image, sound, animation, and other works external to the immediate discourse fashioned. These links, or at least the set of defined pathways, can also evolve or change over time, and be altered by subsequent contributors to the overall hypermedia network, or what Nelson has termed the "docuverse."[5] The end result of hypermedia is the creation of a network of meaning that is polysequential, that easily accommodates a range of media, and, like a Saussurian model of language, constantly shifts its synchronic relations over the diachronic progress of time. [→99]

Certainly, any text from the eleventh century cannot fulfill the condition of hypertext in the true electronic sense. The correspondences in the language of the 1K and 2K metatexts described above do, however, serve as a starting point for a deeper investigation of how "late print" theories of hypertext and hypermedia may clarify the operation of medieval writings. Such consideration helps reveal aspects of pre-print texts that do not necessarily align with the dominant characteristics of print culture, and so have remained obscured and/or unnoticed. Bolter, later seeking to distinguish electronic texts from all previous forms of writing technologies, argues that the roll, the codex, and the printed book could not easily accommodate associative relationships alternative to the linear textualities that inhere in the traditional paperbound forms of writing, and that therefore these technologies "tended to ignore them."[6]

Bolter's point has a material foundation, admittedly, in the broad physical similarities of manuscript and book, but lumping these print and premechanical modes of writing together also ignores the large part that the cultural and economic dominance of the unvaried, mass-produced, and author-friendly print product plays in constructing the relationships of the written word as fixed, linear, and largely closed to alternative textualities. Similar to Bolter's paradigm of hypertextuality, Anselm's devotional texts seek to construct alternative associations, but modern scholarship, traditionally disposed to find in the past what textualities it has in the present, has rarely considered them. Studying such medieval devotions through ideas of hypertext and hypermedia studies, though, highlights the nature of Anselm's innovative work, as well as its place within the textual communities operating in the final, fading years of Anglo-Saxon culture.

ANSELM'S TEXT

Anselm (1033–1109) became a monk at Bec in 1060, prior in 1063, and abbot in 1078. During this time he likely composed the majority of his prayers and meditations, possibly as his first literary endeavor.[7] In 1072 Adelaide, daughter of William the Conqueror, requested that the prior provide her with a selection of psalms for her private use. Anselm's letter of reply mentions that he also included seven prayers of his own making, now identified with some degree of certainty as works in the extant devotional corpus.[8] In 1073–74 Anselm worked to perfect a Marian prayer, creating not one but three versions in the process.[9] And though by 1075, as R. W. Southern puts it, "Anselm had written all the *Prayers* and *Meditations* that are important for the development of devotional theology," the cleric continued to add to and refine the collection for the next three decades, even after his appointment as Archbishop of Canterbury in 1094.[10] Sometime after 1104 Anselm completed what is now considered the final authorial redaction of his prayer collection, adding a few new prayers and the preface for general usage by the laity noted above, and sent this version to the countess Matilda of Tuscany.[11]

The continuous process of the collection's composition, Anselm's habit of compiling different sets of prayers and meditations for individual audiences and contexts, and the tendency of later compilers to inflate Anselmian collections with falsely attributed spiritual exercises, together resulted in a lack of a basic or definitive form of the *OsM* in manuscripts that is notable even by medieval standards. The preservation and transmission of Anselm's prayers remained vigorous, if haphazard, through the medieval period. Subsequent compilations of these texts, all of which differ in order and number of works included, survive in at least a dozen English and seven Continental manuscripts from the twelfth century, and numerous others from subsequent centuries.[12] Most, if not all, manuscripts group Anselm's writings with either apocryphal insertions or devotions of other authors, a tradition that continued and expanded well into the seventeenth century.[13] Indeed, by Gabriel Gerberon's printed edition of 1675, the amount of devotional literature believed to be written by Anselm himself had swollen to 111 pieces, all of which were unhesitatingly included and printed by Migne two centuries later in the *Patrologia Latina*.[14] In 1932, however, André Wilmart carefully disentangled a slim set of nineteen prayers and three meditations as genuine Anselm compositions.[15] The current corpus of "genuine" Anselmian prayers consists of four prayers to God, Christ, the Cross, and the Eucharist, a set of Marian devotions, a group of ten prayers to saints, and a pair of prayers for friends and enemies, respectively. The three extant meditations concern the excitation of the mind to fear, a lament for lost virginity, and, most famously, human redemption.

Modern commentators on the *OsM* usually note a distinctive set of innovative attributes, predominated by unprecedented length, a tendency toward intense verbal elaboration and at times prolix descriptions, and a heavy emphasis on compunctive introspection and emotional frenzy.[16] Additionally, as Thomas Bestul has observed, after Anselm's death the early tradition of reception and transmission of Anselmian devotions constituted "a remarkable break with past tradition" through its specific assignment of authorship of entire collections of texts to the nearly contemporary figure of Anselm rather than, as was standard practice, to "some saint from the patristic era."[17]

These innovations notwithstanding, the *OsM* has received over the past century practically no scholarly attention when compared to such later works as the *Proslogion*'s famous ontological proof of God; by 1999 more than a thousand scholarly works had been published on the *Proslogion* and just thirty-six concerning the *OsM*.[18] And after Wilmart's foundational set of early-twentieth-century manuscript studies, only a literal handful of treatments dedicated specifically to this collection have been written.[19] This neglect stems in no small part from a chronologically driven conception of Anselm's literary career, which first "peaks" with the composition of the *Monologion* and *Proslogion* and then with his later arguments on the human condition culminating with *Cur Deus Homo*.[20] In such a teleological framework, Anselm's devotional works, widely believed to be his first literary efforts, are more often than not relegated to the status of the formative, and as important not for what they are but for where they lead.[21]

Significantly, the "early" characterization of these texts inaccurately portrays the actual *historia* of Anselm's process of composition. As Southern and others note, but then ignore, Anselm continued to work on his collection of devotional writings throughout his professional life, paying more attention to them across his duties as prior, abbot, and then archbishop than to any other of his literary endeavors. The "schoolbook" quality of the majority of Anselm's other literary productions after 1078 (after the completion of the *Proslogion*) led Gregory Schufreider to argue for a shift from the meditative to the rational in his later literary career.[22] But the fact that as late as 1104 the archbishop was still reworking and adding to his devotional collection suggests not so much a shift as a desire to accommodate both the scholastic and the devotional in his writings, with a continuing fondness for the latter in constant evidence.

Throughout the span of these writings, Anselm's concern about reception remained paramount. The longest formulation of this concern, the preface already quoted, would arrive late in his career, in his 1104 letter to Countess Matilda. But in a letter from 1073 to Gundolf, a monk at Bec and later bishop of Rochester, Anselm employs strikingly similar language on the construction and use of a set of three Marian prayers:

> Denique idcirco volui eas ipsas orationes per sententias paragraphis distinguere, ut anticipando longitudinis fastidium, ubi volueris, possis eas legendo incidere.

> [You will find that I have divided the prayers up into paragraphs, as I anticipate that you will become bored by their length, so that it is possible to begin to read anyplace you wish.][23]

Though not as elaborate as the later preface for Matilda, his instructions to Gundolf more than thirty years before attest, in practically the same language, to Anselm's long-term concern with the ways in which his prayers should be structured and read. As the transmission of Anselmian texts continued through the twelfth century and beyond, this close regard for specific instructions on reading resulted in the then-unprecedented practice of including a prologue and letters of instruction in devotional collections.[24] Finally, this strategy of composition and desired reception signifies that even while he wrote a number of ratiocinated arguments that would eventually earn him the sobriquet "the father of scholasticism," he remained committed to a textuality wholly outside and alternative to the burgeoning rational tradition.[25]

TEXTUAL INNOVATION

Anselm's approach to his prayer collection stems in part from a balancing act in the textual practices of his own Benedictine community at Bec. The Benedictine reform of the tenth century resulted in the production of independent prayer books and sets of prayers appended to psalter collections, and the *OsM* easily fits into this category.[26] In addition, the Benedictine Rule emphasized *lectio continua*, orderly and sustained reading, which governed the textual structure of the Benedictine day, from the liturgical cycle of the Scripture, to the rule of silence during mealtime readings, to the strict chanting schedule by which the entire psalter was distributed in rotation between the major and minor hours of the day.[27] Such an ethos in turn informed the *lectio divina*, the daily practice of devotional study as set forth in chapter 48 of the Rule, which also mandated that books in private study be read one at a time over the course of a year, *per ordinem ex integro*, from beginning to end.[28]

By Anselm's time, however, the Benedictine Rule and Office had evolved into a highly corporate and elaborate process that occupied most of a monk's daily schedule, leaving little time for prolonged individual prayer. Further, the meditation explicitly required by the Benedictine Rule had become less reflection and study and more a practical, perhaps bureaucratic, preparation for the highly complicated musical and verbal performances demanded of the Benedictine community on a daily basis.[29] The textuality delineated in the *OsM*, with its de-emphasis of beginnings and endings, serves as an alternative to such rote preparation and the traditional linear progress of *per ordinem ex integro*. In dispensing with a format of continuous reading, Anselm explores a devotional routine situated between the needs for *lectio continua* and *lectio divina*.

Anselm's version of *lectio divina* also differs from other contemporary writings in eschewing the use of explicit quotations of other authoritative texts. Though not adverse to citing biblical or patristic authority in later writings, Anselm appears to have had no interest in writing scriptural commentary or in the recent genre of Sentences; in his early meditations and devotions he often avoids explicit textual references altogether.[30] As Benedicta Ward notes, Anselm's early prayers do not quote Scripture directly, but rather appear to absorb it into their language.[31] A similar approach occurs in the preface to Anselm's *Monologion*, where he notes his desire to provide discussion on the being of God without direct recourse to any scriptural quotation ("quatenus auctoritate Scripturae penitus nihil in ea persuaderetur").[32] This suspension of authoritative texts contrasts sharply with the works of devotional contemporaries such as John of Fécamp, whose *Confessio Theologica* has been described as a "tissue of quotations from the Bible and the Fathers . . . [and] a mosaic of quotations from Augustine to Gregory."[33] While such "networks" of intertextuality may be considered hypertextual to a degree, their referential nature remains rooted both in the logic of linear sequence and in the authority of the written word, and so they stand apart from Anselm's new mode. Anselm's avoidance of explicit intertextuality in his devotional works contrasts with the standard form of contemporary instructional commentaries and arguments (some composed by Anselm in the latter part of his career) that served as the foundation of theological scholasticism. The scholastic tradition of rational discourse relied on a dense skein of intertextuality to build its logical schema, as well as on, as Jesse Gellrich puts it, "the careful subdivision and order of its own procedure."[34]

This is not to say that Anselm did not revere and regularly utilize the authority of Scripture and the Church Fathers; others have already provided ample evidence on this point.[35] But Anselm viewed the potential of text in a different light when it came to crafting *lectio divina*. Anselm's devotional works, along with the *Monologion* and *Proslogion*, constitute a body of writing that in various ways refrains from such careful and ratiocinated organization. The paragraphic divisions described in the preface to the *OsM* are not hierarchical subdivisions but, rather, prayerful statements designed to function independently from deterministic structures. In the *Proslogion*, Anselm, dissatisfied with the fact that the *Monologion* was "composed of a complex sequence of interconnected arguments," set out to fashion a proof of the existence of God that could support itself without reliance on the logic and authority of other proofs.[36]

With its famous ontological proof of the existence of God, the *Proslogion*, of course, functions as a blend of affective spirituality and a "cool and calculating moderation of philosophical rationality," a meditation that arises from a prayer to God but is also carefully constructed with a series of logical syllogisms.[37] But Anselm's description of its origin of desire highlights a theological principle integral to understanding the textuality of his devotion: the primacy of the human capacity for faith over the faculty of reason. For Anselm, Christian faith is not a questionable phenomenon, and therefore, unlike Augustinian faith, it need not be proven by reason.[38]

With regard to writing the link to God, struggles with the limitations and failures of language to represent the divine are common to Anselm and other thinkers of the period. Alan of Lille, for instance, considers the problems of using *verbum* (as word or verb) to denote Christ, when verbs denote motion and God is above all motion. Likewise, Peter Abelard examines the difficulty of using verb tenses and their implication of past, present, or future when describing God, as nothing can apply to God only a part of the time.[39] In the *Proslogion*'s famous example of the fool who proves God's existence by uttering "God does not exist," Anselm exploits a similar gap between grammar and faith.[40] For Anselm, such a statement shows the fool to misunderstand God, an entity defined through its existence outside the mind. As God is also by definition an entity about which nothing greater can be thought, the sentence is correct grammatically only inside the mind of the fool, who does not understand God; outside his mind, the sentence must grammatically fail as "the predicate 'does not exist' contradicts the subject 'God.'"[41] In short, Anselm verifies God's existence through "grammatical clarifications" themselves predicated upon faith in God's necessary operation beyond the logic of traditional grammatical structures.[42]

Unlike the devotional ideologies of his scholastic or Benedictine contemporaries such as John of Fécamp or Hugh of St. Victor, Anselm's approach ultimately seeks not to originate in or conclude through the sustained reading of texts.[43] However, in his earliest instructions on the prayers, to Adelaide in 1072, Anselm portrays the phenomenon of reading in much more traditional terms. Most of these prayers, the monk explains, if read slowly and with complete attention, "tend toward the increase of love." Though the need for deliberate pace and circumspection may be found in later prefatory writings, here the focus remains fixed on the textual content of the prayers, their careful consumption (presumably from start to finish), and what the process of reading them can provide to the supplicant. In the Adelaidean version, the written text is never left behind.

But in his instructions from his letter to Gundolf (1073) onward, instead of viewing the devotional text as both source and telos, Anselm begins to construct a more transitional kind of text, where a concentrated but piecemeal perusal "excites the reader's mind toward the love or fear of God," "encourages the burning desire for prayer," or "pierces [the reader] by contrition or love, through which we reach a concern for heavenly things."[44] Though the goals are perhaps, on the surface, similar to those of the instruction to Adelaide, Anselm's decision to fragment the reading process places these effects not in the realm of the textual but after or, more to the point, beyond it. In breaking the text of the *OsM* into lexia, Anselm desires to dispense with a continual and sequential mode of reading and suggests, instead, that the act of reading disappear through its own operation.

In effect, in his version of *lectio divina* Anselm views reading as a form of what New Media critics term an "obstructive mediator." Anselm seeks a divine discourse that in the end erases its interface and renders the act of reading transparent. But as Bolter and Grusin point out, such efforts to create "transparent technologies"—for example, a photorealistic virtual-reality that uses panoramic photos, sound, and text to immerse the viewer in a "new" world—remain beholden to the double logic of remediation. [→6] As such, they must still define themselves by the standards of the media they seek to erase.[45] As with Anselm's "grammatical clarifications" in the *Proslogion*, where God is explained by rules of grammar he does not technically obey, Anselm's textuality in the *OsM*, while seeking to transparently transcend the written word, must remain defined and articulated by it.

Anselm's attempt at transparency in writing must also contend with what Walter Ong has termed the "alien and external technology" of pre-print writing, a technology that Ong argues separated the practitioners from their language more drastically than either print or computers later did.[46] Indeed, Eadmer of Canterbury's early-twelfth-century biography of Anselm sheds light on the disparity between the technological work of writing and Anselm's own form of private prayer. Early in his *Vita*, Eadmer describes his subject's nightly vigils, and provides some insight into the character of Anselm's own personal devotions. Each night,

> Sanctis meditationibus insistebat; ex contemplatione summae beatitudinis et desiderio vitae perennis immensos lacrimarum imbres effundebet; hujus vitae miserias suaque si qua erant et aliorum peccata amarissime flebat, et vix parum ante nocturnas vigilias sepeque nihil somni capiebat.

> [he occupied himself in holy meditations; and in his contemplation of the final blessedness and in his desire for life everlasting he shed profuse tears. He wept most bitterly for the miseries of his own life, for his own sins (if such there were) and for those of others, and he hardly slept—often slept not at all—before matins.][47]

Eadmer's portrait makes no mention of whether Anselm read during his devotions, though he clearly describes emotional states similar to the ones Anselm desires readers of the *OsM* to reach. Directly before his account of Anselm's nightly devotions, however, Eadmer also notes that Anselm performs a different kind of nightly work with texts, reporting that "Praeterea libros qui ante id temporis nimis corrupti ubique terrarum eant nocte corrigebat" [by night also he corrected books, which in all the land before this time were disfigured by mistakes].[48]

Eadmer's account functions as a distillation of Anselm's devotional impulse and both its distance from and proximity to the study of texts. Anselm's written prayers are evoked by this description of their composite poles: his painstaking textual work, the close reading and correcting of manuscripts for scribal error, which in turn is followed by an elaboration of his own, at times wordless, affective devotions. The former reminds us (and probably Anselm) of the alien, external, and obstructive nature of the media within which he works, while the latter provides a haloed version of the unwritten, theophanic world he seeks. [→23]

Eadmer's report that Anselm often prayed through the night until matins juxtaposes the intensity of the experience with the regimented structure of monastic canonical hours. The fact that what halted the experience of Anselm's prayers was, ironically, the timed schedule of prayers (matins) reminds us that in Anselm's model devotion is associative and not, a priori, a practice that emphasizes the linear or the logical. Similarly, Anselm's prayers tend to thematize the chaotic emotional world of the devout sinner who remains transfixed inside the fragmented space of sin. As Anselm writes in his first prayer to Mary:

> O perturbata, o confusa peccandi conditio! En quippe vos, peccata mea, quomodo discerpendo distrahendo corroditis, corrodendo torquetis praecordia mea. Eadem enim peccata mea, o domina, cognosci a te cupiunt propter curationem, parere tibi fugiunt propter execrationem. Non sanantur sine confessione, nec produntur sine confusione.

> [How disturbed and confused is the state of sin!
> How my sins tear my heart in pieces and divide it,
> gnaw at it and torment it.
> Because of these sins of mine, lady,
> I desire to come to you and be cured,
> but I flee from you for fear of being cursed.
> My sins cannot be cured unless they are confessed,
> but to acknowledge them throws me into confusion.][49]

The sinner's state is unending, full of flux and frenetic, but replete with fragmentation and stasis. Suffering from the fractured confusion of a heart torn to pieces, the narrator/reader/sinner desires both to step toward holiness and to flee from Mary but, inside the poem, goes nowhere. Anselm elsewhere exhibits a tendency to discount such movement, and by relation temporality, when explaining spiritual phenomena. In *De processione spiritus sancti*, for instance, he refutes the Greek Orthodox rejection of the Trinitarian *Filioque* clause, wherein the Holy Spirit is understood to proceed from both the Father and the Son. The Greek position, Anselm argues, misguidedly derives its conception of procession from a natural, linear, and necessarily temporal event, such as the flow of a river descending from its source. According to Anselm, such a natural process cannot be the basis for understanding the eternal procession of the Holy Spirit, which transcends temporality, but rather can only limit it.[50]

Such struggles between the step and the static reaffirms Anselm's own textual struggle between the temporal process of writing and transcendent *contemplatio*, and perhaps develops from his Neoplatonic understanding that human expression exists as a limited version of a higher form. Denying a beginning and end to texts reflects the belief that the divine *Verbum* is synonymous with God, who exists outside temporality, "always" lacking a beginning or end. In the *Monologion*, Anselm addresses the issue of the difference between the worldly language and the divine Word of God, and draws a sharp distinction between the *voces significative* that comprise human language and the *naturala verba* that are spoken or thought by God himself.[51] As God is independent of all matters of time, and exists as the one and universal Word from which all descends, Anselm proposes a function of reading that in its own limited capacity seeks the atemporal and thus aids in linking man and God through a hierarchy of language.

Anselm's three tiers of conceptual and representative language are well documented.[52] For humans, the relationship of sensible (external, linguistic) signs to natural (internal, universal) ones functions as a metaphor for understanding the highest form: divine language. All human creation works from these inner "mental texts," and in relation to God this inner language can become consubstantial with the essence of the Creator—in Brian Stock's phrase, "the expression of the supreme spirit is the spirit itself."[53] Anselm's devotional goal is a form of this final "linguistic" category, or what Gillian Evans has hypothesized constitutes "wordless prayer."[54] In his "Prayer for Enemies," Anselm himself details such expression:

> . . . ad quem invocandum non invenit os meum nomen quod sufficiat cordi meo. Nullum enim verbum hoc mihi sapit, quod te donante affectus meus de te capit. Oravi, domine, ut potui, sed plus volui quam potui.

> [My mouth cannot find any name in invocation
> that will satisfy my heart.
> For no words here have any taste to me
> when my love receives from you what you give.
> I have prayed, Lord, as I can,
> but I wish I could do more.][55]

To reach such a wordless state, Anselm proposes traversing the space between *signa voces* and *signa naturala*. But in the levels of prayer expressed in writing, the body itself also begins to constitute a form of obstructive media. In the prayer above, the gap between the mouth and the heart parallels the distance between technology and transcendence. Anselm here desires the transparency of spiritual communion (the heart) without the *ordo* and syntax of linguistic prayer, but is constantly aware of the shortcomings of his own medium of human expression (the mouth) as it works against that desire.

As Jesse Gellrich has shown, the idea of the book in the Middle Ages as a signifying system often functioned as "a metaphor for divinity: the entire preexistent 'totality' of God's plan was potential in [its] signifying means."[56] Following the scholastic model, medieval writers sought to approach as close to the divine boundary as possible through massive textual undertakings—*summae, operae, sententiae*. The purpose of such texts was to clarify the totality of the divine from the human side through a careful sequential itemization and argumentation of all aspects of an issue. As Gellrich explains,

> such treatises must be composed of adequate *articuli*, constituent "parts" or "members," and subdivided into finer elements; the pattern or ordo of the whole is preserved by proper comparisons, *similitudines*, and sufficient contrasts, *distinctiones*; the inclusion of precise diction, harmonious sentences, and rhyme will foster mnemonic devices for rapid memorization; finally the last item in an argument must affirm the *concordantia* of the whole, the principle that no contradictions remain as all opening objections are conclusively refuted.[57]

The *manifestatio* described by Gellrich sought to textualize all aspects of the universe within human reach, to clarify them by *ordo*, and to contain them within the physical boundaries of the manuscript. While these works serve as a metaphor for the totality of God, they also produce a concrete text to serve as a symbol of the foundational importance of writing and reason to spiritual knowledge, and imply that within the written lies the utmost limit of human knowledge of the divine. Such a belief echoes similar, if more subtle, beliefs engendered in scholarship through the systematic totality of print. [→12] In the *OsM*, Anselm avoids such epistemologies, choosing to approach divine totality not by imitating its form but by exploring how the divine operates beyond the temporal and sequential limits of the written word. What is at stake in such devotions is not a mode of production but a mode of information—instead of replicating the limitless *quantity* of God, Anselm's looser and liminal textuality, in effect, serves as a metaphor for the limitless *quality* of God. Though still in writing—the necessary medium of learning and devotion—Anselm's prayers operate not as an end but as a textual conduit, a map or, better, a *link* to text beyond logocentric texts. In short, as spiritual hypermedia.

HYPERTEXT AND VIRTUAL REALITY

In contrast to nonelectronic writing, a hypertext operates as, in Bolter's words, "a fragmentary and potential text, a series of self-contained units rather than an organic, developing whole."[58] For the reader, the text discovered becomes a notional rather than an actual one, as a physical product and its delineated discourse is replaced with the potential of a highly variable infrastructure where meaning resides in the contingency of the user's navigation between a few or some or, most rarely, all of the individual, hyperlinked lexia of text. [→99] To borrow Nicholas Negroponte's language, in hypertext, meaning is no longer encoded in physical matter but in digital bytes, and this shift away from the concrete correlates with a vastly more elastic system of information delivery.[59]

Negroponte, Bolter, and other theorists of digital media locate the difference between text and hypertext in the microcosmic shift between materiality and its lack; Anselm inversely bases the operation of his devotions on the universal transcendence of the divine over the earthly. But both approaches arrive at the same conclusion: that the linear manifestation of the written word shall (or at least should) be surpassed. In New Media studies, the perception of material difference between text and hypertext has also resulted in challenges to received understanding of the processes of reading and writing, as critics worry the definitions of these functions in light of the electronic age.[60] By analogy, the *OsM* differs from other meditative texts of its time in that it is not "material for reading which can thus become prayer" but is reading and prayer simultaneously.[61] The hybridity of Anselm's text and its presumptive distinction between writing and prayer is revealing. For Anselm, writing does not subsume prayer; it is an expressive medium that bridges to it. That is, prayer uses text, but, in modern terms, it functions as a discursive form that is arguably another type of "media" altogether.

Though hypertext is not linear in its operation, it does not do away with this aspect of printed texts, but instead repurposes it. The traditional linearity of text remains on the most basic level, as any exploration of a hypertext still relies in part on reading connected lexia of text. The remediating function of such hypermedia inevitably contains aspects of both transparent immediacy and hypermediacy.[62] [→8, 16] As a hypertextual expression, Anselm's *OsM* also remediates text in the pursuit of a higher and more contemplative mode of prayer. Importantly, the *OsM* also functions through and within a network of text, image, sound, and even other sensory perceptions. Rather like more recent forms of New Media, these writings seek to blend the "real world" of the individual user with a virtual one, distanced from but assembled out of a sensory palette. This immersive experience—whether a man playing a computer game or a monk reading *and* wordlessly praying—is one which in turn creates a new reality, "the reality of media."[63] This reality embodies the inherent contradiction of remediation, as the "other world" mediated through representative media necessarily also becomes a part of reality in its experiencing. [→117] In the *OsM*, notions of fragmentation, timelessness, and spacelessness function symptomatically as a remediated reality of human-divine interaction.

The remediation of real and virtual spaces in Anselm's devotional texts, and the issues of immediacy, transparent technology, and hypermediacy that it raises, are symptomatic of the main theological belief at the core of Anselmian devotion. The flexible textuality adumbrated in the preface to the *OsM* derives in part from the desire to step closer in *lectio divina* to the nature of the divine *Verbum*, which is expression without beginning or end and so differs greatly from the "real-time" process of human language and text. But in Anselm's Neoplatonic order of belief, what is really real can get a bit confusing. As Gregory Schufreider explains,

> what we at first thought was real, namely, the things themselves, assume the ontological status of images; as if what we ordinarily refer to as "reality" (*res ipsas*) were actually a "likeness" (*similitudo*) of something else.[64]

In Anselm's view, the highest form of reality is divine, and therefore timeless and spaceless. But, for the most part, written language remains the sole method of representing the really real, and so ends up mediating the divine through the human, or virtually real. For Schufreider, Anselm's discussions of the divine wholly collapse these poles:

> Anselm tends to want to have it all ways at once. In the case in point, he insists upon applying what would appear to be the ultimate, even if somewhat paradoxical, spatiotemporal features to this supreme being that would characterize his distinctive existence in terms of a certain

time-spacelessness whose abundance of space and time—we might almost say excessive spatiotemporality—would nonetheless allow one to claim that God exists "everywhere" (*ubique*) and "always" (*semper*).[65]

This is a complex and paradoxical ontology: Anselm's Neoplatonism reduces the "ordinary" real to the status of a "virtual" image; this reduction transforms the represented images of the divine in his writings to images within images. To overcome the limitations of his representations of divinity, then, Anselm injects them with an excessive temporality and spatiality, qualities that they cannot possess and yet also must, as representations of supreme forms, subsume. In his devotional theology, Anselm imagines the physical world in ways not unlike digital notions of virtual reality—compelling, yet ultimately artificed redactions of the "real" real. Immersed in the physical world, Anselm seeks through prayer and meditation a transparent, immediate immersion in the spiritual realm.

The desire for and potential effect of transparent technologies—for instance, the way a video game such as *Doom*, *Quake*, or *Myst* can become immersive and "suck you in"—rank among the most distinctive aspects and desired goals of digital multimedia.[66] So-called virtual reality, the technology of total visual immersion inside a digitally constructed world, joined with the capability of a controlled and roving point of view, may be considered both a new technological telos for digital media and a remediating force for older forms such as film.[67] [→118] In the logic of New Media evolution, the more immediate (or less mediated) the users believe their experiences to be—that is, the more forgotten the technology—then the more virtually real, and successful, the representation is. Of course, discussions of how a new media form's artificial representations of reality strive to approach the real and conceal the formative technology long predate digital media. They also recall the musings of Walter Benjamin on "new media" of the past, such as mechanical reproduction of photos and film, as well as debates about the contrived and mathematical representation of nature occasioned by the rise of perspectival painting in the Renaissance.[68] [→168]

Immersive digital media and Anselm's devotional literature also share overt strategies to deny the analytic distance and frame that exist between the user and the experience. Anselm, we have seen, struggled with hypermediacy in the sequential nature of text and its distanced, ratiocinated pedigree, while digital media must still contend with such obstacles as slow frame rates, compressed audio, variable bandwidth delivery, and, in true virtual-reality systems, bulky headgear and other "wearable" equipment. In the quest for transparency, both immersive forms result in what could be termed the anxiety of (hyper)immediacy.

The computer game *Riven*, the sequel to the wildly successful *Myst*, provides a good example of such anxiety.[69] The success of *Riven*, like *Myst* before it, depended on its ability to draw the user into an alternative world of photorealistic quality, wherein one navigates one's way through a series of environments. In playing these games, the user has a degree of operational freedom, with the ability to move right and left, backward and forward, and often also to look up and down, or to zoom in to closely examine objects or spaces. The games, with their goal of solving a series of complex abstract and spatial puzzles to answer a larger question about the history and fate of this alternative world, can become addictive—but only if the user succumbs to the illusion of the world and, in essence, begins to forget the mediating frame of the computer monitor. To achieve this, the game's designers have provided a careful set of technical and receptory calibrations. The first time the game is played, for instance, the program has the user run through a complicated routine to adjust the color, contrast, and brightness of the monitor and check the computer's audio output levels to ensure the most effective presentation possible of the multimedia content. More telling for the current discussion, however, is what the *Riven* development team writes in the opening of the user's manual, under the rubric "Message from the Creators":

> *Riven* was designed to be an immersive experience. So, shut the door, turn down the lights, turn up the sound, sit in a comfortable chair, and let your self be drawn into the world of *Riven*. And, for goodness sake, use a pair of headphones or a good pair of speakers![70]

This preface from "the Creators," with the anxiety of immediacy evident in its instructions, reads as a scion of Anselm's own instructions for the required immersion of divine meditation. Anselm's preface to the *OsM* also attempts to calibrate and carefully control the space and orientation of the reader *sive* meditator. The preface's instruction that the prayers not be read "in a place where there is noise, but in quiet" does not specifically describe the optimal space for prayer, but it does reveal this place's character as a space in transit between the external noises of the diurnal and the internal locus of divine conversation. The opening of the *Proslogion*, though, elaborates on such a space:

> Eia nunc homuncio, fuge paululum occupationes tuas, absconde te

modicum a tumultuosis cogitationibus tuis. Abjice nunc onerosas cu-
ras, et postpone laboriosas distensiones tuas. Vaca aliquantulum Deo, et
requiesce aliquantulum in eo. Intra in cubiculum mentis tuae; exclude
omnia praeter Deum, et quae te juvent ad quaerendum eum, et, clauso
ostio, quaere eum.

[Up now, little man—flee, for a little while, your occupations; hide
yourself, for a time, from your disturbing thoughts. Cast aside now your
burdensome cares, and put aside your toilsome business. Yield room for
some little time to God; and rest for a little time in him. Enter the inner
chamber of your mind; shut out all thoughts save that of God, and such
as can aid thee in seeking him; close thy door and seek him.][71]

The prefaces of *Riven* and Anselm both reference not one space but two: the
external room that literally surrounds the user/reader and the inner realm in
which that person will become immersed. [→159] Anselm, like *Riven*'s creators, instructs the reader to shut the door; the inner chamber (*cubiculum*)
he mentions conflates the private room of devotion—the place where one
shuts out everyday noise to begin the process of meditation—with the ultimate destination as the inner chamber of one's mind, a place that is actually
a nonplace.[72]

Not surprisingly, the prayers of the *OsM* also contain numerous poetic
images of inner space, mostly describing the supplicant's sinful state through
tropes of descent, burial, and confinement. In the "Prayer to St. John the Bap-
tist," for instance, the sinner finds himself unable to bear the "interior horror
of his face," trapped "by evil on every side"; in the second "Prayer to St. John
the Evangelist," the sinner begs from John entrance into "the wealthy chamber of your mind"; while in the "Prayer to St. Nicholas," the sinner describes
his inner state through a series of metaphors of spatial confinement: a metal
prison of iron, a precipice, a trench, an abyss.[73]

In video games, it is easy to lose oneself within the nonmaterial, nontem-
poral "space" of digital media, where "action follows upon action according
to an internal logic that seems to need no conscious intervention by the actor
. . . [where] there is little distinction between self and environment, between
stimulus and response, or between past, present and future."[74] Players of *Myst*,
Riven, and other games can attest that the experience of playing them becomes eerily immersive and begins to challenge normative notions of space
and time. Speaking from personal experience, I can securely report that in

playing *Myst*, one can explore late into the night, being only dimly aware (but at times much more anxious) of the time that is passing, and moving back and forth between the materiality of the playing space (chair, desk, computer) and the seemingly limitless realm of the internal landscape of the game. Of course, the spiritual devotions of Anselm generally possess more gravitas than the recreational diversions of a commercial computer game, even if both can result in one's staying up far past one's bedtime. Nonetheless, other connections between saint and gamer arise. Early on in his vita of Anselm, Eadmer notes that Anselm became so committed to spiritual exercises while at Bec that he attained a level of divine speculation that enabled him to unravel many obscure questions about God's divinity. Hence, one night as he lay in bed meditating on how prophets could see the past and future as the present, and convincingly set such temporal collapses down in speech or writing, Anselm suddenly found he had the power to see through walls:

> Et ecce cum in his totus esset, et ea intelligere magnopere desideraret defixis oculorum suorum radiis vidit per medias maceries oratorii ac dormitorii monachos quoroum hoc officium erat pro apparatu matutinarum altare et alia loca aecclesiae circumeuntes, luminaria accendentes, at ad ultimum unum eorum sumpta in manibus corda pro excitandis fratribus schillam pulsantem. Ad cujus sonitum conventu fratrum de lectis surgente miratus est de re quae acciderat.

> [And behold, while he was thus absorbed and striving with all his might to understand this problem, he fixed his eyes on the wall and—right through the masonry of the church and dormitory—he saw the monks whose office it was to prepare for matins going about the altar and other parts of the church lighting candles; and finally he saw one of them take in his hands the bell rope and sound the bell to awaken the brethren. At this sound the whole community rose from their beds, and Anselm was astonished at the thing which had happened.][75]

Anselm, meditating upon the ability of the prophets to transcend temporality and to preserve this transcendence in oral or written text, achieves a similar, if temporary, power over the physical barriers of his immediate monastic space. His own divine speculation remediates his enclosed room of meditation, and enables movement beyond material walls (and by implication material texts). His ability to make walls transparent, however, never goes beyond his own "real" monastic enclosure—he views his fellow monks still within their spaces in the church and in their cells, preparing for the canonical hour of lauds. Though through his meditation Anselm restructures the way physical space and time is viewed, these earthly limits likewise inform and re-form and circumscribe his exploration of divine mysteries.

According to Eadmer, Anselm had a second monastic vision that expanded upon the fluidity of space in the devotional experience, and upon the remediating relationship of real walls and divine spaces. [→160] Eadmer reports that during the time Anselm was composing the *Proslogion*, the monk labored to have his whole mind set on the contempt of this world ("totam suae mentis intentionem in contemptum mundi") and his whole desire fixed only on those things that are of God. With his thoughts so focused, Anselm fell into a state Eadmer describes as *per mentis excessum raptus* [beyond the mind] and experienced a series of visions.[76] After viewing a swift-moving, filth-strewn, and turbulent river that swept along both rich and poor alike, symbolic of the torrent of earthly values that can carry men away, Anselm is asked if he wishes to see what it is to be truly monastic ("verus monachatus"). Assenting, Anselm is led to a place "quasi in conseptum cujusdam magni et ampli claustri" [as if into the enclosure of a great and spacious cloister] and ordered to look all around. Gazing about, Anselm sees the walls of the cloister covered with the most pure and brilliant silver. In the middle of the space he finds grass fresh and silvery, delightful beyond human belief ("ultra humanam opinionem"), which bends and spring backs "more alterius herbae"—just like the other (that is, earthly) grass.

Anselm immerses himself in the space of his vision. Unlike the filthy, and linear, river of the worldly, which Anselm in his *contemptum mundi* views from a distance, the ideal space of monastic existence surrounds him. Anselm stands at the center of this space, circumscribed by his vision, scanning it from a 360-degree perspective, possessed of a full range of perceptual movement similar to that sought after in immersive digital media. The world of Anselm's vision is somewhat paradoxical: it is an enclosure within a cloister, yet is "great and spacious." But though this virtual world is formed *per mentis excessum*, it in turn remains enclosed by the structures of real world—the silvery walls are like those of a cloister, and grass is defined by its comparison to actual grass.

Both this vision and the one previously described show how Anselm's glimpses of the divine are remediated through the interaction of real and virtual spaces. In the first devotional vision, real walls lose their substance as the real space of the monastic dormitory dissolves in the inner contemplation of divine mysteries. In the second, the relationship reverses, as the ideal of monasticism is revealed through the virtual space of a monastery cloister with lifelike grass and enclosed in silver-plated walls. In both, however, the importance of space is clear. The rendering of real space transparent in the quest for the inner *cubiculum* of the divine discourse remains a key aspect of Anselm's devotion, as evidenced both in his preface to the *OsM* and in his visions. While this collection of prayers is never supposed to allow its readers to escape earthly existence—every single piece reminds them over and over again of their earthly state of sin and failure—it does wish to usher those readers into an unearthly state in which higher understanding may be attained. However, this inner mental state, cast by Anselm as a divine space, must be received through the material and hypermediate frames Anselm wishes to forgo—the presence of writing, the act of reading, the physical space that contains the reader. As a result, representations of virtual spaces found within Anselm's writings and visions themselves reveal how the desire for transparency never fully escapes the hypermediacy of writing and, indeed, of the physical world. Like digital programs that construct virtual realities out of prior media—photos, recorded sound, text, film—Anselm's inner space of devotion likewise derives from, and yet attempts to suppress/surpass, the written medium that represents it, along with the physical space that contains it.[77]

HYPERMEDIA

New Media theorists are quite fond of pointing out that medieval manuscripts configured text and image into spatial networks second in complexity only to recent iterations of electronic media. [→35] The close integration of text and image on the illuminated page in medieval manuscripts creates a hybrid discourse rarely found in printed texts.[78] Though modern discussions of the *OsM* rarely mention them, most early *OsM* manuscripts contain numerous illuminations to accompany specific pieces. Indeed, as Otto Pächt has argued, it is possible that Anselm himself designed his prayer collection for Matilda of Tuscany to be illustrated.[79]

In early illuminated manuscripts of Anselm's devotional discourse, the collaboration of the technologies of word and image produced a textuality analogous to that now found in digital discourse. MS Bodleian Auct. D.2.6., commonly referred to as the Littlemore Anselm, contains an illuminated copy of the *OsM* written in the mid-twelfth century, some thirty or forty years after

Anselm's death. Pächt has demonstrated, principally on the evidence of its illuminations, that this copy derives from the illustrated exemplar, no longer extant, that Anselm had sent to Matilda. Outside of Pächt's use of them to establish provenance and influence, the images in the Littlemore Anselm have received little notice in Anselm studies. But these illuminations, all initials, are notable for their permeable borders between word and image (see figure 4). As with many medieval illuminations, their shapes resist regularity or standardization; architectural details, human figures, and decorative gestures frequently jut out at odd angles from the main image, forcing the text into visual contours and detours disconcerting to the modern eye. Boundaries between word and image at times nearly disappear as the edges of images clip and cut the beginnings of words placed next to them.

George Landow observes that hypertext systems, particularly those that integrate text and images, by "weakening or reconfiguring the boundaries among them" result in "an open, open-bordered text, a text that cannot shut out other texts."[80] The Littlemore Anselm similarly evokes such ideas in its close interaction of text and image on the manuscript page, and the manner in which (at least in strategies of meditation) the boundaries of the written word are broken open by it. In the manuscript, the letters of the initials function architecturally, creating enclosing spaces to house the images of figures closely tied to the particular prayers they begin. Further, like Anselm's devotional textuality, and his "virtual" visions, these letters become the occasion for the representation of both inclusive and exclusive spaces. Frequently the contour of the initial serves to separate scenes from each other or, more tellingly, to separate divine figures from human ones. The illuminated "S" that begins the Littlemore copy of Anselm's "Prayer to St. Peter" stands as a case in point (see figure 5). The illustration actually consists of two scenes: on the left, under a set of church spires and Romanesque arches, Christ hands the keys of heaven to St. Peter; the initial is attached to the right of this structure, Peter occupying the top curve, keys in hand, while below in the lower curve four naked figures look up, hands clasped in prayer.

Pächt's caption to this scene, "St. Peter Receiving Souls into Heaven," is not quite accurate.[81] The hierarchy set in place by the spatial text—Peter above, souls below—makes it clear that the souls have not quite completed their divine journey. Anselm's prayer mentions the opening of heaven only at the very end of the prayer, and then only as a desire, not an event. Rather, the image appears to support the scenario that opens and constitutes the bulk of the prayer

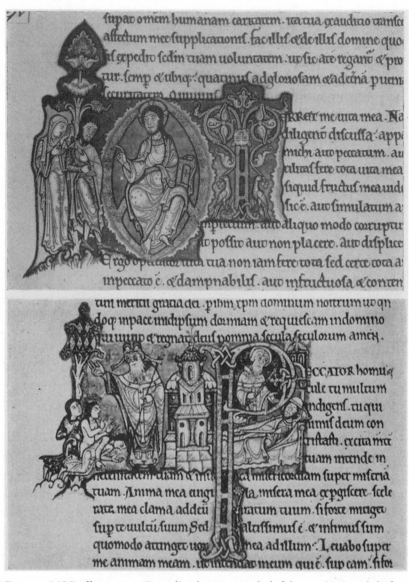

Figure 4. MS Bodleian Auct. D.2.6 (Littlemore Anselm), fol. 189v, "A Couple before Christ," and fol. 180v, "The Legend of St. Nicholas." By permission of the Bodleian Library, University of Oxford.

Figure 5. MS Bodleian Auct. D.2.6 (Littlemore Anselm), fol. 169r, "Christ Giving Peter the Keys to Heaven; Souls Approaching Peter in Heaven." By permission of the Bodleian Library, University of Oxford.

it illustrates: the sinner's call to Peter to send spiritual succor down from on high:

> . . . miserabiliter indigeo auxilio tuae benignae potentiae, sed nec os meum habet verba, quibus necessitatem meam sicut ipsa est exprimat, nec cor meum habet devotionem, quae de tam infimo ad tuam tantam sublimitatem attingat. . . . O magne PETRE, si clamor tribulationis meae non ascendit usque ad te, respectus tuae pietatis descendat usque ad me.

> [In my misery I need the help of your power and kindness,
> but my mouth has no words to translate my actual need,
> nor does my mind have enough devotion to reach
> from such a depth as mine to such a height as yours. . . .
> O great PETER, if the cry of my trouble does not rise up to you,
> let the care of your goodness descend to me.][82]

The image, then, reaffirms the separation of saint and supplicant, here paradoxically expressed in writing as a lack of words ("nec os meum habet verba") as well as devotion. But it also reinforces the mission of Anselm's prayers to nevertheless establish a devotional conversation across this boundary of the human and the divine. In the opening of this prayer, Anselm repeats the twin themes of expressive and devotional lack, emphasizing the distracted state of the sinful reader:

> . . . nec torporis sui tenebras quas contraxit de sordibus peccatorum suorum potest erumpere, nec in eadem intentione diutius valet consistere.
> . . . Quis ergo subveniet misero, qui nec valet exhibere tribulati vocem nec dolentis mentem?

> [Because of the sordidness of my sins,
> I do not have the strength
> to remain for long in this exertion (of the mind). . . .
> Who is there to help a wretch
> who has not the strength to voice his trouble,
> or express the sorrow of his mind?][83]

Images such as the illuminated "S" relate to both reader and represented sinner, providing visual (non-textual) support for a potentially distracted reader's devotional goals. The conflation of image and text within the illuminated initial, in addition to the overlapping quality of the general layout, blurs the boundaries of the physical text and reifies the devotional *telos* of finding the open, borderless text of divine conversation where "the strength to express trouble in words" is no longer necessary.

While the illustrated Littlemore Anselm offers evidence of such virtual desire and effort, it also discovers the self-referential contradictions that arise from remediation. As multimedia geared to spiritual communion, the manuscript is also a material object that hinders attempts to move beyond its limits. Take, as example, the initial of St. Peter in figure 5. The curve of the letter "S" imposes a solid band between the figures and evokes both the help and the hindrance that the written word brings to such devotion. At the same time, the pictorial representation of the letter and its participation in a literally "wordless" visual scene of communication liminally constructs the "S" as not quite text, but not quite nontext. This struggle between the hypermediacy of text and the transparency of desired devotion is precisely what informs Anselm's prefatory comments to his collections, and their manipulation of the media boundaries between text and image. Both devotional strategies seek to remediate the linear operation of the written text. Change the operational logic of the written word, and you move one rung closer to the higher form of the divine *Verbum*.

Though, unlike current digital hypermedia, the technological limits of the late eleventh century prohibited the manifest inclusion of any other media besides the written word and drawn image, the *OsM* nevertheless should be understood as gesturing toward the full range of sensory elements in its execution. Sound, in particular, plays an important role in the formation and reception of Anselm's less ratiocinated writings. While the preface to the *OsM* signals at its beginning the importance of reading "non . . . in tumultu, sed in quiete," this caution should not be understood as demanding the exclusion of all sound in the act of *lectio divina*. Though private reading has of course long since become a mostly silent event, medieval reading, especially prayer was an oral affair; at least four early manuscripts of the *OsM*, including the Littlemore Anselm, have been carefully punctuated for reading aloud.[84] In shutting out the tumult, Anselm seeks quiet as the proper setting to ensure the proper sounds of devotion, which range from voiced reading to inarticulate weeping.

Evidence of Anselm's concern with the sounds of devotional reading is also found in the very title of the collection, culled by editors from the opening of Anselm's letter to Matilda: *Orationes sive meditationes*. *Orationes*, of course, though usually rendered by modern translators as "prayers," has equally strong roots in the orality of "oration" and the long tradition of spoken prayer. The title itself embodies a certain expressive fluidity regarding the nature of the devotions that traverses the full range of teleological steps toward a conversation with God. Editors have been quick to read the opening phrase as a classification. The writings contained within are therefore formally categorized as either a prayer or a meditation, an approach that unintentionally implies these categories are exclusive, and dictates our fundamental understanding of the collection as nineteen prayers followed by three meditations. But the translation of the title as "Prayers and Meditations" is not exactly accurate, and the conjunction *sive* invites a different interpretation. *Sive*, usually translated as "or" (not "and") with shadings of "whether" or "if," connotes a less assured division between the forms it conjoins. As "Prayers *or* Meditations," Anselm's description stresses not the separate but the dual nature of each text: prayers that lead to higher meditation. Additionally, what should be considered the fuller description of the texts, "orationes sive meditationes quae subscriptae sunt," encapsulates a bridge from the earthly to the divine that begins not in writing but in a form of prayer injected with the sense of the oral or spoken (*orationes*). Writing (*quae subscriptae sunt*) remains only as the medium of representation, the site that mediates *orationes* into *meditationes*.

As Brian Stock has argued, Anselm himself viewed his paragraphic texts as reductive forms of mental and/or actual conversations, asserted the superiority of the oral mode, and viewed speaking as "literacy at the highest level."[85] Such privileging of the oral is readily found in early works such the *Monologion*, already mentioned as possessing devotional and rational aspects. The prologue to the text famously begins:

> Quidam fratres saepe me studioseque precati sunt, ut quaedam, quae illis de meditanda divinitatis essentia et quibusdam aliis huiusmodi meditationi cohaerentibus usitato sermone colloquendo protuleram, sub quodam eis meditationis exemplo describerem. Cuius scilicet scribendae meditationis magis secundum suam voluntatem quam secundum rei facilitatem aut meam possibilitatem . . .

> [Certain brothers have often and eagerly urged me to put down in writing some thoughts about meditating on the nature of divinity I have proposed in familiar conversations with them, as well as some other matters related to such meditation, by way of an example of that medi-

tation. It is more in accord with their wish than with the ease of the task or my abilities . . .][86]

In Stock's view, though the written form provides a certain utility of recording, Anselm agrees to the task somewhat unwillingly. His prologue, additionally, "implicitly elevates the interior dialogue over the written product," as the reductive "text produced can never fully recapture the vitality of the original processes of reasoning."[87] In a classic, Phaedrus-like approach, Anselm here views the spoken dialogue as more immediate, natural, and, a priori, closer to the desired mental text that constitutes true meditation. As Anselm develops as part of his discussion later in the *Monologion*, it is the internal *locutio* of what Schufreider translates as "sign-sounds" that moves the expression of an idea or thing closer to its "true" form.[88] Writing, an external image of sign sounds, can mediate—or, more accurately, remediate—the process of meditation for a wider audience, but it cannot be as subtle, or as transparent, as either instructional conversations or actual private prayer.[89]

In contemporary discussions of hypertext, similar aspects of orality within writing may occur. Commenting on the linear structures engendered by traditional forms of writing, Bolter notes that the process of this writing "is an attempt to impose order on verbal ideas that are always prone to subvert that order," and that these ideas form "texts-behind-the-text."[90] New Media provides a more ready access to these underlying "verbal ideas" because such systems likewise resist the linearity and hierarchy of writing. Walter Ong has defined such ideas as the "secondary orality" of electronic communication, which shares a number of attributes with "primary" orality. At the same time, though, this new form "is essentially a more deliberate and self-conscious orality, based permanently on the use of writing and print."[91] Writing came before and was the recirculated foundation of the quasi-oral expressions of New Media; in Anselm's *OsM* we again find secondary orality, and though it seeks to depart from writing, writing still remediates it.

The *OsM*'s recursive filtering of written oral and visual discourses through each other is in turn supported by the collection's emphasis on sensory and affective treatment of the word. As their preface states, the devotional exercises aim most immediately at "exitandam legentis mentem" [exciting the reader's mind]—a mandate repeated in the title of the first chapter of the *Proslogion*.[92] As Southern notes, Anselm believed that the senses "give the mind access to these great realities beyond the senses" and have "a mediating role in leading the mind from earthly things to the knowledge of God," a good explanation for why the saint departed from devotional literary tradition and injected so much descriptive elaboration into his prayers.[93] In the "Prayer to St. Stephen," for instance, Anselm's description of divine text gestures toward the immersive as it expands the text's sensory range to encompass tropes of sight, smell, physical dimension, touch, and sound as well:

> . . . plus videndo plus fulgescit, omni modo tractatum semper ad delectationem crescit. Formam gerit fidei, soliditatem habet patientiae. Simplictatis puritate nitet, benignitatis colore lucet. Caritatem sapit, pietatem olet. Tactu reddit mansuetudinem, sono repraesentat misericordiam.

> [The more this word is seen, the brighter it looks.
> In whatever way one examines it,
> it always grows in delight.
> It carries the form of faith,
> it has the solidity of patience,
> it shines with the purity of simpleness,
> it glows with the colour of kindness,
> its taste is charity, its smell is goodness;
> touched, it gives back gentleness;
> sounded, it responds to mercy.][94]

Similarly, in the "Prayer to St. John the Evangelist," the supplicant desires the meditative text to become wholly ocular in quality:

> Ecce, iubens et habens et coram illo indigens invicem sese aspiciunt. Si igitur, domine, visio tua plus est pia quam oratio mea devota, visio tua sit oratio mea.

> [Behold, here is the one who teaches and possesses,
> in the presence of the one who is in need,
> and they gaze at each other.
> If then, Lord, your gaze has more piety in it
> than my prayer has devotion,
> let your gaze become my prayer.][95]

Here the written prayer envisions the moment of the divine-human gaze as one that will supplant the written and/or spoken devotion. As text, the divine gaze is immediately contained not only by the act of its writing but by a rare citational allusion:

> Non enim scripsisti: "Si quis videns fratrem orare clauserit viscera sua," sed: "Si videns fratrem necessitatem habere." Age ergo, domine, vide necessitatem meam, immo ecce vides eam.
>
> [For you have not written
> "If any see his brother have need and praying,
> and shuts his heart against him,"
> but "If any sees his brother have need!"
> Act, then, sir, seeing my need; for indeed you see just that.][96]

Inside this prayer, the border between the specular and the textual collapses, not unlike the collapse between text and image illustrated in the initials of the Littlemore Anselm. "The Prayer to Saint John," ironically, likely derives from the second and third epistles of John, both of which close with a written refusal to write things that could better be expressed face to face.[97]

Through various integrations of the graphic, the oral, the written, and the sensory, both the *OsM*'s content and its material form promote a higher kind of "text" in the divine realm. Anselm's anticipated transcendence remains constrained by the technical limits of multimedia in the medieval manuscript, but nevertheless rejects its limits. This remediating relationship inevitably results in hypermediacy, while the conviction remains that the immersive experience of this representation of *lectio divina* would inspire true revelation. In the ideal act of devotion, no distinction between the representation of divine *discussus* and the reality of God's presence survives; in the language of Grusin and Bolter, the presence of the medium becomes forgotten, the presence of the represented objects becomes immediate, and the mechanisms of the media employed turn transparent. The virtual reality of prayer becomes virtually real—or, to return to Schufreider's comment, it is for Anselm "as if what we ordinarily refer to as 'reality' (*res ipsas*) were actually a 'likeness' (*similitudo*) of something else."

This belief that what is real is a representation, and what is represented can lead to a higher reality, drives Anselm to push against the technical boundaries of his text. In the *OsM*, Anselm combines aspects of different media to permit access to a higher expression, and an understanding of a higher reality. To this end, he also manipulates notions of real and virtual spaces in his text and visions. The remediating properties of these expressions also illustrate the difficulties of using material practices and representations as a stepping-stone to the spiritual. But in Anselm's ontological structure, the remediation of media and space in his devotional expressions would not remain a paradox. Instead, the desire for devotional immediacy, the obstructive nature of the media used, and the irreconcilable tension between the transparent and the hypermediate would, arguably, fit neatly into Anselm's ontology. For in his discursive struggle to understand, explain, and represent the divine within the limits of human expression, Anselm in the end remediates the real to achieve his goals. As in his famous ontological proof, here the limits and problems found within human expression, and the haphazard and faulty manner in which they try to fathom the divine, would only prove to Anselm its existence.

POST-SCRIPT: ANSELM AFTER ANSELM

Anselm's struggle with traditional textuality and his attempts to fashion an alternative serve as a useful blueprint for his own subsequent critical reception. The quality of Anselm's more devotional writings (sharply) contrasts with his authorial reputation, which at times approaches that of a latter-day patristic infused with the logic of the Enlightenment. Anselm, though, appears to have worked to suppress the textual dissemination of his name and the concomitant authorial status. As archbishop, Anselm ordered his biographer Eadmer to destroy the vita of him that Eadmer had nearly completed, "judging himself unworthy of any such literary monument to posterity."[98] This denial of his literary worth may also be found, ironically, in the preface to his most famous work, the *Proslogion*, where, discussing it and his previous *Monologion*, he writes: "it does not seem to me that either this work or the one I mentioned before deserves to be called a book or to bear the name of its author."[99]

Avoiding *auctoritas* corresponds to the *OsM*'s stated desire to avoid traditional textuality. As Anselm makes clear in his preface, the written prayers are only starting points, designed to inspire the reader toward his or her own prayers, or even wordless devotion.[100] In these writings at least, Anselm regards himself less as an author than as the enabler of other authors, the readers. Even the reader's *auctoritas* is fleeting, though, as Anselm's ultimate devotional goal is not for the readers to fashion text but to lose themselves in textless devotion. As a hypertextual author, Anselm acts more as the architect of a database than as the creator of a narrative; much like the authors of recent hypertext fiction, he constructs a textual network within which a reader makes his own textual choices, and obtains meaning through them. [→99] Anselm, it turns out, rejects the notion of authorial control—indeed, he openly encourages the loss of control, both of his authoritative status and of his reader's reception of his written text.[101] [→91]

In the Middle Ages, Anselm's name became famous more from his prayer collections than from any of his scholastic texts.[102] But this later authorial reputation actually had little to do with his own writings or textual models as he conceived them. Rather, Anselm's *auctoritas* came to rest upon the imitations of other writers, and upon corrupt and inaccurate applications of his model of devotional reading, before being ultimately evaluated and defined by the new scholasticism of print culture. In both medieval and (post)modern treatments, Anselm and his works fell more and more under the regard of the sequential and the logical, leaving behind most, if not all, of his "other" textuality.

The Medieval Anselm

For a short time after Anselm's death, his prayers were collected and used within a manuscript tradition following an older Carolingian model that anthologized prayers anonymously, and without prefaces or titles.[103] At the same time, a new type of devotional anthology developed around Anselm that preserved his authorial attribution as well as his prefatory materials. This was in part due, no doubt, to the stylistic and affective changes that Anselm helped develop and popularize. After Anselm, a number of imitators copied his devotional innovations, beginning with his biographer Eadmer and then Ralph of Battle.[104]

Because these later writings were Anselmian in character if not in quality, they were often silently incorporated into collections and attributed to Anselm.[105] As noted earlier, by the seventeenth century, 111 prayers and mediations were believed to have been written by Anselm, a considerable increase from the 22 pieces securely established as his.[106] Anselm's own redactions of his prayers, unfixed in form and lacking any programmatic cohesion, made it easier for a wide number of imitators to be interpolated into versions of the *OsM*.[107] Within such a burgeoning apocryphal tradition, Anselm ceases to function as a specific, individual author, as his growing "author function" attracts texts he could not, and perhaps would not, write.[108] In each manuscript collection of Anselmian prayers, the name of Anselm becomes literally the nominal head of a literary network of collaborative authorship. This networked collaboration then takes on extratextual dimensions in the compilation, copying, and transmission of these interpolated collections into other collections, with or without ascription to Anselm.

As the Middle Ages progressed, and the authority of Anselm gathered more and more works under its aegis, Anselm's textual model became appropriated and diluted by an increasing number of other writers and deployed for purposes further and further from his stated intent.[109] *A Talkyng of the Love of God* (hereafter *Talkyng*), a mid-fourteenth-century devotional text written in the Middle English vernacular of the West Midlands, provides a particularly good example.[110] The text is primarily a conflation of two earlier meditations written for anchoresses, augmented by borrowings from and translations of other affective texts, including the *OsM*. *Talkyng*, in fact, opens with a paraphrastic translation of Anselm's preface to Matilda:

> This treatise is a talkyng of the love of God, and is mad for to sturen hem that hit reden to love him the more, and to fynde lyking, and to tast in his love. Hit falleth for to reden hit esyliche and soft, so as men may mest in inward felyng and deplich thenkyng savour fynden. And that not beo dene, but biginnen and leten in what paas so men seoth that may for the tyme yiven mest lykynge. And whon men hath conceyved the maters with redyng, inward thenkyng, and deoplich sechyng, without eny redynge uppon the selve maters, and of such othere that God wol senden—hose wole sechen, schal given inward sight and felyng in soule, and swetnes wonderful, yif preyre folwe.[111]

This prologue contains much taken directly from Anselm: the goal of exciting (*sturen*) the reader to a higher contemplative state, the need to read slowly and in quiet (*esyliche and soft*), and especially the explicit rejection of beginnings and endings (*beginnen and leten in what paas . . .*). However, while both introductions focus on the affective goals of the reader, the aim of *Talkyng* differs in small but strategic ways. Anselm's original model emphasizes that the reader should read only enough to be led to prayer, while the author of *Talkyng* stresses that the reading selections should hinge upon how they give pleasure (*mest likynge*) and hold the reader's interest.[112] To facilitate such reading, the preface to *Talkyng* substitutes punctuation for Anselm's structural innovations, noting only at the end of the preface that, "to beo more lovesum," the work has been "riht poynted." The swapping of *paragraphis* for *poynts* highlights the structural differences between the two works; *Talkyng* does not consist of paragraph-like lexia, but rather is a long, tripartite passage of rhythmic and partially rhymed prose that rarely acknowledges its divisions or sources.

The author of *Talkyng* chooses to emphasize only one aspect of Anselmian devotion: the sensory appeal to the emotions of the reader.[113] By doing so, he reveals "a wide difference between the 'inward feeling' of *Talkyng* and the 'deep thinking' of Anselm."[114] When one considers the manuscript context of the surviving copies of *Talkyng*, this singular emphasis on the pleasure of reading takes on a significance that moves the debate far from Anselm's original focus. As Derek Pearsall has shown, the two manuscripts containing versions of *Talkyng* were likely highly politicized compilations, and probably connected to the Lollard controversies over the right to read theology in the vernacular, as well as such readers' ability to understand true theological doctrine.[115]

If the prologue to *Talkyng* charts a shift in Anselmian devotional models toward the inner pleasure of the reader, the prologue to the early-fifteenth-century *Orcherd of Syon* (hereafter *Orcherd*) dispenses with notions of any experience outside the text altogether. The work, a Middle English translation of a Latin translation of Catherine of Sienna's *Dialogues*, was written for the nuns at the convent of Syon.[116] In the preface, the translator presents a unique structural conceit that constructs Catherine's dialogues as a textual orchard:

> In this orcherd, whanne ye wolen be conforted, ye mowe walk and se bothe fruyt and herbis. . . . religious sustren, in this goostli orcherd at resonable tyme ordeyned I wole that ye disporte you and walke about where ye wolen with youre mynde and resoun in what aleye ye wole of XXXV aleyes where ye wolen walke, that is to seye of XXXV chapitres, o tyme in oon, anothir tyme in anothir. But first my counceil is clerely to assaye and serche the hool orcherd and taste of sich fruyt and herbis resonably aftir youre affeccioun, and what you liketh best, aftirward chewe it wel and ete thereof for heelthe of youre soul.[117]

The translator then lays out a *kalender*, a table of contents describing the seven parts and five sections contained within each part (the thirty-five *aleyes* that readers may wander down). The textual structure here presented does descend from the original Anselmian model, but has wandered far from its point of origin. This modified model, however, also highlights other aspects of hypertextuality than we found in the *OsM*. Here the emphasis is placed even more on the writerly act of reading—the reader does not read to be transported to the discourse of the divine, but simply to fulfill an individual purpose. The translator's scheme also makes explicit the divagational manner in which this text is to be explored: "one tyme in oon, anothir tyme in anothir." Though the translator advises the reader to survey the whole textual orchard, the structure welcomes a nonsequential exploration of the text; the order in which such a survey is to be made is left open, as are the process and goals of the reading. The instructions regarding the process of reading is that the reader should return to different sections at different times, depending upon her *lyke*.

More dramatic, however, is the *Orcherd*'s overt spatialization of its textual material. [→96] *Orcherd* provides two spatial approaches to its material, one metaphoric and one literal. The visual conceit of the textual orchard provides a basis for the nonlinear approach the reader should take to the work. The *kalender*, with its thirty-five précis of different sections of Catherine's dialogues, provides a method by which one may take advantage of the nonsequential potential of the codex by jumping to the desired section of the text, much the same way scholars make use of a book's index when returning to (or finding) a relevant passage for citation in a study. In the evolution of Anselmian texts, the *Orcherd of Syon* falls somewhere between the original eleventh-century hypertextual impulses and the realization of actual hypertexts a full millennium later. Still constrained by the visual and physical frame of the page, *Orcherd* nevertheless moves toward the writerly and multisequential dynamics of the hypertextual discourse. [99]

Other late medieval uses of Anselmian models of devotion, however, perform exactly the opposite function, reining in the hypertextual in favor of a model of reading that presages the dominance of the sequential in print culture. The Middle English translation of the *Pseudo-Augustinian Soliloquies*, for instance, provides an accurate paraphrase of Anselm's original preface in its prologue, but its inclusion is somewhat suspect.[118] The material of the *Soliloquies* is actually designed for concentrated intellectual study, and demands for the most part a rigorous attention to sequence and detail. The Anselmian preface, inserted by the Middle English reviser, was likely a spurious addition designed to normalize this text for an audience of nuns typically instructed to approach *lectio divina* affectively, not intellectually. Meanwhile, fourteenth- and fifteenth-century texts like the *Cloud of Unknowing* and Julian of Norwich's *A Revelation of Love* contain explanatory materials that provide reactionary reading models that include but carefully reverse the Anselmian model and attempt to ensure that the reader will read each work in a careful, orderly process. Consider the "Anselmian" prologue to the *Cloud of Unknowing*:

And over this, I charge thee and I beseche thee bi the autorite of charite that yif any soche schal rede it, write it or speke it, or elles here it be red or spokin, that thou charge hem as I do thee for to take hem tyme to rede it, speke it, write it, or here it al over. For paraventure ther is som mater therin, in the beginnyng or in the middel, the whiche is hanging and not fully declared ther it standeth—and yif it be not there, it is sone after or elles in the ende. Wherfore yif a man saw o mater and not another, paraventure he might lightly be led into errour. And therefore, in eschewing of this errour bothe in thiself and in alle other I preye thee par charite do as I sey thee.[119]

Here readers, encouraged to "take hem tyme to rede it, speke it, write it, or here it al over," should read the work comprehensively and continuously, as the sections (beginning, middle, end) do not stand as fragmented *paragraphis* but rather logical sequences to be carefully adhered to and *followed*.

(Post)Modern Anselm: The Effect of Print

Through the *compilatio* of medieval manuscript tradition, Anselm became a spiritual author in name, if not necessarily always in genuine product; through the appropriation of and reaction to his model of devotional reading, he also became something of a literary figure. After the Middle Ages, however, his reputation as a philosophical author all but replaced these earlier notions. With the advent of the Enlightenment, Anselm's ontological proof of God became a veritable cottage industry, and occasioned commentaries by Spinoza, Descartes, Locke, Leibniz, Hegel, and, most famously, Kant.[120] True to the accretive process of print culture, scholarship then sired a flourishing industry in metacommentaries, as more than five hundred scholarly commentaries of such seventeenth-, eighteenth-, and nineteenth-century commentaries on Anselm have been published.[121] [→16] By the nineteenth century, and largely on the strength of his ontological proof, Anselm had risen to a place of primacy in Western thought, viewed as "the pivotal thinker in medieval philosophy . . . both the heir of Augustine and the 'father of Scholasticism,' whose own favorite son is Thomas Aquinas."[122]

In medieval manuscript culture, Anselm's sensory spirituality and alternative modes of reading thrived, but the modern print-driven intellectual culture of the "new scholasticism" championed Anselm's logical treatises. Not surprisingly, the emphasis on the sequential, scholastic aspects of Anselm's thought has flourished even more in the university setting, where the rational inheritance of scholasticism and the Enlightenment predominates.[123] Medieval scholastics such as the *moderni* and the Thomists "conventionalized the themes, plot and shapes of books in a truly rigorous way, as they also structured syllabuses, scripture and debate."[124] Though these scholastics later resisted the advent of print longer than most, the rigid and systemic nature of their ideas and texts also prefigured what print culture and its principal mode of analysis, literary scholarship, has long stressed: order and unity. [→24]

In the twentieth century, what scholarship on Anselm's devotional writing there is has centered almost completely on such issues. André Wilmart's early preoccupation with distilling the true works of Anselm from the amassed tradition of centuries of false attribution exactly matches the trend of stemmatic and best-text editorial studies that to this day dominate medieval editing practices. [→18] F. S. Schmitt continued this purification with his 1943 edition, with scholarly apparatus for the nineteen prayers and three mediations. Schmitt edited the prayers as part of his Herculean effort to edit all of Anselm's work, an effort reminiscent of the summae of the medieval scholastics. Benedicta Ward completed the scholarly cycle with her 1973 translation of the *OsM*. Published by Penguin, this work made Anselm's devotional writings accessible to the modern reading public at large.

Unwittingly, the efforts of Wilmart, Schmitt, and Ward echo the medieval tradition of creating false texts around Anselm. The modern *OsM* constitutes a wholly artificial collection of devotional writings: though Anselm may have indeed written every one of them, they never all appear together, in this order, in any medieval manuscript.[125] [→19] Ward's translation, following the plan of Schmitt's edition, also consolidates and reduces the dense medieval network of innovative textual practices, integrated multimedia, and subsequent transmissions of *compilatio* and *inventio* into a single, standard, and unified expression of print.

In an editorial project informed and ordered by formalist principles, it becomes natural to then find and focus on the development and movement of themes across the collection—my current study certainly practices the same critical approach. In her substantial introduction to the translation, Ward identifies a number of such formal concerns, studying, for instance, the development of Anselm's prayer to Mary over its three versions, arguing that the two prayers to John the Evangelist form a diptych of balanced discussions of fear and love, and hypothesizing that the prayers for friends and enemies may at one time have been joined together, as may have been the first and second meditations.[126] In her discussion of the "Prayer to St. Paul," Ward similarly argues that the text "falls clearly into two parts, the first doctrinal, the second more personal."[127] For Ward, the importance of formal principles in reading Anselm carries through to the level of Anselm's polished rhetorical phrases; she notes that written words "are for him, as for the whole monastic school of *grammatica*, an expression of inner coherence, and their order and balance are vital to his meaning."[128]

Ward is surely correct in such holistic readings; anyone would have a hard time refuting the poetic skill of Anselm's Latin phrasings, or the balanced bi-partite structure of many of the prayers. But valid as they are from the for-malist perspective, these considerations neglect Anselm's own stated, primary concern: *the fact that these texts were also designed for a fragmented reception.* Modern scholarship of the *OsM* has continued, if not finished, the work begun by late medieval appropriations of Anselm's original devotional mode, all but effacing both Anselm's innovative textuality and its medieval reception and compilation. As products of the print age, such scholarship, like the *Cloud of Unknowing*'s prologue, asks that readers approach the prayers as whole and unified entities. While Anselm may have written his prayers with thematic unity and "inner coherence," he was less concerned that they be read with an eye to such principles. *Pace* Anselm's express desire, modern scholarship rarely acknowledges the gap between what is written and what is read in the *OsM*.

In contrast, in a hypertextual assessment of these prayers, the texts operate not only as aggregate wholes but also as self-contained lexia, which need not be connected to the texts around them. Unlike meticulously crafted scholastic arguments of logic, the *paragraphis distinctae per partes* that Anselm carefully builds into his poems work against reading the work as a unified whole. In short, reading in the modern sense guided by a modern edition constructs a modern, not an Anselmian, text.

In the late age of print, critiquing the dominance of linear meaning in the interpretation of medieval texts and texualities also suggests the larger issue of the cultural and hermeneutic milieu into which this technology and scholar-ship has evolved. In his discussion of postmodern expression and new tech-nologies, Frederic Jameson notes that traditional modern aesthetics—"largely, but not exclusively, designed for literary texts—do not require . . . simultane-ous attention to the multiple dimensions of the material, the social, and the aesthetic."[129] For Jameson, the high modern age of "late capitalism," which roughly corresponds with the beginning of Bolter's late age of print, is perhaps the only cultural period not readily open to a reticular arrangement of meaning operating across a text's materiality. Importantly, Jameson proposes that not only postmodern but precapitalist cultural expressions should therefore be reevaluated outside the modernist aesthetic impulse:

> It is because we have had to learn that culture today is a matter of media that we have finally begun to get it through our heads that culture was always that, and that the older forms or genres, or indeed the older spiritual exercises and meditations, thoughts and expressions, were also in their very different ways media products. . . . Mechanization of culture, and the mediation of culture . . . are now everywhere the case, and perhaps it might be interesting to explore the possibility that they were always the case throughout human history, and within even the radical difference of older, precapitalist modes of production.[130]

Bolter's and Jameson's studies of media and expression were published in the same year, late in the previous century. They are simpatico in their consideration of text not as text but as an evolving medium that struggles within and against its prior formal iterations. [→6] They also argue, respectively, that both written discourse and modes of its reception remained largely inscribed within the interpretative ideologies and technologies of the modern, from the Enlightenment forward.

To use Jameson's language, Anselm's "older spiritual exercise" also is a media product, but one that did its job differently than today with respect to writing; and this pre-print, now printed, model possesses certain points of connection with post-print media products. Likewise, alternative conceptions of space have much to do with both medieval devotion and digital media. [→159] Jameson further views the construction of space as a key indicator of how the representational logic of a culture functions, and argues that in the shift from the modern to the postmodern, the space of artistic expression "mutates" beyond orderly arrangements of unity. Examining a range of contemporary art forms—literature, painting, photography, video, and architecture—Jameson sets forth the notion of a postmodern "hyperspace" as the new environment of aesthetic discourse.[131] This hyperspace, as Silvio Gaggi remarks, is "a disjointed and incoherent space in which the individual becomes disoriented and loses his or her sense of clear physical placement in a whole that is comprehensible."[132] [→179] New Media thinkers such as Gaggi,

Bolter, and Grusin have been quick to capitalize on Jameson's use of the term *hyperspace*, pointing out that this new space may also be understood digitally as cyberspace, where the lack of axial organization of discourse and the virtual nature of the subject's participation lead to similar transformations of the self.[133] True to Jameson's hypothesis, though, consideration of Anselm's devotional texts as "media products" reveals a form of hyperspace at play here as well. In the *OsM*, readers are also expected to lose their selves, albeit out of spiritual ecstasy rather than in an alienating departure from modernist *ordinatio*.

All in all, the similarities between pre- and post-print hyperspaces and hypertexts remain striking. The aesthetic response to the disorienting effect of the postmodern condition, Jameson imagines, must assume a new form of art, one that

> will have to hold to the truth of postmodernism, that is to say, to its fundamental object—the world space of multinational capital—at the same time at which it achieves a breakthrough to some as yet unimaginable new mode of representing this last, in which we may again begin to grasp our positioning as individual and collective subjects and regain a capacity to act and struggle.[134]

Substitute "Christianity" for "postmodernism," and replace "multinational capital" with "God," and you have a reasonable restatement of Anselm's project: an attempt to hold on to Christian truths, and to mediate the human individual within the world of the divine. Despite transcendental desires, the technological and remediating text always remains, and the "immediate" point of prayer is not to leave this world behind but to better understand one's place within it. For Anselm, that place was not the place of an individuated subject but that of a participant in a corporate collective of monastic life and worship. His written attempt to negotiate the gap between the earthly life of the sinner and the divine form from which he descended, like Jameson's envisioned response to the confusion of the multinational, networked age of information, places faith in the representational to expedite salvation, whether it be political or spiritual.

Like digital media promoting virtual, immersive environments, Anselm's innovative texts of devotion encouraged users to imagine a transcendent "salvation" through a transparent technological experience—where users left behind the very media they employ. But such desires for transparency remain always-already bound up in the operation of the technologies that embody and ultimately produce them. Transparency, like salvation, never "really" happens in the physical, material wor(l)d. The media designed to disappear can never fully do so, and inevitably encode the remediating struggle between the need for technologies of representation and the longing to move beyond them.

3

Hypertextile: Closure and the Missing End
of the Bayeux Tapestry

Closure is, as in any fiction, a suspect quality, although here it is made manifest. When the story no longer progresses, or when it cycles, or when you tire of the paths, the experience of reading it ends. Even so, there are likely to be more opportunities than you think there are at first. A word that doesn't yield the first time you read a section may take you elsewhere if you choose it when you encounter the section again; and what sometimes seems a loop, like memory, heads off again in another direction.

—Michael Joyce

DESIRING THE SINGULAR END

Both postmodern spaces and pre-print models of medieval devotion do not necessitate clear beginnings and endings. Many other medieval expressions, though, at least superficially conform to our current expectations of concrete endings and narrative closure when we read and study them.[1] No one doubts, for instance, that the Bayeux Tapestry lacks some part of its original ending: the narrative of the textile breaks off in literal raggedness shortly after the death of Harold (see figure 6).[2] In the final extant section, a group of five Normans on horseback pursue an equal number of fleeing English. Below the English, the episode plays out in microcosm as two more riders bear down on a hapless fugitive tangled in vegetation. The fabric here contains huge physical holes, and parts of the upper and lower borders are missing entirely. The Tapestry's inscription notes the obvious: "et fuga verterunt Angli" [and the English have turned in flight].[3] As early reproductions of the work attest, much of what survives has been heavily restored. The 1731 engravings in Bernard Montfaucon's *Les monumens de la monarchie françoise* reveal that many details of both horses and men here are conjectural, while in his 1818 watercolor of the Tapestry, Charles Stothard reconstructs some, but not all, of these figures based on vestigial stitch holes and thread remnants.[4]

No record remains of the Tapestry's original ending, or of when the damage to it and the less substantial injury to the beginning of the work occurred.

Figure 6. The last surviving section of the Bayeux Tapestry, *The Bayeux Tapestry Digital Edition*, panels 172–73. By permission of the author and Scholarly Digital Editions.

Conceivably the damage happened through gradual attrition. When rediscovered by Nicholas-Joseph Foucault in Bayeux in the early eighteenth century, the bulk of the work survived in a remarkable state of preservation, mostly due to the fact that for probably centuries it had been displayed only once a year at the Feast of Relics.[5] Before and after its official rediscovery in the late 1720s, though, the Tapestry survived a series of events that make its relatively well-preserved state all the more serendipitous. If the Tapestry was in Bayeux by the twelfth century, as is likely, it would have had to survive the burning of Bayeux Cathedral in 1106.[6] In the mid-sixteenth century, Calvinists pillaged Bayeux, and royal records note the destruction of several valuable wall hangings and efforts to preserve others, presumably including the Tapestry.[7] In 1792 the textile was appropriated by zealous military volunteers for use as a pack cloth on a munitions wagon before being reclaimed by a civic-minded lawyer, while two years later local officials were forced to stop attempts to

slice up the Tapestry to decorate a holiday float.[8] The translation of the work
to Paris for an exhibition in 1803 for Napoleon may have further damaged the
artifact.

Aside from such sporadic threats to and interventions for the safety of the
Tapestry, its storage also contributed to its destruction. Though the early manner of storage remains unknown, the distressed and torn nature of the end of
the textile suggests that, for most of its history, it was rolled with the end section exposed. In 1812, in response to increasing requests to view and study the
work, the mayor of Bayeux placed the Tapestry on a makeshift mechanism of
two spindles and winches. To view the work, one wound it from one winch to
the other over a table. This method of storage and increased display doubtless
exacerbated the attrition at both the beginning and the end of work. In 1814
the English antiquarian Hudson Gurney described the winch as "a machine
like that lets down buckets into a well," a method of display that prompted
his colleague Dawson Turner to observe with alarm that the end had come to
resemble "a mere bundle of rags," and that if greater care were not taken, the
entire work would be ruined inside of fifty years.[9] It was not until 1842 that
the Tapestry was taken off the spindles and housed behind glass; in the 1860s
restorers then worked to halt and repair the damage to date.[10]

A casual student of Anglo-Saxon history can easily envision the general outlines of what probably comprised the original ending. Almost every contemporary account of the Norman Conquest follows the same formula regarding the
Battle of Hastings, and it would be surprising if the architect of the Tapestry's
narrative deviated from this narrative model. Tapestry scholars generally agree
in their reconstructions of the end of the Tapestry, and the assured tone of
Charles Gibbs-Smith's description may be taken as emblematic:

> There would not appear to have been room for much more of the Tap-
> estry length, and its ending has never been recorded. But, despite some
> dissident opinion, many art historians would feel confident in assum-
> ing that there must have been a bordered ending in harmony with the
> bordered beginning. As Edward the Confessor is seen at the start of
> the story, it would seem natural—if not inevitable—that an enthroned
> William should sit at the end. If the Conqueror did not appear here, it
> leaves the last appearance of so important a character in the thick of the
> battle, which would scarcely commend itself to an artist. Certainly no
> designer would think of completing such an elaborate work without a
> fitting and harmonious end-piece; so the present writer, at any rate, feels
> that it must have been King William the First.[11]

Certainly it is difficult to quibble with the historical and formalist arguments presented here. More than half of the surviving Tapestry concerns preparations for and events during the Battle of Hastings, and it is hard to imagine that the Tapestry would have gone on much longer after William's success at Hastings. The material construction of the textile appears to bear this out. In her study of the Tapestry's manufacture, Simone Bertrand analyzes the length of the eight panels of linen that constitute the work. While the first two panels are about 13.5 meters long, the last five are considerably shorter, measuring between 6.6 and 8.3 meters.[12] The final, damaged piece now measures 5.25 meters, and prior lengths suggest that a little over two meters, or about seven feet, are now missing.

So what ended up in the end? Gibbs-Smith's "fitting and harmonious" extrapolation of the Tapestry's brief closing with a newly crowned and enthroned William has a solid literary basis. Fourteen of fifteen surviving accounts composed in England and Normandy within one hundred years of Hastings record a Christmas Day coronation.[13] Nine of these accounts include after Hastings a rapid denouement of England's surrender and William's accession to the throne, thus providing more textual evidence for the argument that the Tapestry too did not spend much more space "wrapping up" its narrative.[14] Though details vary in each of the literary accounts, twelve of them agree on one other central point: that after Hastings and before his coronation, William made his way to London, and Archbishop Stigand, the *cild* king Edgar, and other nobles capitulated shortly thereafter.[15]

These two moments, the surrender of a city and the coronation of a king, already resonate within the visual language of the Tapestry. The architects of the work had developed a pictorial shorthand for representing cities in the space of two or three feet, as seen in the depictions of Dol, Rennes, Dinan, Bayeux, and Hastings.[16] Further, in the textile's representation of William's Breton campaign—arguably the Tapestry's thematic curtain-raiser for William's conquest of England—the Breton duke Conan surrenders the city of Dinan, a victory unattested to elsewhere.[17] William of Poitiers's account of William's battle with Conan only results in the Breton leader lifting his siege of Dol and fleeing.[18] The Tapestry, though, builds out its version with a pursuit past Rennes and an explicit depiction of the relinquishing of the keys of a city. As many have argued, William's Breton campaign of 1064 historically served as a proving ground for his more ambitious invasion of England two years later.[19] In the Tapestry, the campaign has been understood to glorify William more than in literary accounts, and to foreshadow William's subdual of another, more powerful rebellious vassal, Harold.[20] As the penultimate moment of the Tapestry's narrative, a formal depiction of London's surrender by cowed nobility and ecclesiasts would spring naturally from such iconographic roots.

The idea that the Bayeux Tapestry ended with William's Christmas Day coronation is reinforced by other internal evidence. As Gibbs-Smith noted, the Tapestry commences with Edward on the throne, rendered to evoke his royal seal and with the full iconic trappings of rule: palace, fleur-de-lys crown, throne, scepter, and sapiential beard.[21] As with the formulaic depictions of cities, enthroned rulers recur throughout the Tapestry as symbols of legitimate power. Edward appears enthroned twice, Guy of Ponthieu once, and Harold twice.[22] Harold's enthroned representations come in quick succession. First Harold appears in full regalia, with orb, scepter, and crown, surrounded by a pointing and applauding audience. The next scene, however, challenges this appearance of legitimacy: as Halley's comet streaks above, Harold holds nothing but a spear, he now appears slumped, the sides of his palace and throne likewise sag, and the Latin inscription omits his previously included title REX. William, notably, appears enthroned more than any other figure, fully six times, not counting the conjectured end.[23] The Tapestry portrays Harold's usurpation and its illegitimacy through stylistic elements as an event that interrupts the Norman view of rightful succession from King Edward to William. A third representation of an enthroned and accoutered English king, this time William, would graphically stress the Norman leader's rightful connection to Edward, a connection emphasized throughout the Tapestry by the duke's constant depiction as enthroned. Further, the second representation of the rites of coronation, this time ordained by right and might, would usurp the usurper Harold, canceling out his perjurious accession and providing a neatly structured and fitting close to the Tapestry inside the material space calculated to remain.

This is the ending we want, the ending we believe—Harold dies, the English flee, London surrenders, and the people crown William king. The end. In 1997 Jan Messent finished embroidering a commissioned reconstruction of just such a "finale" for the Bayeux Tapestry (see figure 7).[24] Though Messent draws upon only one historical source, the entry for 1066 in manuscript D of the *Anglo-Saxon Chronicle*, her eight-foot conclusion to the Tapestry includes versions of two key events, the surrender of the nobility of London to William and the duke's coronation as king.[25] Though any number of details in Messent's work could be quibbled with—the dependence on an Anglo-Saxon and not a Norman source, the lack of the iconic representation of the city of London in submission, the failure to name Archbishop Stigand in the group of nobles who surrender—its stylistic and thematic consonance with the surviving sections makes it easy to claim that her work stands as a studied and very fair "best guess" at the contents of the Tapestry's end within the statistically determined missing length. If Messent's work is not *the* end, it certainly remains a good end.

Messent's work also affirms the structuralist belief that the process of a literary narrative inevitably leads a reader not only to an ending but first to the *anticipation* of an ending, whatever it may turn out to be. Messent's best guess at an end reveals that, long after the heyday of New Critical desire to finish unfinished texts, imagining and actually fabricating such ends still has considerable currency. In Gibbs-Smith's "fitting" description and Messent's embroidery that fits, a desire for narrative closure governs the expressed need in both academic argument and whole cloth to reconstruct and therefore finish the Bayeux Tapestry.

Frank Kermode and Barbara Herrnstein Smith have argued from philosophical and psychological approaches, respectively, that despite changing cultural values, narrative forms, and literary ideologies, readers' expectations of closure during the process of reading remain.[26] As Smith notes in regard to poetry,

> The perception of poetic structure is a dynamic process: structural principles produce a state of expectation continuously modified by successive events. Expectation itself, however, is continuously maintained. . . . at some point the state of expectation must be modified so that we are prepared not for continuation but for cessation.[27]

The prolepsis of cessation also functions as a condition of our existence, as most physical phenomena we experience do come to some sort of end.[28] The material context of the printed book, still the dominant mode of literary expression, is no exception; the fact that in a book at some point there must be no more pages to turn demands that, at least on some level, readers understand the book as a closed system of meaning and are in turn conditioned by such a system.[29] Or, as Walter Ong puts it, "Print is comfortable only with finality."[30] Even on the level of grammar, writing arguably mandates that the reader find closure in word order, clausal structure, and punctuation. A sentence fragment is, after all, a would-be sentence that fails to represent a completed thought or action. [→45] From sentences, to the materiality of the books that contain

Figure 7. Jan Messant's reconstruction of the end of the Bayeux Tapestry. By permission of Madeira Threads.

them, to the finite aspects of physical existence, readers experience endings and in turn desire closure in the process of reading. In short, as New Media critic Jane Yellowlees Douglas observes, "the experience of narrative closure numbers among the principal pleasures of reading narratives—the one thing that both prompts and enables us to read."[31]

As a visual and inscribed story composed of three layers of pictorial discourse and spatially displayed, the Bayeux Tapestry differs sharply in form from the late-twentieth-century narratives that are the focus of most critical discussions of closure. Yet modern audiences continue to "read" the Tapestry as they would a novel, secure in the idea that the progression of the textile has been designed with a discrete end in mind. Certainly the Tapestry provides plenty of internal evidence that it conforms to the basic narratal tenets of beginning, middle, and end. The work cleanly divides into three parts: Harold's preparation and journey to Normandy, which culminates in his military campaign with William and the famous oath-swearing at Bayeux; Harold's usurpation of the English throne and William's preparations for and accomplishment of the crossing of the English Channel; and the Norman preparation for battle and then the actual combat with the English, which leaves Harold dead and William victorious.[32]

Another kind of ending in the Tapestry, the false ending, heightens expectations of closure. The Tapestry supports the progression toward an authoritative statement of finality through two moments that possess the form of a conclusion, but act instead as antitheses to what they should represent. Such moments spur the narrative toward its designated and presumably corrective final ending. Logically, both of these false endings concern Harold, as in the Tapestry and in Norman literary accounts the English earl subtends William's rightful succession to Edward.[33] After the victorious end of William's Breton campaign, during which Harold appears to have served heroically, the Tapestry shows Harold first receiving arms from William and then swearing a sacred oath to the duke (see figure 8).[34] Taken together, these episodes represent Harold's political and spiritual submission to William and his subsumption into a Continental model of vassalage.[35] The differences between the representations of these two ceremonies of fealty, however, only emphasize their failure to conclude the narrative.

Framed by groups of horses traveling away from it on both sides, the arms-giving scene appears isolated from everything around it. The figures of William and Harold turn in toward each other, and the gonfanon in Harold's hand extends vertically from border to border, bisecting the narrative and emphasizing the separate and static nature of this first scene. But just a few feet later, the oath-swearing scene completely upsets any sense of resolution established by the arms-giving.[36] Here the design of the Tapestry contrives to defer completely any sense of ending, even while Harold ostensibly "fecit sacramentum Willelmo duci" [swears a sacred oath to Duke William].[37] In contrast with the closed figures of the arms-giving scene, Harold now stands with his body entirely open between two reliquaries, arms gesturing both forward and backward. Harold's second companion to the right walks away from the scene toward the boat leaving for England even as he looks back upon

Figure 8. Arms and oath giving in the Bayeux Tapestry, *The Bayeux Tapestry Digital Edition*, panels 155–158. By permission of the author and Scholarly Digital Editions.

the oath in Bayeux, likewise punctuating the scene's failure to finish what it started, and pulling the viewer on to the development of Harold's perjurious future and William's vengeance. The inscription for the following scene, where Harold sails back to England, explicitly marks the course of Harold's future. By not staying within the prescribed ending of vassalage to William, Harold has now reversed his previously documented political and heroic ascent: "Hic Harold dux reversus est."[38] Far from conclusively becoming William's man, as the visual language of the arms-giving scene promised, Harold is now, as Suzanne Lewis has described him, on "liminal ground, caught in a moment of crucial indeterminacy."[39] In terms of Norman propaganda, this indeterminacy at the moment of supposed closure leads to Harold's treason and the delay of William's political destiny.

But Harold's reversed course more immediately leads to the Tapestry's second and considerably more blatant false ending—Harold's coronation.[40] As with the oath scene before it, the visual language in the coronation reveals the event to be a false ending that promises, and iconographically prefigures, the Tapestry's legitimate end (see figure 9). On its own, the mise en scène of the ceremony evokes the same stability and stasis that the arms-giving scene does. The architecture of the palace here completely interrupts the upper border, and the rigid, parallel lines of both the building and the figures who occupy it recall Harold's border-spanning standard from the arms-giving ceremony. Harold and his officiating archbishop face the viewer squarely, flanked by inward-leaning supporters who frame the moment and draw the viewer's gaze inward, not onward. The inscription "Hic resident Harold rex anglorum" [Here resides Harold, king of the English] likewise indicates a narrative pause—Harold does not simply sit (*sedet*) upon the throne, but has fully settled (*resident*) into his rule.[41]

In a document of Norman political propaganda, the putative finality of Harold's crowning moment is intended to be grotesque, not glorious, as it apes the form of the textile's legitimate and presumed ending: "Hic resident Willelm rex anglorum."[42] Once again, the Tapestry stresses the falseness of Harold's actions through visual clues that tug the narrative forward. Discord in the coronation scene begins with the identification of the presiding archbishop, Stigand, a renegade ecclesiast who himself usurped the Norman Robert of Jumièges' see at Canterbury, who was excommunicated five times by the pope, and whose historical participation in Harold's coronation remains much in doubt.[43] As in Harold's oath, the right-hand audience at the coronation becomes another narrative link that exposes the artificiality of closure. Here five

Figure 9. Harold's coronation in the Bayeux Tapestry, *The Bayeux Tapestry Digital Edition*, panels 72–73. By permission of the author and Scholarly Digital Editions.

supporters look toward Harold, clapping or, as the *Carmen de Hastingae Proelio* relates, "intimating by their hands what they were unable to say."[44] What they would soon say becomes immediately obvious as these five men, joined by a leader, turn 180 degrees away from Harold and now point not at their new king but at the ill omen of Halley's comet streaking through the upper border (see figure 10).[45] The comet itself visually links to a second, slanted portrait of a shaken and subaltern Harold, stripped of his orb, scepter, and his inscription "Rex," and now enthroned upon the watery foundation of an invasion fleet. The narrative economy that refutes Harold's assumption and presumption splits the event of his coronation into two iconic scenes. The first throne scene depicts Harold's attempt to close the line of kingly succession—his desired ending—while the second establishes that a legitimate coronation is still to come.

Figure 10. Halley's comet and Harold in the Bayeux Tapestry, *The Bayeux Tapestry Digital Edition*, panels 74–75. By permission of the author and Scholarly Digital Editions.

The unrelenting linear motion of the Tapestry provides the impetus for such a conclusive ending. With only two significant exceptions, the progression of the textile's central narrative is steadfastly left to right, like the Latin inscriptions that accompany individual episodes; it constantly pulls the viewer forward through the depicted episodes.[46] For example, the last event represented in the extant part of the Tapestry, the Battle of Hastings, is also its longest, and begins with a gradual charge of Norman horsemen toward the English line. This charge continues for more than thirteen feet, as the cavalry build momentum; the horses first walk, then canter, then finally break into full gallop toward the Anglo-Saxon positions.[47] The effect of such a lengthy charge is twofold: inside the episode, viewers find an acceleration toward a climax, in this case the first clash of Norman and Anglo-Saxon troops, where the forward momentum abruptly ends and the fighting begins. But more importantly, the length of this charge relative to the other, much shorter episodes of the work, along with the fact that the actual battle accounts for almost one-quarter of the surviving textile, signals to the viewer that the ultimate conflict of the narrative has been reached. All that remains after the battle, it would seem, is a brief and victorious denouement.

The fact that this pat denouement is inconveniently absent, however, conveniently invites us to reexamine our desire for it through the problematic and contradictory nature of textual closure in the late age of print. Our sense of the closed system of the Tapestry's narrative is not so different from our sense of printed books. As T. E. Hulme presciently noted in 1936, "the covers of a book are responsible for much [interpretative] error. They set a limit around certain convenient groups of ideas, when there are really no limits."[48] [→68] More recent critics have developed such thinking, and argued that the physical limitations of print media and an originative bias toward the text-producing author should give way to the intertextual permeability of textual boundaries and the interpretative plurality found within the reception of a text.[49] In the critical shift from the readerly to the writerly, endings do not effect closure but only remind us that, to paraphrase Roland Barthes, there is no last reading, even if the text is concerned to give us that illusion.[50] Instead, the end of text functions more like a depot than like a terminal, marking the continual process and plurality of meaning, like Barthes' reread *Sarrasine* or Stanley Fish's context-fueled classroom text.[51] Accordingly, the missing end of the Bayeux Tapestry needs also to be reread through such approaches. The Bayeux Tapestry lacks an ending. The Bayeux Tapestry lacks AN ending. The Bayeux Tapestry has endings.

THE ENDINGS OF THE TAPESTRY

Of course, much recent scholarship has already argued for readings of the Bayeux Tapestry that privilege the reception of the work over authorial intention, thereby multiplying possible interpretations by a factor of specular or conversational contingency.[52] But more simply, the very fact that the Tapestry does not conclusively finish provides the work with two ends, what it is and what it is thought to have been. Even though one can (as Messent did) re-create the latter through an educated guess, the ending of the Bayeux Tapestry, at this point, cannot possibly be known, any more than the conclusions to Chaucer's *House of Fame* or Chrétien de Troyes' *Perceval* can be known. The difference between the Bayeux Tapestry and these famously unfinished works is that modern audiences believe the end of the Tapestry did exist at some point. The belief in the lost ending then moves attempts to close the narrative from the area of pure invention to one of studied reconstruction. The belief that the end did in fact exist fixes the idea of "*the* end" in the viewer/reader's mind more firmly.

But the accepted argument for the missing ending of the textile presumes a correspondence between the original work and a formalist concern with balance and resolution, a concern that has as much to do with modern reception as it might with medieval production. [→24, 73] At second glance the statistical assurance that on average only another eight feet should be missing—just enough to show the capitulation of the English and William's coronation—seems less secure. The modern approach of customizing the Tapestry's narrative to fit predetermined material length could easily be reversing the actual compositional process. That is to say, the narrative of the Tapestry did not have to be woven to fit any length, as any excess material on the eighth or even a ninth section of canvas could simply have been cut off. Norman and English accounts contain plenty of other episodes for inclusion: William surveying the carnage and offering thanks, William burying his dead, the recovery and burial of Harold, the Norman attacks on Romney and Dover, the capitulation of Canterbury, and a skirmish near London all appear in contemporary accounts of the aftermath of Hastings.

And though Rosemarie McGerr has argued that much medieval narrative theory and practice espoused a particular type of closure in which the end includes "a sense of recapitulation of the whole, framed to have the greatest impact on the audience," her study also considers a number of texts that evidence the "playfulness" of literary inconclusiveness, as well as scribal anxieties about such missing endings. Elsewhere others have argued that medieval writers often demonstrate a lack of concern for conclusivity in their writings.[53] Even when works were designed to resolve, they often did not because of lengthy compositional processes and abbreviated life spans. In his *Ars versificatoria*, written a century after the production of the Tapestry, Matthew of Vendôme makes sure to distinguish between a *conclusio* and a *terminatio*—the latter being the end of a work brought about by the death of the author.[54]

It is possible, of course, that the Bayeux Tapestry was never finished, though modern commentators rarely entertain the possibility.[55] Conversely, a few scholars through the centuries have considered the work essentially complete as it stands with the death of Harold and the fleeing English. In 1817 Hudson Gurney sought to redress claims that the Tapestry was incomplete by arguing that "whereas it is an apologetical History of the Claims of William to the Crown of England, and of the breach of faith and fall of Harold, [the Tapestry] is a perfect and finished action."[56] One hundred years later, W. R. Lethaby would echo this sentiment, writing that an image of William enthroned, while not necessarily out of place, "would be anti-climax to Harold's terrible doom and those stark corpses."[57] And on the cusp of this century, Suzanne Lewis argues that the "quasi-oral" nature of the piece and its relation to its audience demands, not such a fixed ending, but rather a more "open-ended" narration that more readily accommodates the fluctuation of performance and reception.[58]

Such arguments reside in the minority, but should not be dismissed completely. As we have seen in the previous two chapters, medieval texts often operate through models that do not necessarily accommodate modern notions of either the structure of narrative or the sequential progression of writing. Close to the content of the Tapestry, historical projects such as the *Anglo-Saxon Chronicle*, an updatable compilation of current events, were actually designed as unending narratives. As it survives, the Tapestry's narrative now also participates in a form of unending process, and invites further investigation, not only of the pat and ornamental ending we imagine, but of the physical, "ongoing" ending we have.

The Tapestry now ends in the middle of an action: remnants of the defeated English army flee, pursued by Norman horsemen. At this point the Tapestry is heavily restored, so much so that the quality of the content of the end itself has been questioned, further complicating readings of the surviving section.[59] Assuming, however, that the prerestoration engravings of the final part of the Tapestry from the late 1720s fairly reflect the original material, some observations on the ending as it survives may safely be made.[60]

In the final extant moments of the Tapestry, the English run and the Normans chase. In the tattered end, the English never stop fleeing; no new narrative episode cuts off—or, perhaps more appropriately, finishes off—these figures. Instead, the linear architecture of the central narrative here does something unexpected: it splits into two separate layers, defined by a landscape line that springs from a branch of a tree and runs the length of the pursuit. In the stacked progression, fearful English hotfoot it up above while whip-wielding Normans spur their horses down below.[61] Though scene splitting occasionally occurs in other parts of the textile, notably in Edward's deathbed and Norman shipbuilding scenes, no other section divides the landscape and the narrative in a linear progression.[62] Jan Messent's woven finale neatly ends the scene by quickly running the floating landscape line down to the bottom of another tree, thus opening up the entire canvas for the next scene, the English submission at Berkhamstead (see figure 7.).[63]

But by remaining open and bifurcated, the surviving "ending" provides a divided social reading, an account where the threat of the defeated but fleeing English branches off from but never rejoins the narrative of Norman triumph. This is not to suggest, as others have, that the Tapestry contains within it explicit codes of Anglo-Saxon subversion.[64] But the current openness of the Tapestry's end does translate the final moments of the work from the realm of ornamented political orchestration to the social reality of conquest.

In his discussion of Chaucer's fragmented *Cook's Tale*, Paul Strohm locates closure within the larger symbolic field of the 1381 revolt. Strohm notes that the lack of narrative containment for the Cook's riotous Perkyn parallels the English authorities' desired, but ultimately unattainable, quick and orderly disposal of Wat Tyler and his revolutionary agenda:

> The aspirations of 1381 were not really brought to an end by the death of Tyler or by the return of the rebels to their homes or by the multiple judicial processes of 1382. Redirected and associated with other arenas of struggle, they resurfaced as parliamentary acknowledgement of the burden of taxation on the working poor, as local impetus for manumission, as religious dissent. Associated . . . with the most turbulent social energies of its day . . . Perkyn's story could hardly be finished in any satisfactory sense.[65]

In Strohm's analysis, the lack of a controlling frame around the social decay of the Cook's narrative exposes the impossibility of such frames in the social reality of such narratives. It also shows a concomitant desire to foster such control through the creation of historical texts that report, fictively, on the orderly resolution, containment, and rehabilitation of social dissent.

Similarly, the end of the Bayeux Tapestry has as much to do with a desire for containment as it does with closure. Like the 1381 Peasants' Revolt, the Norman Conquest was not a painless political event. Though William was crowned king on Christmas Day 1066, rebellion and dissent persisted until almost the end of his reign some twenty years later.[66] At the current end of the Tapestry, the English flee but are never caught. Uncorrected by images of the English aristocrats submitting to William at Berkhamstead or Wallingford, and of the Norman duke enthroned at Westminster, the uncaptured English reify the fear of ongoing subversion that Norman propaganda seeks to stop.

Ironically, other complete Norman historical accounts that explicitly cap the Norman invasion of England with William's coronation also betray such a fear. In William of Poitiers's *Gesta Guillelmi*, for instance, the coronation ceremony is interrupted by jittery guards:

> Die ordinationi decreto, elocutus ad Anglos condecenti sermone Eboracensis archiepiscopus aequitatem valde amans, aevo maturus, sapiens, bonus, eloquens, an consentirent eum sibi dominum coronari, inquisivit. Protestati sunt hilarem consensum universi minime haesitantes, ac si caelitus una mente data unaque voce. Anglorum voluntati quam facillime Normanni consonuerunt, sermocinato ad eos ac sententiam percunctato Constantiniensi praesule. Ceterum, qui circa monasterium in armis et equis praesidio dispositi fuerunt, ignotae [linguae] nimio strepitu accepto, rem sinistram arbitrati, prope civitati imprudentia flammam iniecerunt.

> [On the day fixed for the coronation, the archbishop of York, a great lover of justice and a man of mature years, wise, good, and eloquent, addressed the English, and asked them in appropriate words whether they would consent to him being crowned as their lord. They all shouted their joyful assent, with no hesitation, as if heaven had granted them one mind and one voice. The Normans added their voice most readily to the wish of the English, after the bishop of Coutances had addressed them and asked their wishes. But the men who, armed and mounted, had been placed as a guard round the minster, on hearing the loud clamour in an unknown tongue, thought that some treachery was afoot and rashly set fire to houses near to the city].⁶⁷

What is striking about this account is the separation between the closure that the narrative of the coronation seeks to achieve and the revelation of Norman anxiety about immediate rebellion that underwrites such propagandic texts. Poitiers depicts the English in a completely positive and accepting light. Their spiritual leader, Archbishop Ealdred of York, unlike the perfidious Stigand, is a man just, mature, wise, good, and eloquent, and under his guidance the English people joyfully assent as one.

In contrast, the mounted troops outside the ceremony, presumably Norman, react as figures who are also outside the smoothing intent of propaganda. The curious aspect of Poitiers's account is that the soldiers, not privy to the revisionism of the historical text, assume the political worst and misread not the clamor of the Anglo-Saxons but *the noise of cultural assimilation*. Importantly, the unknown tongue that the guards hear is not the foreign cadence of English but the cacophonous admixture of both English and Norman adulation of King William. In short, at the first report of Anglo-Norman synthesis, symbolized by the literal amalgamation of the two cultures' languages, the guards mistrust their ears and set fire to the city. In Poitiers's telling, the English are wise and the Normans are rash; this temporary inversion discovers the difference and confusion between the disruptive reality of cultural conquest and the socially corrective and pacifying work that renarrations such as Poitiers's *Gesta* and the Bayeux Tapestry seek to enact.

SPACE, CYCLE, AND HYPERTEXTILES

Poitiers's account also notes the detail that William's coronation took place "in basilica sancti Petri apostoli, quae regis Edwardi sepulchro gaudebat" [in the basilica of St. Peter the apostle, which boasted of possessing the tomb of King Edward].[68] The *Gesta*'s linking of William's kingship to Edward's through the latter's death further affirms the textual goal of legitimizing William as Edward's successor. The Tapestry, of course, opens with an enthroned King Edward, and may, in a sense, have intended to end with an evocation of this figure as well.

Within the Tapestry, all three appearances of King Edward are marked by a temporal discontinuity, which builds with each successive depiction. The historical time of the king's meeting with Harold, seen at the opening of the Tapestry, is not chronicled elsewhere and has been the subject of some conjecture. The only time that such a meeting and Harold's subsequent mission to Normandy could have taken place is 1064, but no literary source provides a date, and all the versions of the *Anglo-Saxon Chronicle*, usually one of the best sources for the activities of both Harold and Edward, uniformly omit any entry for this year.[69] In his second appearance, upon Harold's return from Normandy, Edward appears hunched and sickly, an odd portraiture given that in 1064 Edward's sudden and fatal illness was still nearly two years away and, in the meantime, he had the strength to go hunting with Harold and to combat a rebellion in Northumbria.[70] But Edward's third and literally final appearance, on his deathbed, is the most chronologically challenging of all. In one of the few split-level narratives in the work, Edward appears twice in the same space of his palace: above we see Edward on his deathbed surrounded by companions, while directly below, a clergyman and aides shroud his body for the funeral.[71] This vertical juxtaposition of events is minor, however, when compared to the fact that the scene immediately preceding Edward's final moments is the funeral procession of Edward's corpse into Westminster.[72] Critics have dedicated much effort to explaining the "curious dislocation of events" whereby the Tapestry first buries Edward and then shows him alive.[73] Speculations range from a simple mistake of embroidering, to setting Edward's death in dramatic counterpoint to Harold's subsequent acceptance of the crown, to narrative devices of flashback or simultaneity, to deliberate narrative ambiguity.[74] Regardless of the intentions of the designer, though, the Tapestry's representation of Edward's death and burial disrupts an expected sequence of narrative through an extranarratal manipulation of space.[75]

This manipulation also recalls the literary theory of spatial form pioneered by Joseph Frank and subsequently developed by narratologists such as W.J.T. Mitchell.[76] Frank's study found that certain forms of modern literature "undermine the inherent consecutiveness of language, forcing the reader to perceive the elements of the [work] not as unrolling in time but juxtaposed in space."[77] For readers of such texts, meaning inheres not in linear progressions but in a momentary and simultaneous grasp of nonlinear elements, which the reader arranges in a spatial relationship in order to produce a unity of meaning.

Unlike its literary analogues, the Tapestry is not metaphorically but manifestly a spatial document, most likely designed to be hung around the walls of a hall or other building. As such, medieval audiences experienced the work not only in a linear fashion but in an instantaneous, monumental, and, to use Susanne Langer's phrase, *presentational* mode.[78] Langer distinguishes between the discursive—the word-based sequential meaning of literary texts—and the presentational mode of visual art, which transcends temporal limitations of sequence. The Bayeux Tapestry's narrative pushes the limits of such categories, through the conflation of an inscripted linear progression and its spatial display. The temporal incongruities of Edward's appearances—his extranarratal iconicity at the Tapestry's opening, the telescoping of the two years between his health and death, and the reversal of his death and burial—all point toward Edward's being invested with a spatial meaning that operates outside temporal sequences. Edward is not simply a player in a narrative sequence, he is a figure imprinted with an extratemporal significance that supports the narrative sequence even as it works outside it.[79] In other words, the space of the Tapestry provides synchronic meaning that works concurrently with the textile's diachronic sequence of events.

Our imagined ending of the Tapestry—William on the throne—iconically echoes Edward on the throne at the beginning. Such a relation of beginning to end also resists traditional print-driven notions of cessation in the narrative. If we imagine the Tapestry not as it is reproduced in books, as a single forward-moving line, but as an enclosed space of presentational discourse, the textile no longer functions as exclusively linear, but cyclically as well.[80] Set on or inside the walls of a building, the Tapestry would end where it begins, with the enthroned William coming full circle back to Edward. Here closure in the Tapestry is not a narrative end but a continuing cycle of legitimate rule—a political succession that relies on recession. In this mode, the "line" of the narrative advances, but only to emphasize William's place in a closed and ongoing circuit of succession and selection. This extranarratal, spatial expression ultimately derives not from ideas about narrative but from the social need to conceal tumultuous political change in the guise of sameness. In the propagandistic end traditionally imagined for the Tapestry, the Norman Conquest is not a new beginning, a cultural shift of power, a subjugation of an island nation by an upstart Continental powerhouse. Rather, it is a *nonevent* heralded by the message that nothing, in fact, has changed, and certainly nothing has ended but Harold's treacherous interruption.

Indeed, the unique material nature of the Tapestry's narrative only reinforces a political economy of space that occurs in more conventional and literary accounts of the Norman Conquest. We have already seen how William of Poitiers places the grave of Edward and the throne of William in the same space of the St. Peter's Abbey, an account copied almost verbatim fifty years later by Orderic Vitalis.[81] Writing a century after Hastings, Wace also associates William and Edward, but in a different mode. According to Wace, after his coronation the new king William

> pois fist toz les barons mander e toz les Engleis assembler, a chois les mist quels leis tendreient e quels costumes il voldreient, ou des Normanz ou des Engleis, de quels seignors e de quels reis; e cil distrent del rei Ewart, les soes leis lor tienge e gart . . . celes lor plorent, celes pristrent. Issi lor fu a voenté e li reis lor a graanté.

> [called together all the barons, and assembled all the English, and put it to their choice, what laws they would hold to, and what customs they chose to observe, whether the Norman or the English, those of which lord and which king; and they all said, King Edward's—let his laws be kept and held . . . these pleased them well, and they therefore chose

them. And it was done according to their desire, the king consenting to their wish.][82]

Wace, who also probably used the Bayeux Tapestry as a source for parts of his chronicle, replaces earlier literary conflations of past and present in physical space with a more overt linkage to both Edward's rule and the will of the conquered populace. Though the space, and the body, of Edward are absent in his narrative, Wace maintains a spatial sense of the political cycle by the more direct, if blatant, reference to the continuation of Edward's rule through his laws, and by the tacit omission of any reference to Harold. Like the Tapestry's representation of Edward's burial and then final moments of life, Wace's account resurrects Edward and, through a closed narrative circuit, attempts to ensure William's survival through, at least juridically, Edward's.

The concept of closure itself remains closely connected to space. David Hult remarks that "as a spatial description, 'closure' initially encompasses all the coordinates appertaining to a circumscribed territory: the 'enclosed place' itself."[83] The Tapestry's enclosed circuit of narrative space defines the "end" and the closure of the work. But the layers of conclusions in the final physical moments of the textile today caution us to distinguish carefully between ending and closure in the Tapestry, and to recognize that the different ends found within the work suggest both decisive and more indeterminate senses of closure. They also encourage us to realize that forms of closure enacted by the narrative may correspond to, but do not necessarily function in the same capacity as, the narrative end of the work, a discursive element that denotes discrete stoppage or completion.

A formalist reconstruction of the end of the Tapestry remains convincing, indeed probable, though as we have seen, its current absence allows a more unobstructed view of other cultural discourses operating *sub imagos*. In the past, the unique nature of the Bayeux Tapestry has led commentators to discuss the operation of its narrative through analogies to other, more common narrative forms—literary epic, historical chronicle, chanson de geste, comic strip, film.[84] However, the linked nature of the determinate and indeterminate grades of closure found within the missing end to the textile suggest another and more recent model: hypertext fiction. [→40] Hypertext fiction has of late generated a good deal of theoretical discussion, much of which has centered on the capability of the medium to offer the reader a shifting base of narrative progression and closure.[85] As the opening epigraph of this chapter suggests, at any given point in hypertext, readers face dozens of shifting narrative options, each leading to other interactive lexia. The active negotiation of these links is what guides the progression and orders the meaning of the narrative.

Though viewers of the Bayeux Tapestry are not presented with multiple and branching lines of hyperlinked narrative at any given moment, the spatial nature of the textile does at times hypermedially link in ways that break the boundaries of its own sequential, unfolding, and inscripted register. Surrounded by the narrative on all sides, medieval viewers would have been able to connect narrative moments of the Tapestry across the story-space that they literally occupied. Richard Brilliant, for instance, has schematized the physical dimensions of a hypothetical hall in which the Tapestry could have hung. Reconstructively arranging the textile around a hall with a length-to-width ratio of 7:2, Brilliant argues for separate sets of "visual and thematic relationships" to a "narrative core" for audiences viewing the work from key perspectives, such as from the hall's entrance, or from a master's high table.[86] Of course, such visual relationships would change even more in accordance with the shifting perspectives of a mobile audience.

Moreover, the space in which the Tapestry was shown need not have been of a fixed dimension. The Tapestry was not a delicate product, but made of heavy woolen threads worked upon thick linen. The constitution of the Tapestry, coupled with the fact that the entire work could be folded up and stored in a box no bigger than a funeral casket, suggests the textile may have been designed for portable display.[87] The portability of the Tapestry would result in its display in different-dimensioned spaces, and therefore provide a system of visual links dependent upon individuated environments. In short, the presentational aspects of the Tapestry's visual narrative are contingent first upon the dimensions of the display space, and second on the viewers' itinerant perspectives within this space.

Space, especially with reference to narrative beginnings and endings, plays a major role in hypertext theory. As with recent treatments of the interpretative contexts of the Tapestry, conceptualizations of multilinear hypertext narratives have centered on the principle of arrangement and, accordingly, distilled the structural relationships across perceived narrative linearities into topographic representations.[88] Once the networked space of a hypertext is mapped, the narrative hyperstructure often also takes a circular form.[89]

The circular, networked, and nonaxial organization of hypertexts returns us to the issues of the Tapestry's endings. The architecture of digital literature alters the notion of the narrative end; in such fiction, as Bolter writes, "the story itself does and does not end," as through a compilation of interactive choices unique to each navigation of the hypertext, readers experience related, but substantially different, versions and endings of the narrative.[90] Hypertexts have permeable borders where both discrete beginnings and endings become questionable. In some hypertexts, readers may choose from any of a number of points of entry. In most, readers will exhaust their own participation before they run out of space in which to read, but also will lack the final physical point beyond which there is simply no more, which must be found in a printed book, and which drives traditional readers on to the satisfaction of preordained closure.[91] [→38]

Lacking a physical ending, and operating in part through a spatial network of visual meaning, the narrative of the Bayeux Tapestry now arguably has at least as much connection to hypertext theory as it does to the traditional theories of literary narrative through which it has long been read. Simone Bertrand has gone as far as to hypothesize that the Tapestry may also lack its beginning, on the evidence that the beginning border of the textile is largely reconstructed.[92] This claim is tentative at best, but the idea that the Tapestry has a reconstructed beginning as well as a missing end does further the notion of the work's permeable boundaries.

Though hypertexts necessarily lack a physical end, the reality of a reader's need for an ending is harder to leave behind. Readers of hypertext fiction, like their analog counterparts, still seek fulfillment in the process—in other words, closure. But if a hypertext lacks an end, how is closure determined? The answer lies in the ability of hypertext to reconfigure closure in terms of reception and to distance it from authorial design. As Jane Yellowlees Douglas writes, "Once we dispense with closure as an entity that is always determined by an author and always consumed by a reader . . . we can clear for ourselves a bit of neutral ground to examine what defines an ending beyond the blank space accompanying it."[93] In place of the blank space determined by the print author who writes no more, who forces readers to stop, hypertextual closure instead is dictated by readers when they are sated by a certain participation in the narrative process—when enough becomes recognized as enough.[94]

Hypertext fiction occupies a new space between traditional linear narratives and repetitive, multilinear experiences of sequential navigation, such as old-fashioned board games or modern video games. The moment the Bayeux Tapestry lost its ending, it joined the ranks of such texts, as only the reader, and not the author, can construct the possible ending. Like a hypertext, the work is now, to paraphrase Douglas, a narrative about its own structure and about its suspension of closure; its hypertextual elements—its missing end and spatial linkages—also serve as a link to understanding the critical and technological plurality in which the visual narrative now exists.[95]

PRINT CULTURE AND THE TAPESTRY

Since the Bayeux Tapestry was rediscovered and "published" in the early eighteenth century, editions and other scholarly treatments of the Tapestry have necessarily operated in the closed, static system of print. The notion of the modern scholarly edition has long depended upon the assumption of producing a common or unified text. The desire for unity, along with the expectation that scholarly meaning derives from words, not images, has had great consequences for the study and reproduction of the Tapestry. [→18] The forces and contingencies of print culture have, in effect, textualized the textile and, like the work's missing end, compromised its study as much as they encouraged it.

Print culture and technology have long mandated how we understand the Bayeux Tapestry. In 1818, while traveling through France on what he termed a bibliographical tour, the Reverend Thomas Frognall Dibdin decided to try to view the embroidery. Access, it turned out, was rather difficult; letters 14 and 15 of his travelogue detail Dibdin's efforts to negotiate permission from French officials to obtain a glimpse of the famous textile. In particular, the parson had to press his case with the mayor and chief magistrate of Bayeux, a "priggish" gentleman who struck Dibdin as "a very Caesar in miniature."[96] At first the mayor was reluctant to grant the Englishman's request, observing that Dibdin's "countryman, Mr. STOTHARD, had been already there for six months, upon the same errand, and what could [Dibdin] want further?"[97] Dibdin managed to make his case convincing, and eventually viewed the work.

The mayor made waves for Dibdin because of the cultural rift between England and France, and because of the sensitive political nature of the Tapestry—a documentation of the Norman conquest of England that, only fifteen years before, Napoleon had studied in anticipation of a repeat performance.[98] But the explicit reason the mayor gave for denying Dibdin entrance was the efforts of his compatriot Charles Stothard, who had spent the better part of 1818 completing the first color reproduction of the Tapestry for the Society of Antiquaries of London.[99] The mayor's point here was clear: if the English now had a color reproduction of the Tapestry, why need the actual Tapestry be examined? Given the method by which the 850-year-old textile was then stored and studied, the mayor also had a legitimate worry—each viewing of the work further damaged its fabric. At the time, the city archives still kept the Tapestry wound around a spindle; to view the Tapestry one turned a winch and drew the narrative material out across the table.[100] Dibdin even includes an engraving of this mechanism, ironically the only illustration in his account of the Tapestry.[101]

Dibdin's report of trying to view the Tapestry reveals two issues still central to modern study of the artifact: the formal parameters of its reproduction and its erosion. In the past 180 years conservators have developed increasingly sophisticated ways of showcasing and protecting the Tapestry through technology; its current home at the Centre Guillaume le Conquérant boasts centralized atmosphere control and curved glass that actually magnifies the textile for the viewer. In tandem, modern critics have viewed and elucidated the work through interpretative lenses of increasing refinement, now aided by mass-produced color reproductions of the Tapestry more accessible, detailed, and accurate than Stothard's early watercolors. But, as with the formal reconstructions of the Tapestry's missing end, the material and critical processes of Tapestry scholarship and reproduction have also combined to substantially revise the received nature of the textile. In short, textual treatments of the Tapestry reproduce the work in a medium alien to its source, and translate the narrative operation of the Tapestry, so rooted in *imagos*, through *logos*. Such treatments do not generally allow for an experience of the Tapestry, but rather a reading of it removed from the physical and spatial medium of its narrative expression.

For a century and a half after the rediscovery of the Bayeux Tapestry in the late 1720s, the technological limitations of the print medium required that the Tapestry be reproduced, for the most part, as text. Though engravings of the Tapestry were published in 1731, 1733, 1823, 1838, and 1853, circulation was limited, and most notices of the Tapestry took forms similar to Dibdin's account: unable to visually represent the pictorial narrative easily, reports resorted to words alone.[102] Such *ekphrasis* simplifies and reduces the graphic nature and content of the work considerably, often shrinking 230 feet of woven discourse to one or two dozen printed pages. Throughout the nineteenth and early twentieth centuries, accounts from antiquarians such as Dibdin and Stothard and discussions of the Tapestry in popular periodicals such as the *Gentleman's Magazine*, the *National Repository*, and *Scribner's* did, in effect, bring an awareness of the textile to an increasing number of readers—but simultaneously alienated such audiences from its graphic and spatial identity and character.[103] Some early-nineteenth-century writing on the Tapestry explicitly separates the content of the work from the image of its expression. Anna Stothard, the wife of Charles Stothard, reports in her *Letters Written during a Tour through Normandy, Britanny and Other Parts of France, in 1818*:

> The tapestry is worked with different-color worsteds, upon white cloth, to which time has given the tinge of brown holland. The drawing of the figures is rude and barbarous, no attention has been paid to correctness of color in the objects depicted. The horses are blue, green, red, or yellow: this circumstance may arise from the limited number of worsteds employed in the work. . . . The Tapestry represents, in regular succession, the events which preceded the Conquest, and the principal circumstances connected with it. As I have minutely examined the whole, and copied the inscriptions that are beneath the border on the upper part, I shall give you an account of them as they follow in succession.[104]

Though she recounts that she has examined the "whole" of the Tapestry, Stothard only provides the reader with the fifty-seven Latin inscriptions that run the length of the Tapestry. The wording of the final sentences of the quoted passage also reveals, unwittingly, the logocentric translation of the textile. What, exactly, does "account of them" in the last sentence mean? Most likely, the phrase refers to the "events and circumstances" of the preceding sentence, but remains closer in proximity to "the inscriptions that are below the border." Stothard dismisses the "rude and barbarous" drawings of the textile, but she includes at the conclusion of her letter a complete transcription of the inscriptions that run through the work. The message here is clear: the meaning of the Tapestry technologically and critically defaults to the Latin *scriptio*. The learned letter, easily reproduced, holds meaning, while the crude image, difficult to represent, need not. [→33] Such sentiment also occurs in an early-nineteenth-century report that public officials at Bayeux deposited in their archives—a copy of the Tapestry's inscriptions, but not a copy of the Tapestry itself.[105] Not surprisingly, such "reproduction" also results in the invocation of other writings. Much of Anna Stothard's subsequent discussion of the Tapestry relates the aforementioned "events and circumstances" of the work to the written histories of William of Poitiers, William of Jumièges, William of Malmesbury, and the Domesday Book. In their use of textual affinity to define the Tapestry by what it is not, such early historicist accounts cast the mold for the next 150 years of interpretation.

Though its first photographic reproduction tempered such strident textualizations of the Tapestry, this new medium also contributed to the continuing gap between the physical document and its textual representation. In his 1875 publication *The Bayeux Tapestry*, Frank Rede Fowke, working from negatives, reduced the photographs taken for the Victoria and Albert Museum, already half-scale, to one-sixth their original size.[106] Significantly, Fowke included these reproductions at the end of the book, a format that the majority of full scholarly treatments of the Tapestry that followed have emulated. This format of text-first-image-after is usually adopted for economic reasons of production; it also softens the fragmentation that must result from printing the continuous visual narrative across printed pages by at least keeping the material all in one place. But while such a layout was, and is, perhaps the best option available to the print medium, it also continued and intensified the textual transformation of the Tapestry.

In editions such as Fowke's, the placement of the Tapestry at the end of the texts relegates it to the status of an appendix or, better yet, a visual index that helps to explicate the preceding written commentary, as opposed to the other way around. Fowke emphasizes his reliance on text to shape the meaning of the Tapestry by starting each of his commentaries with the inscription nearest to the represented scene printed in big, bold type. Of course, not all visual scenes in the Tapestry have accompanying inscriptions, but for Fowke and many subsequent "readers" of the Tapestry, the inscriptions and not the images signal the proper semantic divisions of the textile's narrative. Even the physical composition of the book contributes to this bias, as the written word accounts for 70, 80, 90 percent of an edition; the reproduction squeezes in at the end, a slim margin to a thick page. Referring to the actual, albeit reduced, Tapestry in such scholarly treatments requires an exiting, a departure, a voyage across a sharp divide between printed text and image. [→58]

In the twentieth century, more commercial publications on the Tapestry almost always return to the Tapestry's relationship between text and image. In such works the Tapestry itself occupies each page; words, like the inscriptions inside the textile, crowd around the image.[107] But the printed context of modern criticism continues to polarize the Tapestry's meaning and form. The 1997 *Study of the Bayeux Tapestry*, for instance, is an impressive collection of seminal essays but, no doubt for economic reasons, it reproduces the Tapestry only as a series of black-and-white photographs, of mismatched scale, as an appendix to the scholarship.[108] And while methodologies of inquiry have evolved, the hermeneutic assumptions from which many "new readings" of the Tapestry proceed are little changed from Anna Stothard's.[109] As Richard Gameson comments, "scholars have been surprisingly reluctant to allow a visual narrative its own, independent authority, and the 'Search for the Text underlying the Tapestry' has been pursued with [considerable] zeal."[110]

HYPERCRITICISM

As this discussion of the missing end has shown, interpreting the Bayeux Tapestry through modern criticism and the print culture that houses it can usefully clarify some aspects of the Tapestry's discursive functionality, but such approaches inevitably shortchange other aspects by reproducing the textile through the text. Only a few critics have recently begun to consider the Tapestry from what could be called an ideology of reception and space—an approach that, as we have seen, significantly connects with the hypertextual aspects of the Tapestry's narrative operation. Richard Brilliant, Michael Swanton, and to a lesser degree Richard Gameson develop such considerations by examining the Tapestry less as a text than as a matrix of discursive elements. For these critics, the Tapestry functions not as or from written discourse but rather as an intersection of word, image, space, sound, border, audience, and monument. In the Tapestry, words are only one of many factors; the Tapestry makes meaning through interwoven and oscillating layers of multimedia expression, received across the physical space of display and possibly through oral performance by an interlocutor. [→196] Written texts still inform and function within the narrative of the work, but in such a model they no longer dominate.[111]

By its nature, digital technology allows for more open-ended systems of critical edition, in which the unknown plurality of variants, reconstructions, and interpretations of a given text may be housed within a fluid matrix of electronic reference.[112] If our critical understanding of the Bayeux Tapestry is to progress, reproductions and reception of this unique visual narrative must also be freed in both theory *and* praxis from the printed page. Issues of interpretation and reproduction of this graphic, woven, continuous 230-foot narrative of text, image, and expressive borders remain inextricably combined. Though the mayor of Bayeux who haggled with Thomas Frognall Dibdin believed that reproductions of the Bayeux Tapestry would save it from further harm, from a critical standpoint the reverse is true. The print medium tends to fragment and reduce the work it intends to represent; print has also marginalized the Tapestry, and more often than not condenses its narrative of multiple media to the single medium of the written word.

Given both the limitations of the print medium and the privileging of the word in the study of the Tapestry, the next phase of study lies not on the page but on the screen. As well-developed applications of literary theory have the potential to define more clearly the discursive nature and operation of the Bayeux Tapestry, hypertextual and hypermedial technologies have already begun to demonstrate their power to position interpretation in proper reference to the presentation of the object of study itself. A "medium" by nature is a presentational mode situated *in the middle*, caught between the subject and object, and a key *media*tor in the process of signification. The rigidly linear, splintered medium of print, however, has proven to be a rather opaque middleman, obstructing more than clarifying our view of the Bayeux Tapestry.

With hypermedia one can recenter the visual object of study and can format textual commentary to remain hidden until a user requires/desires to view it. Reproducing the Tapestry digitally also enables a spatialization of the textile that, though certainly not identical to the presence of the original work, provides for a more utile representation. Such display allows for a seamless presentation of the continuous narrative on any number of resolutions of detail, in marked contrast to the traditional conundrum of the print medium: show longer sections of the Tapestry only at the expense of close detail, or vice versa. Though my recently published *Digital Edition of the Bayeux Tapestry* contains such features, and others for a more fluid study of the Tapestry, this two-dimensional electronic edition is only the first and most rudimentary step along the path to realizing the potential of digital technology in the treatment of such objects.[113] [→193]

Ironically, digitizing the Bayeux Tapestry might now be the closest one can come to recapturing the original spatial environment of the monumental textile. For reasons of preservation and safety, the Centre Guillaume le Conquérant now displays the Tapestry in a single horseshoe-shaped case; the textile curves around centralized air-conditioning and security machinery. Viewers, then, experience the Tapestry as a long visual line, always on their left, bent in the middle. This method of display almost certainly contradicts the original vision of the work's spatial context, be it cathedral nave or aristocratic hall. Original viewers of the Tapestry entered *into* the Tapestry, and were immersed in the narrative as they followed it. [→53, 118] Digital technology espouses such networked webs of meaning, and with current technology it is now possible to create three-dimensional virtual environments in which audiences of the Tapestry may experience it inside the nave, inside the hall, making similar connections across the space of the visual narrative. Inside the

Digital Edition of the Bayeux Tapestry, for example, users may link to discourse on the Tapestry in a similar fashion, making new connections across a database of traditionally linear textual arguments.

Digital technology and hypertext theory herald a reduction, if not a rejection, of the physical and hermeneutic influence of printed scholarship. But in the study of the Bayeux Tapestry, as in the study of all medieval discourse, the fulfillment of critical closure, like the eventual cessation of reading in hypertext fiction, remains both open and desired. Given the literary and phenomenological conditioning that things must end, we still must consider narratives in terms of their ending, even when, as with hypertext fiction or the Bayeux Tapestry, texts lack determinable ends or interpretations. In hypertexts without discrete ends, users find closure in the work when they feel it—closure is intuited, not dictated. Users/readers explore a networked text until they feel no more must be done, no more can be learned.

At this point, traditional motion toward the physical end of the text translates into closure itself in the form of achieving the satisfaction of going as far as one might and understanding the realms of possible and feasible meanings. This sense of completion can derive from finding what one believes is *the* singular meaning of the work, or from prioritizing the meanings found within this search and settling on something that most nearly satisfies, that provides the greatest sense of completion.[114] In hypertextual discourse, narrative satisfaction revolves around readerly perspective and an active participation in the drive toward closure. In such texts, then, the closure does not come with the end; rather, the end comes with the discovery of closure.

The same reversal of end and closure holds true for a hypercritical interpretation of the Bayeux Tapestry. Viewers of the textile now must find closure according to individuated needs and desires. Admittedly, most come to the Tapestry's unfinished end, whether in a book or on screen or in Bayeux, and accept the formalist thesis of the structural balance of the submission of London nobles and the coronation of William; fewer argue for the applicability of the open-ended and unfinished quality of the textile's current end, and fewer still understand the work as hypertextual. The Tapestry's hypertextuality functions as an epistemological analogy for the 250-year process of its critical reception. To return to Bolter's phrase, both the narrative and the interpretation of the Bayeux Tapestry "do and do not end." Likewise, this hypercritical study does and does not end. The bulk of this chapter reads like a simple genealogy of medieval studies: it begins with what amounts to a codicological description of the object, continues with the object's history or reception, provides readings from the applications of formalist modern theory to the postmodern leanings of New Historicism, and finishes with the poststructural flourish of understanding the medieval as digital. [→35]

The process of reception of the Tapestry only starts with the Anglo-Norman audiences the textile surrounded, and today continues figuratively in academic efforts to unwrap the work's content. What connects these efforts is technology. The Tapestry remains a unique medieval survival of technological innovation, a new medium, a new way to broadcast social or political content to separate groups or communities. The term *broadcast* itself, now an indicator of electronic transmission, has an agrarian origin in the physical scattering of seeds; conversely, the integration of the technologies of electronic transmission and physical texts, the new digital modes of broad-casting, now can reveal much about the older forms of similar purpose. If anything, the technological operation of the Tapestry now stands as a distant ancestor to that of the hypertext.

The Bayeux Tapestry is not a structure of meaning but a *hyperstructure* of meanings—a set of variegated interpretations of the same document that result in a collective, synthetic matrix of meaning inside which the reader determines, not the end of the work, but an understanding of the end that satisfies. This hyperstructure functions hypercritically as a model for the interrelation of the various interpretive endings of the Tapestry presented above. Inevitably, this study here must function as my closure of the Bayeux Tapestry's missing end. The recognition of the matrix of social, structural, circular, indeterminate, false, and reconstructed endings, and of the contingent quality of their existence to individual contexts, is the method that satisfies my own reading of the Tapestry. This conclusion, fittingly, both acknowledges in the study of the Bayeux Tapestry the material, critical, and technological impossibility of a steady and singular understanding of its ending, and brings this chapter, *finally*, to a close.

The Virtual Reality of the Anglo-Saxon *Mappamundi*

Geometric projection is the best instance of a perfectly faithful representation which, without knowledge of some logical rule, appears to be a misrepresentation. A child looking at a map of the world in Mercator projection cannot help believing that Greenland is larger than Australia; he simply finds it larger. The projection employed is not the usual principle of copying which we use in all visual comparisons or translations, and his training in the usual rule makes him unable to "see" by the new one. It takes sophistication to "see" the relative sizes of Greenland and Australia on a Mercator map. Yet a mind educated to appreciate the projected image brings the eye's habit with it. After a while, we genuinely "see" the thing as we apprehend it.

—Susanne K. Langer

The computer makes possible a kind of historical atlas in which invasions and battles, colonization, and the growth of populations and cities are shown in time as well as space.

—Jay David Bolter

England . . . Just a conspiracy of cartographers.

—Tom Stoppard

As the previous examination of the Bayeux Tapestry has suggested, the study, formation, and reproduction of medieval expression often need to add a healthy consideration of the spatial to the textual modes of interpretation that—by default, almost by instinct—drive most modern criticism. As this chapter and the next will show, the "space" of a medieval expression should not be limited to the internal physical space it occupies, but should include also the more expansive, outer medieval spaces, real or imagined, that it helps define and ultimately produce. Representational technologies of the Middle Ages translated the medieval world into media and, like print culture and like today's New Media, continuously and variably reformulated the ways in which the "real" world was understood.

In today's level four age of information, transparent and immediate access to massive amounts of data has fostered what is now commonly called the "global economy" [→34]; while the law of the conservation of mass more or less dictates that the physical breadth of our world remain the same, our sense of the scale of this world has shrunk dramatically. Indeed, it is safe to say that our notion of the world "out there" is now subject to constant re-configuration, as through technology (digital or otherwise) we can more and more quickly connect to other parts of the world in all sorts of ways. In early medieval society, the geographic and cultural sense of the world "out there" may have shifted at a different pace and scale, but technologies of representa-tion played an equally important role in shaping the perceived world, and revealing the values of those who recorded their views of the world. Maps, of course, are literal worldviews. Medieval world maps, or *mappaemundi*, are also technological productions, medieval multimedia of text, image, theology, science, and received classical and local lore, which can reveal much about the culture that produced them.

In the first edition of the first volume of J. B. Harley and David Woodward's ongoing and magisterial project, *The History of Cartography*, a printing error reverses its color reproduction of the only surviving nonschematic Anglo-Saxon map of the world.[1] Such an error is perhaps understandable, as this world map, commonly known as the Cotton Map (see figure 11), looks nothing like the graphic representations of the world to which modern readers are accus-tomed.[2] To make sense of this Anglo-Saxon worldview, one must overcome many perceptual hurdles as, even correctly aligned, the Cotton Map defies and distorts our modern notions of how the earth looks. Like most medieval *map-paemundi*, the Anglo-Saxon map is literally *orient*ed, with the east at the top. But unlike most of its medieval counterparts, the Cotton Map presents the known world inside a vertical rectangle, squaring the traditionally circular con-vention of medieval (and, to some degree, modern) cartography. For a viewer more used to modern maps, the initial experience of the Cotton Map is one of extreme disorientation (and not just in *The History of Cartography*); sense can be made of this world, but only eventually, after some serious cognitive reset-ting. To modern eyes, these medieval worlds never seem quite right.

Because of perceptual problems, studies of cartography until very recently have not been very kind to medieval world maps, leveling such charges as that "fancy runs riot and the facts are badly distorted" and that they "become more and more removed from reality."[3] Ironically, *The History of Cartography* now distorts the Cotton Map in turn, reversing the way the map should be seen. The unintentional reorientation highlights, quite by accident, the longstand-

Figure 11. The Anglo-Saxon map of the world, MS Cotton Tiberius B.V, fol. 56v (Cotton Map). By permission of the British Library.

ing cartographic biases against medieval maps that the work of Harley and Woodward, and others in the recent school of what could be called critical cartography, seek to combat.[4] As these editors remark,

> Cartographic history [has now become] the study of needs and wants rather than of just the ability to make maps in the technical sense. . . . it follows that the capacity of cartography to influence actions or to mold mental worlds must depend not only on the extent to which maps were actually seen but also on the way they, or their messages, were understood.[5]

Maps are attempts to represent the physical world—the "real world," if you will. [→52] But all maps, medieval or modern, also "mold mental worlds," shaping reality by overtly dictating how the actual world is to be charted and quantified. For us today, at least in quotidian experience, maps stand as the reproduction of geographic reality; unless we physically travel the terrain, map in hand, maps remain largely signifying objects that create an assumed, virtual understanding of reality.

Today "virtual reality," of course, means the digital technology of simulacra of physical environments that may then be experienced as if they were real. Exploring the depicted world of the Cotton Map through both critical cartography and virtual reality (VR), reveals much about the representational strategies of this Anglo-Saxon fashioning of the world, and what role these strategies in turn play in defining aspects of Anglo-Saxon reality.

THE WORLD OF THE COTTON MAP

The Cotton Map survives as folio 56v of Brit. Lib. MS Cotton Tiberius B.V, though its current place in the manuscript is not its original one, and it measures 21 cm × 17 cm (about 8.5" × 7").[6] Patrick McGurk roughly dates the work to 1050 and tentatively traces its composition to Christ Church, Canterbury, though N. R. Ker dates it slightly earlier, to the first quarter of the eleventh century, and hypothesizes that the entire manuscript may have been produced at Winchester.[7] Because of the map's "true" orientation, the British Isles occupy the lower left-hand corner, while the Mediterranean runs straight up the middle, passing a distended Italy and linking up with the Black Sea, which separates northeastern Europe from Asia Minor. Asia and India run across the top of the map, while below these regions Asia Minor, Syria, and Palestine appear, full of scriptural place-names, neatly compartmentalized into quadrilateral sections. The Persian Gulf and the Red Sea dominate the southeast of the map, while what would today be considered North Africa and a trifur-cated Nile River, colored red, run down the entire right side of the map; all bodies of water in the southern regions are likewise colored red or orange. The map contains some 147 inscriptions, numerous geographic features—rivers, mountains, lakes—and one delicately drawn lion in northeast Asia. Land-masses themselves rest inside a surrounding wash of gray ocean, which in turn resides inside a thin, double-lined rectangular frame.

Surprisingly, despite such past descriptions as "famous and oft-quoted" and "justly famous," the Cotton Map has received scant critical attention over the past century.[8] In 1895 Konrad Miller provided a nine-page commentary, and almost a century later Patrick McGurk updated Miller with an analysis of similar length and character.[9] But in his "Famous Maps in the British Mu-seum," J.A.J. De Villiers barely touches on the Cotton Map, while the work does not merit even a mention in any of the three essays presented jointly as a treatment of medieval maps in "Landmarks of British Cartography."[10] In other scholarship, when the map is mentioned, it is almost always discussed only tangentially in reference to Anglo-Saxon literature or to later medieval *mappaemundi*.[11]

The general lack of scholarly interest in the oldest detailed English map of the world doubtless stems, at least indirectly, from a traditional prejudice against medieval *mappaemundi*. Such maps were long considered the "bar-barous offspring" of their more scientific parents from Greece and Rome, and viewed until recently as little more than "passive" interruptions to the evolution of accuracy in mapmaking begun in antiquity and resumed with the advent of portolan charts and the rediscovery of Ptolemy in the early fif-teenth century.[12] Though the majority of later map scholars might not employ words as harsh as De Villiers' 1914 assessment that the "crude and primitive" medieval world maps are evidence that "the science of cartography had sunk to a low ebb," most at least tacitly concurred that such maps contained "little geographic value."[13]

Similar views of medieval cartography flourished in the age of exploration directly following the Middle Ages, when maps became indispensable for safe travel across vast and uninhabited distances. Columbus and his early succes-sors may have examined late medieval *mappaemundi* for theoretical support for a western route to the East, or for the existence of a New World, but the political exigencies that followed demanded increasingly accurate maps, and so rapidly rendered the vague inspiration of these medieval *mappaemundi* passé.[14] Bias against *mappaemundi* arose even in the medieval period; in the early thirteenth century Gervase of Tilbury, who worked on a cartographic reconstruction based on Roman administrative maps, also lambasted those "lying pictures which the vulgar called *mappaemundi*."[15] Many modern views, however more refined in their approach, subtly echo Gervase's sentiments. McGurk's survey of the Cotton Map, one of the most recent in scholarship, focuses chiefly on the map's level of geographic (in)accuracy, usually by describing the work's distortion or disproportional treatments of this region or that.[16]

In the past, cartographic critics have appeared at a loss to understand the Cotton Map, as it refuses to fit neatly into the classificatory and stemmatic schemes laid out for medieval *mappaemundi*. Of the 1,100 or so extant *mappaemundi*, only 103 are detailed maps, and only four (including the Cotton Map) date from before the twelfth century.[17] Most maps from the period read more as simple diagrams than as depictions of geography; the most common model is the "T-O" scheme (see figure 12), which displays a tripartite world with Asia above Europe and Africa, divided by the crossbars of the Don and Nile rivers, and the Mediterranean (the "T"), and surrounded by a circular ocean (the "O").[18]

In contrast, the Anglo-Saxon map fashions a world that evokes the contours of actual landscape; in the words of one commentator, the map "shows with a rare degree of accuracy places and features not illustrated elsewhere and in its coastal delineation surpasses any map prepared before the fourteenth century."[19] The map also only loosely delineates the separation of Asia from Europe and Africa—in the north the horizontal bar of the Don is not readily apparent, while in the south the Nile curves eastward (upward) as on *mappaemundi* from the later Middle Ages. In color, as well, the map contrasts with its cartographic peers, as the map's use of heavy gray and bright orange has no known analogue.[20] In his comprehensive assessment of the categories of *mappaemundi*, David Woodward also has trouble classifying the map. He considers it "nonschematic tripartite"—that is, a scheme that lacks a scheme—but even then is forced to group the Cotton Map with maps largely originating a century or more later.[21] Unless one groups it with much later maps, the Anglo-Saxon map of the world ends up, more or less, in a class by itself, only tangentially and tentatively attached to categories of better understood and more closely related groups of maps.

In its 147 geographic, biblical, and historical inscriptions, the Cotton Map likewise defies easy textual classification. Woodward considers the map to be "directly based" on Paulus Orosius's fifth-century description of the world

Figure 12. Sample T-O map, MS Royal 6C.1, fol. 108v. By permission of the British Library.

contained in his *Historia adversum paganos*.[22] It is true that large parts of the map, especially in Asia, do appear to derive wholesale from Orosius, but this text accounts for only half of the inscriptions included.[23] Sources for the other half cannot be identified with any certainty. Many of them reside within a dense intertextual network of sources and/or analogues, and could variously derive from combinations or redactions of several possible candidates, including Pliny, Mela, Solinus, Æthicus Ister, pilgrimage lists, and scriptural commentaries by Jerome, Isidore, and Beatus, while the bulk of the inscriptions for northeastern Europe and Britain do not appear to derive from any standard literary text.[24]

The Cotton Map, therefore, stands as a work of both art and writing for which no easy stemmatic reconstruction or source study is possible. [→18] If, as has been written, medieval maps "have a family relationship just as human beings," with "distinct parentage and origin in common stock," the Cotton Map stands as at best an orphan and at worst a bastard child.[25] Inaccessible to traditional approaches of medieval literary and art historical studies, it is not surprising, in retrospect, that this map has garnered so little attention. As we have seen in the previous chapter, the Bayeux Tapestry, another "famous" early English document combining text and image, has a dozen or so sure literary analogues, makes reference to places and people easily identified and studied, and contains a specific and progressive narrative. It also boasts some six hundred critical treatments in the past two hundred years.[26] In contrast, the Cotton Map remains caught in a scholarly vicious circle. Difficult to make sense of from a geographic, artistic, or literary perspective, the map has never acquired a foundation of commentary to keep it circulating in the academic mainstream, in order to generate further scholarly discourse. For all practical purposes, the "justly famous" map remains opaque, largely untaught and un-studied.

As noted, recent "spatial turns" in cartographic studies have softened the critical stance toward medieval *mappaemundi*.[27] Such maps, we find, are "no longer judged against classical or modern models of representing geographical space" but are instead "studied in terms of the cultures that produced them."[28] This new critical model ceases to censure medieval maps for moving further and further from reality, and instead starts with the understanding that *map-paemundi* are merely an extreme function of reality, that is, of the cultural subjectivity that all maps contain. Most recently, treatments of the relation-ship between maps and reality have taken a further step into the realm of the poststructural. In *Mapping Reality*, Geoff King notes that while cartographers now concede that "maps inevitably distort reality," this critical shift itself is te-leologically suspect, "suggesting as it does the possibility of some kind of pure, undistorted representation" of the real world.[29] As maps become more and more accurate in their schematized signification, then, they become further and further divorced from "real" perception of the space they reproduce. Or, in the words of novelist Jeanette Winterson,

> A map can tell me how to find a place I have not seen but have often imagined . . . but when I get there, following the map faithfully, the place is not the place of my imagination. Maps, growing evermore real, are much less true.[30]

Theorists like King doubt the "traditional distinctions between map and territory, image and reality." Drawing on such critics as McLuhan and Baudrillard, King supports the postmodern distrust of a notional and essentialist doctrine of the real. Rather, in the words of Baudrillard, "the real is not only that which can be reproduced, *but that which is always already reproduced*: the hyperreal."[31] As such, maps end up occupying an uneasy liminal space between representation and reality, at least in part constructing the world they seek to represent. [→168]

Medieval authors, consciously or not, also acknowledged that the depiction of the world could become the world; the Middle English word *mappamonde* sometimes referred not to a map but to the world itself.[32] The creation and viewing of maps are acts that "translate one's position in space"; traces of such acts may be found in maps in order to better understand the world in which such cultural performances took place.[33] The Cotton Map's lack of coherent textual and geographic formulae points to its own *hyperreal* quality and a lack of concern with issues of traceable origins. The Cotton Map, an Anglo-Saxon attempt to represent reality, is also then a representation that *forms* Anglo-Saxon reality—in other words, it is *hyperreality*.

VIRTUAL WORLDS

Not surprisingly, the role that the digital technology of virtual reality (VR) plays in hyperreal blurring of representation and reality comes up quite frequently in both postmodern critiques of the real and nascent theorizing about New Media.[34] VR encompasses a broad set of computer-generated representations of reality that provide the user with the ability to interact with and navigate through a simulated environment. Such systems can range from two-dimensional, 360-degree video panoramas to four-wall "immersive" virtual environments wherein the user wears goggles and uses a control stick to "walk" through a perceived space and manipulate represented objects found inside the space. David Rothenberg describes such systems as "virtual" because their "location or features cannot be pinpointed in the tangible world. . . . [They exist] within the relation between the machine and the user." A virtual reality does not exist wholly in the computer, nor wholly in the mind of the user. Rather, in such environments, as Rothenberg puts it, we "move through a constructed universe of our own making."[35]

Maps and VR share the notion that manufactured representations of geography are able to conveniently provide an understanding of the world represented. The very first VR environment, created in the MIT labs in 1972, presented on laserdisc a "surrogate travel application," a topographical tour of the town of Aspen, Colorado, where users could virtually drive through the streets of the town, turning this way or that at will, choose to stop in front of major buildings and go inside, and even select the time of year for the simulation through a "season knob."[36] As another technology that creates simulacra of what New Media theorists commonly call the "primary world," VR, like maps, parallels and conditions reality rather than simply representing it.[37] In their analysis of "apparent boundary disputes between the real and virtual," Marcus Doel and David Clarke argue that virtual environments must not be understood as subordinate forms of reality, akin to skiagraphic patterns on Plato's cave.[38] Instead, Doel and Clarke maintain, "by way of the virtual, one is able to realise (actualise) the latent potential of the world . . . no virtuality without reality, and no reality without virtuality."[39] [→8]

The rhetoric of virtual technology has become heady, ambitious in character, promising all sorts of pellucid access to worlds physical or otherwise. One recent print advertisement for multimedia technology shows a man, his suit and tie covered in projected text, passing his hand through a semitransparent school of dolphins against a backdrop of the curve of the earth. The ad copy promises: "At the rate we're advancing multimedia, soon you won't be flipping through this magazine, you'll be walking through it."[40] The language of this ad highlights another key precept of VR: that liquidity of information will be accessed and experienced as some sort of terrain (as also indicated in the ad by the background of the planet). The utopian vision of the ad merges knowledge with travel—readers apparently someday will not read, but will virtually walk through information, as the man does, crossing both the text projected upon him and the dolphins that virtually swim around him.[41] [→55]

These two aspects of VR—the synthesis of physical distance, and the understanding that information itself can be rendered into space and "traveled"—have much to do with understanding Anglo-Saxon maps of the world. Even commentators who have disdained medieval maps have acknowledged their elastic framework: *mappaemundi*, like VR, are multimedia products that through their technology can represent that which is physically impossible. Medieval mapmakers also understood that their products needed to combine different media to succeed. In the early fourteenth century, Fra Paolino Veneto noted that the best *mappaemundi* came in the form of

> a two-fold map [composed] of painting and writing. Nor will you deem one sufficient without the other, because painting without writing indicates regions or nations unclearly, [and] writing without the aid of

painting truly does not mark the boundaries of the provinces of a region in their various parts sufficiently for them to be described.[42]

Veneto further stresses that world maps are valued because they codify hard-to-grasp knowledge and allow the mind to "make an image" of what is known of the descendants of biblical peoples and their past and present nations and regions, as reported in "divine and human writings."

Typical assessments of the Cotton Map's gaps in geographic reality often fail to consider the map's "intellectual landscape"—what the Anglo-Saxons did know, as opposed to what they did not.[43] As Naomi Kline notes, medieval maps of the world must be understood to function less as an accurate indicator of physical space than as "conceptual enclosures for stored information."[44] In New Media terms, the map should therefore be understood as a *datascape*—a cartographic product that need not have correspondence "with any real place on earth, but rather with imaginary places and circumstances made to seem real enough by an appeal to aspects of visual perception."[45] Analogous to such a theory of virtual environments, the representational technology of a medieval world map provides an areal and visual simulation of physical terrain, only distantly related to the "real world," and more explicitly encoded with specific symbolic data that both create and affirm the viewer's sense of the world. In short, as information in the digital age tends to be understood in terms of landscape, terrain, or distance—as in "cyberspace" and the much-touted "information superhighway" of the 1990s—so should the geography of the Cotton Map be read as an Anglo-Saxon datascape.[46] [→159]

Today much of medieval map scholarship tends to read *mappaemundi* through the singular lens of Christian theology.[47] While spiritual matters play a central role in the content of the Anglo-Saxon *mappamundi*, this religious content did not operate in a vacuum. Sylvia Tomasch notes that medieval representations of the physical world are packed with broader cultural impulses and "geographical anxieties and desires."[48] When evaluating cartographic discourse, Tomasch warns of "reifying the image with such precision that no space remains between the signifier and the signified, between the simulacrum and the thing itself—between, that is, the text and the territory."[49] With regard to the Cotton Map, the traditional approach of cartography need not be reinvented by substituting theology for topographic accuracy. Desires and anxieties of medieval maps certainly may be spiritual, but they can also be political, historical, economic, or literary.[50] The three studies of the Cotton Map presented below provide a series of close rhetorical readings that start by defining functions of the map through theories of VR and finish by understanding the content and meaning of the map not as an index of geographic reality but rather as a map of Anglo-Saxon hyperreality.[51]

THE LINES ON THE MAP

When we think of maps today, we primarily consider them in terms of lines. On a local scale, maps give us the roads we follow to other roads, the rivers we might cross on the way, the contours of elevations, and the boundaries between neighborhoods, towns, counties, states, and so forth. On the global level, lines can become even more abstract: the time zones, longitudes and latitudes, the International Dateline. Overall, the lines on a modern map function as an index of its accuracy; we look to them to reveal the natural and constructed world as it actually is, much as Renaissance practitioners of Cartesian perspective relied on linear projections to better reproduce in two dimensions what the eye perceived in three. [→8, 167]

The Cotton Map is an image drawn from lines, but it is also a set of expressions drawn from texts, the lines of which intersect within the page of the map, itself contained within the manuscript of a larger Anglo-Saxon anthology of texts and images. Arguably, maps such as the Cotton Map become more than images or illustrations of texts; they create cultural narratives in their own right.[52] The form of the Cotton Map is both built and largely understood through linear means—through physical line and linear text, and then through stemmatic study and textual analysis in its interpretation. At the same time, while the Cotton Map (like VR) may be constructed upon grids of geographic and textual lines, it defies the operational expectations of linear expression and creates meaning in ways that the predominant methodologies of academic study, themselves overwhelmingly linear, are not set up to recognize or perpetuate easily.

The Cotton Map's depiction of Asia and Africa, as mentioned, draws heavily from Orosius. Konrad Miller, while acknowledging this debt, argues that "the positions of the rendered countries do not agree with Orosius's text at all."[53] Proving such a claim would be a difficult endeavor at best, as no map illustrating Orosius's description of the world survives from classical times.[54] In his surveys of medieval maps, Miller drew his own versions, based on actual medieval prototypes, to illustrate his idealized conception of accurate maps of geographic literature such as Orosius. Such maps, to be sure, tell us nothing about classical maps and much about Miller's modern desire to privilege literary accounts in his assessment of medieval maps.

Orosius, of course, is connected more famously to the Anglo-Saxon world by way of the late-ninth-century Old English translation of *Historiarum adversum paganos libri VII* (often attributed to King Alfred), in which contemporary accounts of Ohthere's and Wulfstan's voyages around the coasts of northeast Europe are interpolated into Orosius's geographic description.[55] Comparing the Alfredian translation to its classical source, Sealy Gilles observes that while Orosius appears to take "an entirely physical" approach to the world he describes, the Anglo-Saxon version "consistently subordinates physical to political geography and carefully delineates the juxtaposition of peoples," an effect no doubt due in part to the Old English text's function not as a description of a studied world but instead as a subsequent translation (in the textual and geographic sense), a representation of a representation of a now-less-familiar world.[56] [→33]

In the Cotton Map, similar remnants of an attempted literal delineation of Orosian material may still be found, garbled by geographic unfamiliarity and the incompatibility of literary and visual mappings of the same geographic terrain. For example, the map inscribes the Taurus or Taurian mountain range in Eurasia twice, to groups of mountains separated by a considerable distance (see figure 13). In Asia Minor, south and east of the region labeled Cappadocia and under the Armenian gap, an image of Noah's ark, and the city of *Docusa* (Dascusa), a short group of mountains bears the inscription "Mons Taurus." Further east in Asia Major, a longer chain of mountains has been titled "Taurini montes" and stands as a northern reference point for the region containing Mesopotamia and the rivers likely meant to represent the Tigris and the Euphrates. Approaching the map through Orosius's text, the double listing of the Taurian range makes some kind of sense, however, as Orosius uses this range four different times to locate other geographic areas.[57] In one place, the inscriptions of the Cotton Map more or less reproduce part of a geographic sequence described by Orosius, where Cappadocia is bounded to the west by Asia Minor, to the east by Armenia (where Orosius additionally marks the border with the city of Docusa), and to the south by the Taurian Mountains (here the range marked "Mons Taurus").[58] In the Cotton Map, however, unfamiliarity with the precise geography of Asia leads to certain problems with layout, with the result that the western set of mountains could not then also be identified as the mountain range bordering the Mesopotamian region farther to the east. Consequently, just as the text of Orosius lists the mountain range more than once, so does the Cotton Map, thereby preserving the vestiges of the Orosian textual order of representation, and the attempt to follow it.

Figure 13. Taurian Mountains in the Cotton Map. By permission of the British Library.

But text is not really the same thing as territory. The example of the Cotton Map's treatment of the Taurian range demonstrates how writing can parse geographic representation, lexically breaking continuous terrain into small pieces of necessarily linear description, and at times demand that a specific location be mentioned several times. Maps, on the other hand, promote a one-to-one correspondence of visual signifier to location signified, simultaneously showing a point's spatial relationship to all other places represented. [→100] The Cotton Map's duplication of the Taurian Mountains ultimately stems from the retranslation of geographic text back into visual terrain.

In his description of the Mesopotamian region, Orosius states that from the Taurian and Caucasian mountains, Mesopotamia begins in the north between the Tigris and Euphrates rivers, and then "to the south follows, in succession, first Babylonia, then Chaldea and lastly Arabia Eudaemon, a narrow strip of land that faces east and lies between the Persian and Arabian gulfs."[59] The syntax of Orosius's Latin text emphasizes the linearity of this description: "succedit Babylonia, deinde Chaldea, novissime Arabia Eudaemon," the *succession* of Babylonia, *then* Chaldea, and *lastly* Arabia Eudemon. The Cotton Map reproduces this progression closely: working southward from the perpendicular line of mountains, centered more or less on the inscription "Taurini montes," the viewer finds in order "Mesopotamia," "Babilonia," and "Chaldea," all directly above or below a line probably meant to represent the Euphrates River (see figure 14).[60] Significantly, though, "Arabia eudemon" (a region corresponding roughly to present-day Yemen) does not occur next on this lateral line, or even in its standard place between the Persian Gulf and the Red Sea (or Arabian Gulf). Instead, the Cotton Map places "Arabia" and "eudemon" into regions east of the Orosian line of progression, and before, not between, the twin red bodies representing the Persian and Arabian gulfs. In the Orosian place between these gulfs, the Cotton Map lists two items: "mons Sina" and "Arabica deserta."

Of course, a number of possible explanations exist for why the Cotton Map shifts Arabia Eudemon out of the gulf area, among them a misinterpretation of the Latin source, the influence of an alternative source or analogue, or a competing representative tradition in Old English texts. While not corresponding closely to most of the Cotton Map, the *Old English Orosius*, for instance, omits Arabia Eudemon from its Orosian grouping and instead includes it a few lines further on: "Ondlong þæs Redan Seas, þæs dæles þe þær norð scyt, ligeð þæt land Arabia ¬ Sabei ¬ Eudomane" [Along the Red Sea, in the region spreading to the north, lies that land of Arabia and the Sabei and Eudaemon].[61] The

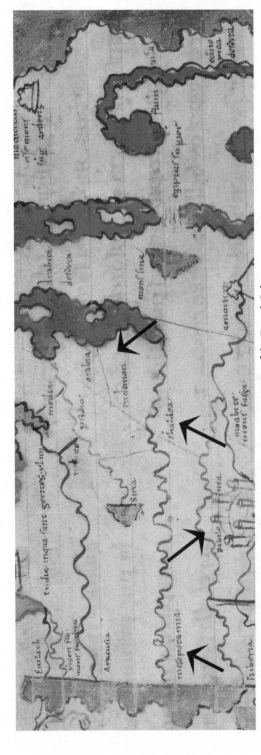

Figure 14. The Mesopotamian region in the Cotton Map. By permission of the British Library.

Cotton Map gives the narrow area between the two bodies of water over to the Arabian Desert, a tradition later seen in more detailed *mappaemundi* such as the Sawley Map and the Hereford Map.[62] The "Arabica deserta" ultimately refers to the desert of the Arabahe, wherein the tribes of Israel wandered for forty years and where, as described in Deuteronomy 1, Moses delivered his last speech to his people after forty years of peripateticism.[63] Below (to the west and inland from) this desert, the map displays Mount Sinai, where, famously, Moses received the tablets of the Ten Commandments.[64]

The two items that displace Orosian material, therefore, represent landmarks, or milestones, if you will, from another textual account: that of Moses and the exodus of the Israelites. South of Mount Sinai, unmarked, the map shows a clear break in the Red Sea meant to mark Moses' parting of the waters (see right-hand side of figure 14). Continuing this line to the south, the map then displays the inscription "egiptus superior," marking the beginning point of the Israelites' journey. Beyond this toponym, still continuing in a straight line, the next inscription, "flum(en) Nilus," marks the Nile River, which has several Mosaic attributions but mostly famously serves as the reedy refuge of the infant Moses.[65]

Opposite the southerly motion of the Orosian description, then, runs a northerly summary of Scripture, from Moses' birth to the flight from Egypt through the Red Sea and onto Sinai. At the point where the lines of biblical and Orosian narrative meet, they turn upward (eastward) to finish—the Orosian with the misplaced "Arabia eudemon," and the Mosaic with the "Arabica deserta." In short, within the space of the map's visual geography, two opposing lines of textual geography collide, and are accommodated by a rewriting of represented space.

The cartographic representation of biblical travel itineraries is nothing novel; many, and especially ones with a Mosaic theme, turn up in *mappae-mundi*, and a map of the Exodus has elsewhere been found with Orosian material.[66] Additionally, Anglo-Saxon culture has been shown to have an especial affinity for the migratory aspects of the Exodus narrative, and for Moses, whose laws King Alfred singled out as an important basis for his own.[67] One must, of course, be careful not to overdetermine the plan of these opposing lines of travel within the Cotton Map, if only because other places with Old Testament and even Mosaic significance may be found elsewhere on the map, complicating the perceived lines of progression. But this example still serves to show how literary texts do not simply frame and fill this Anglo-Saxon world, but actively dictate how medieval mapmakers arranged the represented world, and negotiated overlaps of textual delineation by plotting them region by region.

The intersection of Orosian and Mosaic narratives within the Cotton Map also demonstrates the difficulty in representing the linearity of written narrative inside the visual space of a *mappaemundi*. Hayden White observes the tendency to privilege the narrativization of reality and the world through historical discourse, but questions if "the world, even the social world, ever really comes to us already narrativized, already 'speaking itself' from beyond the horizon of our capacity to make scientific sense of it?"[68] White further wonders if any realism is possible without its narration. The nature of written texts, and the ways they are subsequently read and rewritten through medieval maps and then modern scholarship, certainly suggests that continuous narration and renarration constructs much of the representation of reality. But maps like the Cotton Map function less like a linear narrative than like a discourse from beyond the narrativized horizon of "scientific sense" and the conventions of print, though perhaps not in a manner that White ever imagined.

If anything, these maps express meaning more like digital expressions than traditional print. John Lienhard's description of how cyberspace has transformed the way history is known provides a useful corollary. For Lienhard, cyberspace

> makes a grand resource, but it's a resource that fits no model of information transmittal we were raised with. . . . And history's story takes shape in a new form. We're used to stories that unfold from the printed page. On the Web, the story builds up like a mosaic.[69] [→38]

As the conflict between the Orosian and Mosaic narratives indicates, the "social world" of the Cotton Map is in some ways an uncomfortable frame for the narratives written—or, rather, drawn and labeled—within it. The mosaic of the map accommodates them, it seeks to use them to reference lines of the written word, but it also complicates their representation. The plotting of narrative lines on geographic lines (and vice versa) calls attention to how the narratives of written histories and geographies construct a reality at least one plane removed from the "primary world."

This is not to deny the function of narratives within maps. Indeed, the primary use of maps today is to trace sequences of progress (our routes) through the represented world. But while a written narrative guides the reader through meaning, line by line, on a course from which it is difficult to deviate, "a good map allows for more than one line of thought."[70] *Mappaemundi* tend to bewilder because they deny narrative lines even as they use them, functioning not simply in terms of the writings from which they are constructed but rather, to return to Kline's phrase, as "conceptual enclosures for information." In this way, they operate much more like digital databases, or hypermedial discourse, presenting multiple lines of meaning as previously fixed lines of narrative are simultaneously presented inside the frame page of a worldview.

But as a database of meaning, the *mappamundi* also relates an impression of the physical reality of the world outside the familiar limits of the viewer's localized knowledge/experience. In doing so, maps disclose efforts to organize space through linear structures very similar to those of virtual reality. As Woodward notes and as we have seen, *mappaemundi* can systematically plot content and attempt to chart textual itineraries.[71] The Cotton Map exhibits a strong affinity for the line and the corner; the map, or at least its geographic contours, may well derive from a circular model that became "stretched" over the rectilinear format of the manuscript folio. Most *mappaemundi* are circular, of course, as they relate the form of the world Platonically to the spherical cosmography of the heavens. In books and manuscripts, such a form creates a shapely resistance to the hard and physical edges of the page—the world these images suggest does not fit easily on the written page. Stylistically, these maps incorporate circular figures with great frequency; indeed, the majority of *mappaemundi* feature schema of circles within circles. In contrast, few circular forms appear anywhere in the Cotton Map. Rather, most of this *mappamundi* emphasizes the straight and angular line, perhaps identifying a symbolic bond between the angular representation of England and the ethnographic perception that the land of the Anglii stood set off as an "angle to continental Europe and the rest of the world, both known and imagined."[72]

In contrast to other parts of the map, England itself appears downright curvaceous. As one travels east from England, the cultural, productive center of the map, toward its physical center, unnaturally straight lines begin to dominate. Most obviously, as a sense of local and regional geography gives way to the unfamiliar, the mapmaker resorts more and more to quadrilateral compartments to define geographic regions (see figure 11). These lines first tentatively appear to mark the jumbled regions around the Danube River, and become thick and certain once the elongated Aegean Sea is crossed. Even if, as has been hypothesized, these lines may ultimately descend from province markings on a Roman map, the Cotton Map's use of such lines transforms them.[73] For the most part, the lines occur in a broad band that runs straight through the center third of the map, encompassing the area above the Black Sea in the north, Asia Minor, Syria and Palestine in the center, and Egypt in the south. Much more than the bent shape of England, these lines stress that angularity and geometric uniformity arise not in England, and not on the unknown edges of the world, but primarily in regions covered by scriptural matters. Gog and Magog occupy the north-easternmost compartment of this central band, while scriptural items predominate in the center and south, as far south and west as Pentapolis and Carthage in Africa. But on either side of this band, in the realm of the familiar or the utterly unfamiliar, the regional compartments disappear, almost as if when the authoritative writing of Scripture cannot "rule" the area, then no such lines are employed. Scott Westrem describes the map's pictorial character as "spare, with lines boxing in most 'countries,' [while] waterways offer vermiform contrast to the straight lines of human boundaries."[74] Through its boxy "human boundaries," the Cotton Map anticipates the grid systems of later maps that permit what King calls "the heterogeneity of the world to be reduced to a geometrical uniformity"; Miller notes that early scholars of the map sought to interpret these boxes as parallels and meridians or vestiges of a Greek geographical grid.[75]

The gridlike representation of these regions on the Anglo-Saxon world map also punctuates the map's virtuality. VR relies on a geometric grid to create a credible version of absolute space that is still flexible enough to allow users to manipulate their position and perspective in space relative to other objects and/or locations.[76] In VR (and in popular home video games) millions of coordinate points are plotted on a Cartesian grid; objects and landscape are drawn as huge collections of tiny polygonal shapes on this grid, and the user's perspective of his or her virtual environment is constantly calculated using these coordinates. Essentially, no natural appearance of reality could exist without the massive machinery of engineered, "human" lines operating just out of virtual sight.

Like the Cotton Map, VR also seeks to represent geography by merging text and vision, and this process sheds light on how text and geographical desire intersect in the manufacture or representation of the world. Ken Hillis notes that virtual realities "manifest postmodern sensibilities" concerning the textual production of reality, down to the basic idea that even the most complex virtual environments must be plotted out to a Cartesian grid, and that beneath these representations lurks a controlling text, in the form of thousands of lines of written code. The phenomenon of virtual reality, Hillis argues, arises out of "a conscious awareness that humans have, or wish to, become the authors of their own ontological ground."[77] The boxy boundaries of the Cotton Map represent reality in similar terms—ontological and, for that matter, epistemological *ground* is exactly what is at stake in the Cottonian map. What is authored, what is coded, in the map is the struggle to understand the place of Anglo-Saxon reality in a worldly frame largely constructed by texts and learning—a world, to return to our earlier definition of virtual reality, whose "location or features cannot be pinpointed in the tangible world [that exists] within the relation between the machine and the user." Substitute "text" (really just another technological medium) for "machine" and we have defined the cultural process that drove both the production and the reception of medieval graphing of the world. [→159]

The rectilinear shapes that dominate the center strip of the Cotton Map also cannot be pinpointed in the tangible world, but these shapes' presence on the map reveals much about how the Anglo-Saxon makers constructed the world outside England. In examining these delineated areas, one can see that the map's "sense of geography is defined less by the contours of the world than by bonds of language and culture."[78] Like the representative paradox of virtual reality, where calculated lines and grids undergird the hyperreal representation of landscape and geography, the boxy human boundaries of the Cotton Map are just that: depictions of the natural world that both articulate the distance of the Anglo-Saxons from the physical reality of the represented regions and reveal the Anglo-Saxon attempt to understand, control, and in effect translate these territories into something known and familiar.

Like most other features of the Cotton Map, it is nearly impossible to chart the specific literature for the biblical locations it integrates. Bede, Jerome, Augustine, Isidore, Eusubius, and the Bible itself, or glosses of any of these works, could easily have served as the immediate source.[79] These additions stand as a sort of scriptural "greatest hits" collection, recording the geographic locations of many biblical events, including the route of the Mosaic Exodus already noted, the landfall of Noah's ark, Jericho, Gog and Magog, and, dominating the area, most of the tribes of Israel—the earliest such representation on an extant *mappamundi*.[80] Though the map includes the obligatory high points of New Testament geography as well—Bethlehem, Jerusalem, St. Paul's birthplace Tarsus—the work's overwhelming emphasis on the Old Testament matches with the notion that, while early Scripture remained rooted in this life, the teachings of Christ tended to downplay the physical world in favor of the spiritual.[81]

Theologically these locations play an important role. For medieval exegetics, the study of biblical geography was deemed essential to the proper interpretation of certain scriptural passages.[82] Many biblical locations, cities in particular, are sited with a fair degree of accuracy, or at the very least show an effort at precise plotting. The depicted tribes of Israel, however, stand out from such representations, as there appears to have been little attempt to locate these tribes anywhere near their original homes.[83] Instead, the map artificially locates *terrae incognitae* in a world where no "real" location was known. The division is abstract, but reveals the locative desire and necessity for at least the appearance of geographic knowledge about the area. On one level, the artificial boundaries ascribed to the tribes of Israel make explicit the conflict between human and natural geography debated by classical authors such as Herodotus, who questioned the naming of regions in a single landmass as a process that in effect divided an essentially undivided reality.[84] These tribal lines also oppose notions of geographical determinism traditionally ascribed to maps, as they fail to represent any real sense of the historical place of the Israelites or the contemporary social divisions of the region.

But as unreal as these divisions appear, they also create something very real in terms of the Anglo-Saxon sense of the world. In his examination of the Old English poetic version of the Book of Exodus, Nicholas Howe notes the particular and unusual attention paid to the topography of the Israelites' journey, as for Anglo-Saxon readers the terrain of Exodus could stand "as much for cultural identity as for geographical place."[85] For Howe, the Old English *Exodus* does much more than preserve the allegorical meaning of the Old Testament episode. Rather, the vernacular poem linguistically, thematically, and culturally translates the migrations of the Israelites into a revised narrative that supports and contributes to an Anglo-Saxon sense of origin and identity. In Howe's words, the poet's

> recasting of Exodus into a sea crossing should be read as his most daring attempt to contain ancestral history. For there lies the inescapable correspondence between Israelites and Anglo-Saxons. . . . The poet valued the most elemental possible version of the Exodus story: that a people found its homeland on the far shore of a sea.[86]

This particular brand of geographic desire also finds expression in the Cotton Map. Though the surviving section of the Old English *Exodus* is less concerned with the actual migration and settlement than with the crossing of the Red Sea, the *mappamundi* emphasizes both the process of the migration and the successful establishment of a homeland. But because no precise detail was available regarding the geographic location of each tribe, the map contains invented boundaries of each tribe's homeland, underscoring not only the artificiality of the representation but the anxiousness of the mapmakers to render these locations real to Anglo-Saxon viewers. In doing so, the Cotton Map reminds us that it is a datascape, as much a political map as a physical map, articulating not only physical terrain but assumed "national" boundaries as well. In this map, the gridding of Israel and similar areas thus fashions a virtual world out of a lack of specific knowledge. The divisions into unnatural boxes hyperrealize the world for Anglo-Saxon viewers; as the map combines information and space in a curious blend of the seen and the unseen, it promotes a hyperreal omniscience reminiscent of what contemporary digital critics describe as the new "reality" of cyberspace.[87]

The drawing of such arbitrary lines across the physical world can also, of course, have very real implications. When I first wrote these sentences in March of 2003, thousands of troops from the United States were fighting their way across the deserts of Iraq, on their way to Baghdad to depose that country's leader. Iraq, like much of the Middle East, has national boundaries drawn by western European powers after World War I. The establishment of such virtual boundaries often ignored the migratory reality of tribal geography and split cohesive cultural groups across fabricated national borders, but the boundaries have become real and, almost a century later, continue to contribute to geopolitical crises of international proportions.[88] Modern-day Israel, of course, remains a prime example of how imaginary lines are drawn on maps to very real and continuing effect. As some have argued, the lines marking the internal and external borders of modern Israel carved up Palestinian land "on the basis of a biblical mapping taken from a period of some sixty years [that happened] two thousand years ago."[89] Such a geographic division of the land by following historical lines drawn from texts recalls the Cotton Map's use of Orosius to manufacture its view of the world. And though they have had very real consequences for both Arabs and Israelis who live within them, the lines drawn at the founding of modern Israel remain virtual, hyperreal expressions of geographic desire, if only because both the Israeli and Palestinian states continuously work through diplomacy, violence, and resettlement to redraw them in their respective favors. In some ways, the modern lines of Israel and Palestine are no more substantive than the virtual grid an Anglo-Saxon mapmaker drew over what he thought was Israel almost one thousand years ago; in other ways, as walls continue to be constructed and whole communities attacked or rerouted one way or another, these lines simply embody another, often terribly real, form of desired reality.

Like VR, the lines on the Anglo-Saxon *mappamundi* engage, and confuse, multiple notions of textuality, narrative, and reality that in turn blur the line between the primary world and the world of representation. Paul Starrs's description of the virtual world of cyberspace as "the place where everyone is but nobody lives" is particularly apt here.[90] The end result of this eleventh-century map is a form of Anglo-Saxon virtual reality—the production of an unreal world populated with lines, not people, that also plays a vital role in reflecting Anglo-Saxon desire and fashioning Anglo-Saxon "reality."

The neat and controlled lines that dominate the center of this map also indicate the shifting nature of Anglo-Saxon England's own geopolitical boundaries. As noted, the Cotton Map's *Brittannia* contains no straight lines. Volatility of both territorial and culture definition plagued Anglo-Saxon England throughout the eleventh century, and how the Cotton Map represents England and its European neighbors potentially frames this geocultural anxiety. In contrast, the neat, unnatural compartments of Israeli tribes may indicate the very natural desire for a simple, salvific division of the world, a mapping of society based on the classificatory lines of Scripture and God's authority rather than the unruly, chaotic, and very real mapping and remapping of Anglo-Saxon England that occurred through Scandinavian and Norman invasion and/or perceptions and fears of cultural attrition throughout the eleventh century. [→ 174]

LIVING ON THE EDGE: CORNERS, BORDERS AND CENTERS

In virtual worlds, one of the defining features is the potential to modify one's perception of what is real by creating geographic worlds that emulate primary reality, but that are constructed with an emphasis on encoded information, data, rather than physical surroundings. Such virtual environments are not necessarily wholly digital—Disneyland, for example, is a very real place, yet functions as a world that contains virtual environments (rides in computer-generated simulations) nested inside other virtual environments (re-presentations of Bavarian castles, foreign cultures, or historical periods) in which nobody actually lives.[91] [→76] But "pure," or wholly digital, versions of VR perhaps provide some of the clearest examples of how an understanding of physical reality can be reconfigured, as these simulations do not need to operate within the confines or restrictions of natural space. To begin with, digital VR necessarily challenges the notion of the unique nature of the real; at the very minimum, Paul Virilio argues, with such VR "we are entering a world where there won't be one but two realities."[92]

Further, regarding maps as a function of VR exposes "the socially constructed character of the mappings within which . . . lives are oriented."[93] Like digital VR, maps exist as a material framework that nevertheless can allow a movement away from the material world it evokes, and therefore encourage the user, the viewer, to understand the physical earth from a multitude of perspectives in the same moment of representation.[94] As not only a measurement but a creation of the world known to Anglo-Saxon England, the Cotton Map exhibits a number of struggles between the twin realities of England's marginal locus in the early medieval world and the Anglo-Saxon impulse to recenter the world on their own island. In reflexive representations, early medieval societies such as Anglo-Saxon England have been understood to lack the veneer of ideological unity that comes with later examples of more modern and overtly ratiocinated expressions of national identity. Ernest Gellner, for instance, employs explicitly spatial figures to describe such conflicting realities; for Gellner, "pre-modern and pre-rational" visions of the world lack "a single continuous logical space" and instead consist of "multiple, not properly united, but hierarchically related sub-worlds" and "special privileged facts, sacralized and exempt from ordinary treatment."[95] We have already seen how the Cotton Map challenges the idea of a "single, continuous logical space" in the way it graphically distributes text, narrative, and line across its geography. Similarly, this Anglo-Saxon worldview reports the hierarchical nature of the subworlds and sacred places it contains. Rome and Jerusalem appear prominently (Rome with its six towers is one of the two largest cities shown, along with the historically huge Babylon), biblical lands occupy the center band of the map, holy waterways are distinctively colored, and a paradisiacally described island crowns the top center. England, in the meantime, occupies the lower left corner, its cities tiny and its terrain free of distinctive straight lines. However, the Cotton Map encodes a certain cultural unease with this represented order, a discomfort revealed by how the map's virtual nature allows what is edge and what is center to fluctuate across its surface, and how this fluctuation articulates an Anglo-Saxon challenge to its homeland's traditional place in the geographical order of the world.

When I first began working on the Cotton Map, an obscure inscription to the south of Noah's ark in Armenia, "Docusa civitas," caught my attention (see figure 15). What was fascinating about this unknown city was that, though the artist had provided it with a clear iconic marker, usually an indication of status, the city of Docusa was anything but well known. I eventually identified the place-name as Dascusa, a town on the Euphrates River mentioned by Orosius as being on the boundary between Armenia and Cappadocia at the northern boundary of Syria. Subsequent research revealed little of import attached to this town, from either a Roman or a Christian point of view. Indeed, the *Princeton Encyclopedia of Classical Sites* summarizes the city with unusual bluntness, reporting that "Dascusa does not figure in history."[96] Perhaps, but Dascusa does figure in this Anglo-Saxon representation of the world. Orosius records Dascusa as the easternmost city in southern Asia, marking not only the boundary between three cultural regions, Syria, Armenia, and Cappadocia, but the line between southern and northern Asia. In the Roman world of Orosius, Dascusa signified the line between known and unknown lands. In Orosius's time, the city formed a link in the *limes* of fortifications that delimited the easternmost areas of control of the Roman Empire—a sort of intermittent Hadrian's Wall for the east that Stephen Mitchell has termed the Euphrates Frontier.[97] Orosius, himself well-traveled, used the insignificant outpost of Dascusa as a convenient marker between the several established Roman regions and the unsettled northeastern frontier, known to him only through other accounts.[98] The Anglo-Saxon designer or copyist of the Cotton Map likely knew no more about Dascusa than what he read in Orosius—an outpost, a boundary between two wholly literary and equally unknown worlds—but as a boundary Dascusa held an important place. In the larger grid of Asia Minor, Dascusa also occupies a regional corner; north and east of Dascusa, the ruled lines end and the represented world begins to become less sure, and more fantastic, when known at all.

Like Dascusa, Anglo-Saxon England was seen by much of Europe, and to some degree still saw itself, as a remote corner of the physical, political, and spiritual world. In the Roman Empire, Britain was the mirror image of the eastern Euphrates frontier, a last outpost before the unknown of the west. On the map, "Brittannia" resides literally in the corner of the world, bounded first by water and then, to the north and the west, by the double-ruled lines of the border and then by the blank expanse of the margins—an *angulus Anglorum*, an angle in an Anglo-Saxon corner of the world.[99]

Anglo-Saxons inherited a long historical tradition of Britain's inferior status as a remote corner of the world. In the first century, the Roman geographer Pomponius Mela described the inhabitants of the island as "inculti omnes" [all uncivilized] and "ita magnis aliarum opum ignari" [moreover ignorant of

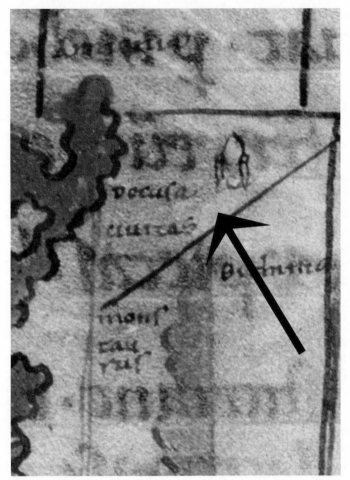

Figure 15. Docusa (Dascusa) in the Cotton Map. By permission of the British Library.

a great many other things].[100] Mela correlates the ignorance of Britons with the island's extreme distance from Rome and the Continent, and rounds out his description by noting that the British "pecore ac finibus dites" [are rich only in cattle and land].[101] Mela's use of *finibus* for "land" may contain a further joke about Britain's remoteness: *finis* commonly carries connotations of limits, ends, or borders. The people of Britain, therefore, were rich only in livestock and their own marginal status.

Three hundred years later, the Roman historian Solinus repeated this view, noting that for all practical purposes the coastline of Gaul stood as the edge

of the known world, while Britain represented a land beyond the periphery
—"paene orbis alterius" [almost an other world].[102] Such sentiments continued through early medieval writers such as Isidore, and early native writers
remained substantially invested in this perception of their home. In the sixth
century, Gildas wrote "Brittannia insula in extremo ferme orbis limite circium
occidentemque" [the island of Britain lies practically at the extreme limit of
the world, toward the west and the northwest]. By the eighth century, Bede
had softened but not erased this perception:

> Brittania Oceani insula, cui quondam Albion nomen fuit, inter septen-
> trionem et occidentem locata est, Germaniae Galliae Hispaniae, maxi-
> mis Europae partibus, multo intervallo adversa
>
> [Britain, once called Albion, is an island of the ocean and lies to the
> northwest, being opposite Germany, Gaul, and Spain, which form
> the greater part of Europe, though at a considerable distance from
> them].[103]

Positioning insular *Brittannia* in the northwest demonstrates the historical
influence of the Roman vantage point, but in the shift from imperial Rome
to medieval Rome, this distantiated perspective assumes Christian as well as
geographical significance.[104] In Gildas, one finds a striking example of spiritual calibration, as the historian initially refers to the island as "divina statera"
[in the divine scales] and then describes its conversion as the sun's warming
of "glaciali frigore rigenti insulae et velut longiore terrarum secessu soli visi-
bili non proximae" [an island frozen with lifeless ice and quite remote from
the visible sun—recessed from the world].[105] This sense of Britain's spiritual
isolation ultimately carries eschatological weight. In the words of Margaret
Bridges,

> If the boundaries of the world as it was known to the Anglo-Saxons
> through classical cosmography effectively placed them in the shabbi-
> est of margins, the tendency of Christian geographers to interpret geo-
> graphical space in terms of the temporal sequence of salvation history
> similarly placed England at the spatio-temporal end of the world.[106]

If, as Orosius describes in *Historarum adversum paganos*, world history did
move from east to west, then readers of the Old English translation could
easily have viewed themselves as on the very edge of one of "feower endum
þyses midangeardes"—at the edge of the physical world and at the end of the

processes of history and salvation.[107] To return to the discussion of England as "angle," the Orosian "four ends of this earth" derives from the common scriptural phrase "the four corners of the earth," a phrase directly translated (*feowerum foldan sceatum*) or alluded to many times in Anglo-Saxon writing.[108]

In the Cotton Map, Anglo-Saxons find a sure statement of their cultural paradox: a major part of Anglo-Saxon identity is particularly rooted in Christian authority, whether shaped by fears of pagan conquest or a desire to prove ethnic superiority by converting others,[109] but this ideology historically has in turn viewed England as the edge of, literally, nowhere. At least on the surface, English cosmography does not "develop strategies for recuperating *auctoritas*" until well into the thirteenth century.[110] But in its depiction of England, the Cotton Map anticipates later strategies for transforming the cosmographical *auctoritas* of the Anglo-Saxon homeland, and pushes back against the traditions that have relegated it to the edge. The edge of geographic knowledge, Mary Campbell reminds us, can be a location charged with "moral significance" and even "divine dangerousness."[111] Living on the edge, as it were, Anglo-Saxons keenly felt the danger of their borders throughout their history. The time of the Cotton Map was no different, as the Anglo-Saxon state began the eleventh century unsuccessfully fighting off one set of invasions and fell to another before the century was out. But from at least the time of King Alfred, as the Anglo-Saxon nation-state formed, it also coalesced around a cultural center other than Rome or Jerusalem.[112] And even as the Cotton Map acknowledges the liminal world that is the origin of the *Angelcynn*, it exhibits the geographic desire and determination that England, ultimately, be a center even as it remains a corner.

In early cartography, societies "placed their own territories at the center of their cosmographies or world maps" when possible,[113] but the Cotton Map in its presentation of the world could not physically center Anglo-Saxon England. [→172] As far as Anglo-Saxons were concerned, precious little existed west of the island, so centering England was impossible from the simple standpoint of layout. But more than that, the Cotton Map as a product of late Anglo-Saxon culture also embraces aspects of the traditional marginalization of England. While Anglo-Saxon England possessed a coherent national identity by the ninth century, this eleventh-century depiction refers to the island by the Roman name *Brittannia*, and does not include the more contemporary *Angelcynn*.[114] In the "big picture" of the *mappamundi*, England appears literally at one of the *feowerum foldan sceatum*, tucked far away from the center of

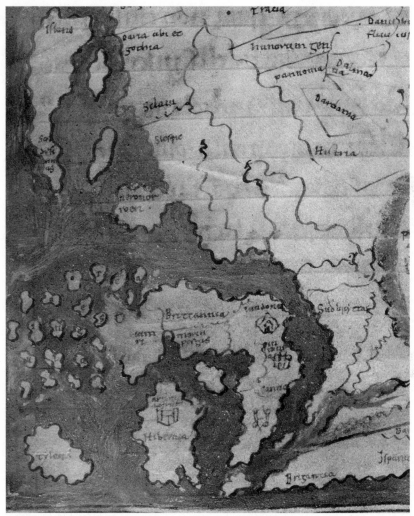

Figure 16. England and Scandinavia in the Cotton Map. By permission of the British Library.

the map, with only Ireland and *Tylen*, or ultima Thule, closer to the physical corner of the manuscript page (see figure 16).

From a literary standpoint, the Cotton Map remains "centered" on its inheritance of Roman geography and theology.[115] However, it is not uncommon for critics to assume that, as a *mappamundi*, the map depicts Jerusalem as its physical center.[116] Jerusalem has a long scriptural and exegetic tradition (including Anglo-Saxon writers such as Bede) as the exact center of the earth, and it appears as the precise center of a number of famous *mappaemundi*, most notably the Hereford, Ebstorf, Psalter, and Higden maps.[117] Importantly, though, the Cotton Map should be considered centered on Jerusalem in only the loosest sense of the term, as the map locates the city down (west) and far to the right (south) of center. Recent commentators have noted that most early medieval world maps actually do not center Jerusalem, and that this convention likely derives from the later political context of the Crusades' quest for the Holy City.[118] It is tempting, however, to consider the decentering of Jerusalem in the Cotton Map as a function of the map's own textual convention and the way it responds to and ultimately rejects notions of England's marginalized state.

Unlike most *mappaemundi*, the Cotton Map is rectangular rather than round. Church writers long agreed that the earth was spherical, but had a tough job reconciling the circular form of the earth and the scriptural concept of the world's four corners. In *mappaemundi*, the usual solution was to place a spherical map inside a square, and fill the "corners" with iconographically suitable adornment.[119] The Cotton Map, in contrast, has the look of a round map that has been deliberately stretched to fit the dimensions of the manuscript page. Fitting the world more accurately to the page allows the mapmaker more space in the lower left-hand corner to depict "the angle of England." In the traditional circular format of such maps, including the majority of later and more elaborate English *mappaemundi*, the British Isles end up squished into the curvature of the border, with most distinguishing features of the islands wholly effaced.[120]

However, cornering the world adds space to the world. Consequently, in the Cotton Map, eastern Europe and Asia Minor expand considerably, creating vast empty spaces that in turn push Constantinople further north than it is normally found on medieval maps, and Jerusalem further south.[121] In comparison to later *mappaemundi*, such a layout actually deemphasizes the center as it creates room in the corners. In the Cotton Map, the physical center of the world appears rather sparse, consisting of mostly empty sections of lower Syria and the eastern Mediterranean. By contrast, each of the corners is set apart with distinctive details: the separate landmass of the British Isles in the northwest, the giant drawing of the lion in the northeast, and the fiery waters and mountains of the southern corners.

The British Isles are, as noted, rather well represented in the map—the one cartographic detail that has occasioned comment in the past. The contoured coastlines fairly approximate the main islands' shapes, which contain icons of three named cities—London, Winchester, and Armagh—and a number of delineated regions, including named regions for Ireland ("Hibernia") and Scotland ("Camri"). The Orkney Islands also make an appearance, as likely does the Isle of Man. One city in the southwest lacks an inscription, perhaps an indication of the provenance of the map or mapmaker.

More striking, however, is the map's use of water to frame England in the world. In keeping with classical convention, the map circumscribes the earth with a gray wash of ocean that in effect presents a third frame inside the double-lined border and then the margins of the manuscript page. Unlike in any other *mappamundi*, though, water similarly frames the British Isles, creating in effect the same representation of the world in microcosm. To no small degree, the curve of the Channel and North Sea echo the form of the Mediterranean and Black seas, which clearly demarcate Europe from the rest of the world. Looking at the map in this fashion, one can then see a succession of three nested L-shaped frames, designed to draw the eye of the viewer from the whole world to Europe and then finally to England (see figure 11). In this scheme, Britain then maps its own marginality onto Ireland, which ends up inside a fourth L-shaped frame of water northwest of Britain. In other words, in the uniquely framed physical and perceptual world of the Cotton Map, Hibernia becomes the territory that displaces Britannia as one of *feowerum foldan sceatum*, and necessarily moves England further in from the edge.

And as the center of the Cotton Map's world presents the general impression of empty space rather than *loci medii*, the center of Europe likewise appears largely blank, prompting one commentator to hypothesize that the confused jumble of regions and tribes thrown into central Europe represent an attempt to break up "the largest blank area in the map."[122] In Europe major cities appear only on its periphery: Constantinople in the east, and Rome and a number of other Italian cities in the south. The broad strip of western Europe that borders England is remarkably devoid of any inscription or detail. Unlike the *mappaemundi* closest in time to it, the Cotton Map completely ignores lower Germany and France, and from what appears to be Jutland to the Pyrenees Mountains, the map includes exactly one inscription, "suðbryttas" (discussed below).[123] Of course, because of a greater degree of familiarity with the contemporary state of Frankish and Gaulish regions, the Anglo-Saxon mapmaker may have simply omitted the Orosian and/or source map description of this region as inaccurate. However, why would not the classical geography then be replaced with something else? The blankness of this area functions in two ways. First, it reinforces the map's accentuation of England by providing another curving blank space, this time of land, to frame the British Isles. The map's omission of England's closest Continental neighbors also supplies additional evidence of an eagerness to distance Anglo-Saxon England from its classical definitions, and perhaps to deny a particular aspect of its current political situation.

Returning to classical and early medieval definitions of *Britannia*, we see that England has long been defined as a cosmographic and cultural Other to Continental territories. In his *Etymologies*, Isidore of Seville, in language closely matching Orosius, explains that Britain is an island within sight of Spain, but literally opposite Gaul: "Brittania Oceani insula . . . haec adversa Galliarum parte ad prospectum Hispaniae sita est."[124] Bede echoes this sentiment, noting that in relation to Spain, Gaul, and Germany, or "greater Europe" (*maximis Europae*), Britain stands "at a great distance against them" (*multo intervallo adversa*). From Isidore and Orosius, Bede specifically preserves the term *adversa*, the word fraught with not only locative but potentially negative connotations—refutation, misfortune, hostility, or punishment, as in the title of Orosius's own work *Historiarum adversum paganos*. Additionally, "Gallia" commonly occurs in most other medieval maps of this region, both earlier and later, precisely because of this marginalizing textual tradition.[125] The Cotton Map, however, largely turns against being defined *adversa maximis Europae*, choosing not only to elide the classical inscriptions of Gaul and Germany but to then leave the region almost entirely vacant.

What remains fascinating about this depiction is the sole inscription that is allowed in the area, "suðbryttas," presumably meant to represent Brittany. The very form of the inscription reveals much about the Anglo-Saxon attitudes behind it: *suðbryttas* contains a unique use of the Anglo-Saxon "ð," one of the only distinctively Old English characters in the text of the map.[126] The literal meaning of the inscription, "south Britain," assumes a somewhat colonialist attitude toward Brittany, and onomastically centers the perspective of the region squarely on England. Such an attitude also references one of the first major cultural events of post-Roman Britain, namely, the defeat by Anglo-Saxon invaders of native Britons, and their subsequent late-fifth-century settlement as Bretons in northwestern Gaul.[127] Without reference to the territories of classical Gaul, or contemporary France, Normandy, Flanders, Maine, and Burgundy, then, the Cotton Map depicts a period both after the fall of Rome and before the rise of the western European political states that would by the middle of the eleventh century definitively end Anglo-Saxon power. In this sense, the *mappamundi* eerily refuses to recognize the very regions poised to directly enable the Norman Conquest of Anglo-Saxon England, only decades (perhaps less) after the making of the map.[128]

Rejecting classical Otherness, the map denies the geography of the pre- and early Anglo-Saxon literary history that was invested with what Homi Bhabha calls "colonial mimicry"—the desire of the colonized to present themselves as "a reformed, recognizable Other."[129] Ironically, Bhabha discusses this effect in relation to the Anglicization of colonies of modern England. In the Cotton Map, Anglo-Saxon England resists the past Romanization inherent in its textual and cartographic descriptions. Instead, this version of the Anglo-Saxon world celebrates the origin of Anglo-Saxon culture, and in turn highlights northern, not southern Continental connections. In contrast to its treatment of western Europe, the Cotton Map lavishes attention on the Scandinavian north and provides seven names for the area (mostly absent from Orosius), including names for tribes in Norway, Finland, and possibly Iceland.[130] The one inscription from Orosius retained in this area, "Daria (Dacia) ubi et Gothia," only intensifies the Cotton Map's regard for the Nordic. McGurk notes that the map pulls Dacia considerably out of position: Orosius places "Dacia et Gothia" in the middle of eastern Europe, between the territories of Alania and Germania, while the Cotton Map moves them much further north.[131] Anglo-Saxons likely viewed the Daci as synonymous with Dani (the Danes), and Gothi (derived from *Getæ*) as the same as the Geats, the Scandinavian tribe that *Beowulf* made famous. [132] Likewise, "Scithia," here positioned east and slightly north of the island containing the "Scridefinnas" (who are also mentioned in the *Old English Orosius*), might have a Scandinavian affiliation.[133]

The Scandinavian elements of the Cotton Map are not surprising, of course, given the sustained presence and development of Anglo-Scandinavian culture in England from the early ninth century into the eleventh century, culminating with the accession of King Cnut, a Dane, to the English throne in 1016. The cumulative effect of all these Scandinavian, or reputedly Scandinavian, references resembles the famous interpolation of the voyages of Ohthere and Wulfstan in the Alfredian Old English translation of Orosius.[134] Traditionally, the interpolation of allegedly firsthand accounts of explorations of Scandinavia and the Baltic region into Orosius's classical geography has been viewed as a natural extension of ninth-century England's connection with and interest in things Scandinavian. Further, as Sealy Gilles observes, the Anglo-Saxon Wulfstan's

> account of pagan customs persisting on the margins of European Christendom is reminiscent of the ancient customs of the English themselves. ... his exploration of a Baltic people authenticates his own heritage and blunts the thrust of Orosius's Christian apologetic, explicitly written *adversum paganos*.[135]

Like the Cotton Map, the interpolations in the *Old English Orosius* also present a cultural perspective that centers Anglo-Saxon England while offering up other regions to be marginalized in its place.[136] And though these pagan insertions do qualify the original intent of Orosius, Stephen Harris has argued that other Old English alterations to Orosius's history do not refute Christianity, but rather present "a sense of Germanic community [that] shapes the Latin into an Old English story of the origins of Christendom."[137] Harris's chief example of this reshaping, namely how the Old English version substantively alters the Gothic sack of Rome, is particularly relevant to the Cotton Map.[138]

As Harris shows, the Old English rewriting of the sack of Rome carefully excises from the original text any emphasis on the political power and spiritual centrality of Rome. Instead, the Anglo-Saxon version uses the occasion of the sacking of Rome to manifest a distinctly Germanic notion of Christendom and kingship, one that, in Harris's words, "permits vernacular access to and Anglo-Saxon identification with ... an order of identity that has left the senate and people of Rome far behind."[139]

The *Old English Orosius*, in effect, decenters Rome from a distinctly Roman history of the world. In a like manner, the Cotton Map shifts focus away from two traditional centers of the spiritual and geographic worlds on whose margins Anglo-Saxon England existed. The physical world of the map does not place Jerusalem in the center—a position it will not occupy for centuries in English *mappaemundi*—while likewise marginalizing the effect of Rome upon England. To be sure, one cannot deny Rome a certain presence in the Cotton Map. Italy alone contains seven cities including Rome—more than any other region of the map—and the result is a visual mass pointing back to the former empire, no doubt left over from a Roman antecedent in the Cotton Map's lineage. At the same time, though, the Cotton Map enacts a strategy similar to that found in the *Old English Orosius*, and emphasizes the

Anglo-Saxon world even as it works from and to a degree within distinctly colonial sources. As noted, the L-shaped England echoes the forms of the larger geographies that contain it, that of Europe and then that of the world. In England, likewise, the cities of Winchester and London, the twin capitals of the Anglo-Saxon world, hold the same relative position as Rome and its lesser cities do in the shape of Europe. Rome may still dominate the cartography of Europe, but in the framed world of England, London and Winchester occupy the same space, and suggest a willingness and desire to have a similar role. Earlier in Anglo-Saxon history, King Alfred's political victories over Danish enemies in England validated Anglo-Saxon Christendom over pagan beliefs from another edge of the world.[140] Similarly, Anglo-Saxon missionaries journeyed "back" to Germanic heathendom, replicating and superseding the pattern of Augustine's original mission from Rome to Canterbury.[141] In both examples, Anglo-Saxon activities work to define new cultural edges in relation to an understood English center.

In the eleventh-century "real time" of the Cotton Map, the imperial glory of Rome is no more real than that of Babylon. The temporal aspects of the map are no more rooted in the primary world than its spatial aspects. Rather, the Cotton Map presents several versions of Rome, and of England, all at once. For Anglo-Saxon England, Rome meant many things, and the map should be understood as simultaneously embodying all of them: the past imperial power, responsible for the historical view of England, as well as a present fallen Rome, along with its present spiritual role as center of Christian belief. Similarly, the map produces many Englands: the past, Othered colony of Roman conquest and then missionaries, the present geographic island, and, most important, the desired stable political entity, which has come in from the edge of the world and assumed a centric role in, at the very least, a larger corner of Europe.

The collapse of space and time in the Anglo-Saxon map, and the ability of the map to represent not one but many worlds at once, reinforces the ways in which the map may be understood in turn as a virtual world. Of course, on the most basic level, the map does not operate as we expect modern maps to; it fundamentally fails to offer a stable representation of the primary world of physical terrain, or of the geopolitical contours of the world at a given point in time. Rather, like VR, the map provides a much more fluid and malleable environment that mimics, but fundamentally differs from, the experience of primary reality. [→186] But the Anglo-Saxon geographic desire in evidence here also reveals the hyperreality of this world by emphasizing not its actuality but its potentiality. In other words, the re-vision of Anglo-Saxon England that this map deploys to reflect and then shape Anglo-Saxon reality depends less on what is than on what could be, and, in the language of Pierre Lévy, *virtualizes* the primary world. For Lévy,

> The virtual is by no means the opposite of the real. On the contrary, it is a fecund and powerful mode of being that expands the process of creation, opens up the future, injects a core of meaning beneath the platitude of immediate physical presence.[142]

The Cotton Map's expression of something fundamentally more than just a sequential or diachronic formulation of past and present, then, marks the process by which the map itself becomes an actualized expression of Anglo-Saxon reality. As Marie-Laure Ryan, elaborating on Lévy's concept of the virtual, notes, "the virtual is not anchored in space and time. Actualization is the passage from a state of timelessness and deterritorialization to an existence rooted in the here and now."[143] The Anglo-Saxon *mappamundi* performs precisely this passage. By simultaneously maintaining and rejecting the geographic and historical notions of England's marginality, the Cotton Map first dissolves temporal distinctions and the geopolitical limitations placed upon it as a territory of alterity. However, the mapping of this virtual state, the mediation of this notional existence by the cartographic (and technological) act, actualizes represented anxiety and desire, and "roots it in the here and now" of early-eleventh-century Anglo-Saxon England. In sum, the virtual world of the Cotton Map expands the reality of its Anglo-Saxon counterpart, and attempts to open up its future, a future ironically to be foreclosed in just a few short decades. [→94]

The map's fluid treatment of space also marks its virtual character in terms of absolute and relative space. Modern bias toward accuracy in maps derives from the perception that maps faithfully reproduce micro- or macrocosmic aspects of physical space and primary reality. Space commonly is conceived in terms of the absolute or the relational, where absolute space proposes a stable relationship to a fixed and measurable physical reality, while relational space imagines that the experience of space depends largely on the relative position of objects within the space.[144] [→167] But like virtual reality, maps by their nature merge or synthesize absolute and relational conceptions of space. Maps can represent to the viewer a world that might appear fixed and finite, but the medium of representation makes possible the extension of physical space in ways not subject to the limitations of space and time in the primary world. Michael Benedikt reports that "the existence and nature of space seems to be a truly basic, fundamental, and universal quality of reality," while "space and time, combined, appear to constitute a level of reality below which no fundamental layers can be discerned, a field without natural parts."[145] But virtual environments possess the ability to add layers of reality that need not be contained by the laws of physical existence, while still simulating the physical world. We have already seen as much in the Cotton Map as it reproduces several realities within the same geography. [→56] Of course, the degree to which this occurs varies with the degree of virtuality contained within the representation. To some extent, the synthetic space found in virtual environments has long been understood to operate in the visual arts.[146] As Ryan writes, "as a real object inscribed in space and time, the work of art is *in* the real world, but as a virtual object that creates its own space and time, it is not *of* the world."[147] The same should be said for medieval *mappaemundi*—like contemporary virtual environments, they are not simply representations of the world, or objects in the world. They are instead simulations that define *worlds* of values beyond the geographic—worlds still waiting to be explored, navigated, and learned.

NORTH LOOKING SOUTH

While the "cornered" design and layout of the map emphasizes England in the lower left corner, and uses the country's marginal location as a distinguishing feature, the map also encourages the eye to focus on a completely opposite region. Up and down its southernmost (right-hand) third, the map presents an array of seven bright red or orange bodies of water. Though not named, the upper two, surrounding "Arabica deserta," must represent the Persian and Arabian Gulfs, more loosely known then as parts of the Red Sea. The three red tendrils running westward along the southern edge of the map are all parts of the Nile River, and represent the mapmaker's attempt to follow Orosius's assessment of the confused and contrary positions of classical geographers as to the source and exact route of the river.[148] Two small, circular lakes, Lake Chalearzus ("lacus Calearsum") and the Lake of Salt ("lacus Salinarum," probably the Dead Sea), in Lower Egypt and in East Africa, respectively, are also colored bright red.[149] Though many other medieval *mappaemundi* color the Red Sea and accompanying gulfs red, no other world map I have seen colors any other Asian or African body of water red. Other medieval maps either color only the Red Sea area red or, alternatively, use red as an indiscriminate feature in geographic regions all over the world. The Cotton Map is rare, if not unique, in confining its use of red to the southern section.

The Red Sea is colored red for obvious reasons, but why the other bodies? The Nile's redness could be a further indication of the Mosaic emphasis discussed above; in his contest with the Pharaoh's magicians, Moses at God's command does turn the Nile—along with all the other streams, pools, and canals in Egypt—to blood.[150] Conceivably the Anglo-Saxon mapmaker could have colored most of the southern waters red in reference to the sweeping nature of Moses' miracle, though such a reading is tentative at best. Regardless, the overall visual effect sharply distinguishes the southern regions of the world from the rest. So as the map presents its northwest corner as a world in miniature, it also highlights the south as another kind of margin, another kind of Other, though markedly different.

Such a differentiation may be a reaction to traditional notions of the north. Notions that Paradise existed in the far east, at the "top of the world," and that both history and final judgment moved westward fed classical and early medieval perceptions of a western hinterland. But in the extremity of both west *and* north, Britain received a double dose of geographical slight, as the north incurred its own prejudices. Churches in medieval Europe often were constructed with "true" orientations, with altars facing to the east, while early in Britain's written history, the icy climate of the north served as a chilly metaphor for the country's spiritual barrenness.[151] Being classically positioned to the left on maps, the north also held associations of evil; in the twelfth century, writers such as Hugh of St. Victor promoted the popular idea that hell occupied the icy regions of the north.[152] And throughout the Middle Ages, zonal maps of climate listed England as the northernmost zone of the world. In John of Wallingford's mid-thirteenth-century map, he crams an eighth zone just for "Anglia," "Hibernia," and "Scotia" into the bottom of the world—in the words of one commentator, "practically at the North Pole."[153]

With its gradual rejection of a Roman perspective, however, late Anglo-Saxon England stopped seeing itself from the south and instead, in Howe's phrase, began to "close that distance by looking, and writing, south."[154] As Howe describes it, by the

> mid-eleventh century, Christian writers in Anglo-Saxon England had learned to make a home for themselves on the map. If these writers gained a certain edge by casting themselves on the north, along the periphery, it was because that gave both drama and spiritual coherence to their history. But they also looked south, and that set them in a neces-

sary relation to the sources of their Christian faith, history, and learning.[155]

The Cotton Map enacts Howe's epistemological notion of "looking south" by literally creating the map used to "make a home for themselves on." Regionally, the map's use of *suðbryttas* points to a similar process, as the map looks to a land both south of Britain and one created by the displacement of native Britons by the force of Anglo-Saxon settlement. Similarly, the line of cities along the map's depiction of Italy recalls the orderly and southern-looking progression of pilgrimage itineraries for journeys moving from England to Rome. One late-tenth-century list from Archbishop Sigbert is included in the Cotton Tiberius B.V manuscript as well.[156]

But the Cotton Map does not simply shift perspectives; rather, it looks to a south that is far past Rome, and through its representation it writes the regions of Africa and southern Asia as the peripheral zone that is in Anglo-Saxon eyes truly remote. In part, the map responds to the received notion from classical geography that both northern and southern extremes of the world, the *ante-* and *ultra-climata*, were home to primitive and savage tribes, a belief that continued in medieval texts and maps as writers desired to put monsters as far away as possible from Jerusalem.[157] To some degree, the Cotton Map preserves this practice in the north, and places on its center northern edge such figures as Gog and Magog, and tribes such as the Turchi (recorded elsewhere as "a filthy people who eat the flesh of youths and miscarried fetuses") and the griffin people ("griphorum gens").[158] However, such northern references are relatively sparse, and they literally pale when compared to the florid visual and textual detail lavished on the southern edge of the world.

More simply, the red coloration to the south could contribute a sensory quality to the map, and signify the hotter climate of the region. John Friedman has noted the climatological bias of medieval cultures, as each medieval nation attempted to situate itself as the "middle people" in the world—the place with the superior climate and therefore morals.[159] In the northwest corner of the world, Anglcynn would of course have a difficult time making such moderating claims, but the Cotton Map exhibits similar desires by charging the southern part of the world with climatological and cultural difference. Read in terms of temperature, the abundance of red only in the southern regions of the map marks these places as truly different. Likewise, in the map the abundance of textual description points to the intrinsic strangeness of the southern regions. The northern sections of the map contain only inscriptions. In the south, text threatens to overrun some regions, as several sentences, phrases, and descriptive modifiers culled from Orosius and possibly Isidore are found scattered throughout Africa and southern Asia.[160] The sheer visual mass of text crammed into the space sends a clear message to the viewer: this place is not like the rest of the world, it needs to be explained, and it is the real Other on this map.

One of the earliest known *mappaemundi*, a Beatus map from the early tenth century, describes Africa as the border to Egypt, inhabited by a monstrous race of people and infested with snakes and wild beasts.[161] The map's inscription derives from Isidore's *Etymologies*, and it is in part reproduced on the Cotton Map.[162] The Beatus map, so called because it often (and likely originally) accompanied St. Beatus's late-eight-century *Commentary on the Apocalypse of St. John*, includes another distinctive feature: a fourth continent, separated from the known world by a fiery hot ocean, colored on the map as a thick, arrow-straight red band.[163] Isidore, working from sources as early as Macrobius, wrote of the "fabled" existence of a fourth continent to the south of the known world, across a fiery sea, and almost every Beatus map includes such a land, either uninhabited or stocked with monstrous races, usually separated from the rest of the world by a straight red line of torrid water.[164]

The possibility of the existence of another landmass to the south was not unknown to Anglo-Saxons. The Old English *Boethius*, for instance, reviews the argument that the known and habitable world was only a part of the whole earth.[165] The Anglo-Saxon *mappamundi* does not depict a fourth continent per se, but its portrayal of the Nile furthers the notion of the southern regions as a distinct and even separate land from the northern realm. Like the torrid red ocean in the southern regions of Beatus maps, the long red branches of the Nile in the Cotton Map suggest a similarly broad band of fiery water that separates the farthest land from the known world.

Medieval beliefs about the climates in other parts of the world found specific articulation in a subset of *mappaemundi* called zonal maps, which divided a spherical world into five or more zones, running from extreme north ("articus") to extreme south ("antarticus").[166] In addition to the Cotton Map, Cotton Tiberius B.V happens to contain a second, zonal, *mappamundi*, rarely mentioned or studied. Folio 29r displays a Macrobian zonal map of the world, that is, a map divided into five zones according to Macrobius's theory of climate (see figure 17). Moving southward, the map depicts the *articus*, the *aestivus* (northern temperate zone), the *aequinoctialis* (torrid zone), the *hiemalis* (southern temperate zone), and the *antarticus*.[167] Only the northern temperate zone and the torrid zone have anything in them—the rest are completely blank. Into the *aestivus* the map squeezes the contours of the *ecumene*, complete with two cities (presumably Rome and Jerusalem), the Pillars of Hercules (which also appear on the Cotton Map), inscriptions and outlines for the three continents, and a semicircular shape in the northeast that likely stands for Britain. In contrast, the central zone consists of a dense mass of Macrobian text describing the quality of the torrid zone, as well as the general condition of the earth, and gives the measurement of the earth's circumference as 252,000 *stades*, a figure that ultimately derives from Eratosthenes' second-century-B.C. *Geographia*. The Macrobean text reads:

> Aequinoctalis zona hic incipiens pene tota alluit(ur) superius et inferius mari, quod dum per medium taerre circumlabitur in IIII(or) quasi insulas totus orbis dividitur; qu(a)e inhabitentur est enim solstitialis superior et inferior habitabitabilis, similiter superior et inferior hiemalis. Sicque fit ut per medium et in circuitu(m) orbis mare currat, quod calore vel frigore est intransmeabile. Est que deprehensus totius orbis ambitus in stadiis ducentis quinquaginta duobus milibus.

> [The equinoctial zone begins here, completely covered by the wash of greater and lesser seas that flow through the middle of the earth, as if the whole earth was divided into four islands; of that which is inhabited, that above and below the summer solstice zone is habitable, and likewise for the winter solstice zone. Thus the sea runs through the middle and around the orb, and is impassable due to the heat and cold. And it is thought that the circumference of the whole earth is 252,000 *stades*].[168]

Medieval writers shied away from declaring that the lands thought to be beyond the impassable torrid zone were actually inhabited by people, as this might contradict the scriptural proclamation that the Gospel has been preached to all people of all races.[169] The text of this zonal map carefully dances around this belief, allowing that the region is habitable, without stating that it actually *is* inhabited.[170] On the graphic level, the zonal map makes clear the inhabited nature of the land north of the fiery, impassable water: close examination of the region's smaller city reveals two tiny heads, one blond and one brunette, peering out from behind the city walls—a human figuration that contrasts sharply with the vast blankness of the southern regions.[171]

Figure 17. The zonal map in MS Cotton Tiberius B.V, fol. 29r. By permission of the British Library.

These tiny figures in the northern region (specifically Rome) of the zonal map signal to the viewer that it is from this region that the rest of the world is perceived, drawn, and defined. One of these figures even sports a tonsure, an authorial indication, intended or no, of the very composition of this outside world within a manuscript within the walls of a monastery.

As the text gathered on the border of the southern region allows for the possibility of some other life, if only in theory, the zonal map of the world predicates two centers. The textual surrogate for the impassible waters to the south, which block the sure rejection of other life on other landmasses, occupies the visual center of this world. But this text is in turn the product of the perceptual center of this world, further north, and symbolized by the specular, the gazing inhabitants cloistered behind walls and towers.

Significantly, the inscriptions of the zonal map are in the same hand as the Cotton Map's text, and provide a cosmographical link between these two worldviews. The Cotton Map must be understood not as the entire world, but as an exploded and virtual view of only the known world of the temperate northern zone, contextualized within the frame of the greater world of the known *and* unknown. Like the text of the zonal map, the inscriptions massed on the other side of the fiery red dividing line suggest much more past the frame of the map, and in turn encourage by comparison the perception of Anglo-Saxon England, as the *locus operis*, as part of the known, central world, and as anything but marginal. Anglo-Saxon England, after all, has ultimately produced these maps, and their southern-looking perspective. In a sense, these maps show the process by which Anglo-Saxon England now writes the world and the texts, refuting its historical identity in the larger world and representing itself not as an unknown quantity on the border of the great known world but rather as a prominent feature of the known world, defined against the borders of a vast unknown.

In another sense, the Cotton Map's reconfiguration of the world and *Brittannia*'s place within it may be viewed as the very beginning of a long cartographic and historical process that would literally move England from its lower left corner to the top and center of the world. In the thirteenth century, in his map of England, Matthew Paris reoriented the direction of the world by putting north at the top.[172] By the end of the medieval period, writers began to comment on the historical belief that the north always defeated the south, and to make the case through classical authorities that "the northwest corner of the world . . . is that most favored by nature."[173] Early modern explorers relied on medieval *mappaemundi* and theories of an inhabitable fourth continent as proof that a "new world" was out there to be found.[174] And the discovery of the New World in the west, of course, provided a whole new set of lands to be mapped.

Through both the New World and the advent of print, England was also, finally, able to convincingly center itself on the map. In the Age of Discovery, the proliferation of printed maps of the world invariably moved England out of the lower corner and toward the top center of the framed space—a happy, or at least ironic, accident, as the top-center position in medieval *mappaemundi* was often reserved for Paradise. Eventually the mapping of the world through England transformed not only space but time as well. Since 1884 the prime meridian in Greenwich has set the temporal center of the world in England, and provided an imaginary (and yet again very real) line to which, as Jan-Willem Broekhuysen described it, the "tide, like the sea itself, still ebbs and flows."[175] In the modern age, at last, England's place on the map would reflect its economic and imperial might: on top of the world and at the center of everything.

SYNTHETIC CONCLUSIONS

Medieval *mappaemundi* have been described as "graphic epitomes" of the earth, and as the physical and ideological relationships between man and material reality.[176] The above analyses of the Cotton Map, framed and inspired by notions of virtual reality, show how *mappaemundi* express these relationships through the virtual nature of maps—that is, through their conceptualization of a fluid geographic reality not bound by the rules of the primary world they purport, at least on the surface, to represent. It is precisely this fluidity and virtuality, though, that resulted in traditional condemnations of medieval maps as inferior maps. Alan Hodgkiss's 1981 assessment specifies the epistemological scheme of such dismissals:

> In the western world cartography was virtually extinguished as a scientific study during the Dark Ages and world maps produced at this time were merely vehicles for subjective speculation and the graphic displays of theological teachings rather than the outcome of systematic reasoning.[177]

Hodgkiss's critique presents the classic cartographic opposite pair: good maps are systematic, scientific, and reasoned, while bad maps are subjective, speculative, and spiritual. [→73] In the history of cartography, the end of the medieval period saw the reemergence of accurate maps, chiefly characterized by a carefully plotted linearity. Portolan charts, for instance, were drawn as navigational charts and made possible a greater detail and accuracy of coastlines. As marine maps, portolan charts also became dense matrices of crisscrossing loxodromes, designed to help shipmen plot courses between positions.[178] Such cartographic practices, together with the rediscovery of Ptolemaic geography, informed and in turn were informed by the development of Renaissance linear perspective as the chief mode of representing the visual world.[179] [→167] At the same time, the development of the printing press permitted more accurate reproductions of these more accurate maps, as the new technology ensured "that the human errors of the copyist were obviated."[180]

As Woodward observes, "it was the historians of science who developed the framework for the history of medieval cosmological concepts." Accordingly, the field of cartographic studies has defined itself largely through the principles it prizes in its subject, namely, scientific reasoning and linearity. Woodward's own assessment of the current state of medieval *mappaemundi* employs linear language as he bemoans that, in the study of medieval maps, "lines of inquiry" are continually frustrated by "gaps and discontinuities" in the genealogies of medieval maps. On the Hereford Map, for instance, Woodward writes, "In short, the convoluted lineage of surviving map images, or reference to such images, has so many discontinuities that in most cases it simply does not allow either the divination of the details of their original construction or confident extrapolation across gaps in the record."[181]

The impossibility of complete knowledge and accuracy in both maps and the study of maps has always existed, however, and must further be recognized not as antithetical to cartography but rather as an intrinsic part of it. In the sixth book of the fifth-century *The Marriage of Philology and Mercury*, Martianus Capella describes the discipline of Geometry, a distinguished lady with "a geometer's rod in her right hand a solid globe in her left" [radium dextra, altera sphaeram solidam]. Geometry, Capella informs us, has beautiful hair, but her shoes are torn to shreds from treading across the entire surface of the earth [crepidas peragrandae telluris causa easdemquae permenso orbe contritas viatrix infatigat gestabat]. [182]

Lady Geometry is called so because she has "traversed and measured out the earth" and can

> offer calculations and proofs for its shape, size, position, regions, and dimensions. There is no portion of the earth's surface that [she] could not describe from memory.

> [Geometria dicor, quod permeateam crebro admensamque tellurem eiusque figuram, magnitudinem, locum, partes et stadia possim cum suis rationibus explicare, neque ulla sit in totius terrae diversitate partitio, quam non memoris cursa descriptionis absolvam].

Yet something in the description of Lady Geometry resists this claim. Capella initially presents this figure holding a globe in one hand—her literal grasp of the world—and a geometer's rod in the other, a device Sylvia Tomasch considers "a symbol of intellectual order, whereby the earth's irregularities are rationalized by the instruments of human mensuration."[183] Capella also reports in this description that servants bring Geometry a third instrument, an abacus board, a device

> designed for delineating figures; upon it the straightness of lines, the curves of circles, and the angles of triangles are drawn. This board can represent the entire circumference and the circles of the world, the shapes of the elements, and the very depths of the earth; *you will see there represented anything you could not explain in words.*
>
> [res depingendis designandisque opportune formis; quippe ibi vel lineares ductus vel circulares flexus vel triangulares arraduntur anfractus. Hic totum potis est ambitum et circus formare mundi, elementorum facies ipsamque profunditatem adumbrare telluris; videbis istic depingi, quicquid verbus visum non valeas explicare].[184]

While the abacus is a rational, scientific device, it also represents the ineffable qualities of measuring the world, that is, what can be seen, but not expressed in words alone.

The pursuit of cartographic accuracy "is misleadingly logical."[185] Lady Geometry possesses the power to systematically conceive of the world, but science and words, Capella reminds us, are not always enough when it comes to representing the world. Modern cartography, like Lady Geometry, aspires to faithful renditions of reality through rational and scientific structures, yet must inevitably fail in some fashion, and render instead only a virtual form of the world it seeks to hold in its hand. In his essay "Deconstructing Maps," Harley charts cartography's fixation with "the history of more precise instrumentation and measurement," resulting in "the growth of institutions and a 'professional' literature designed to monitor the applications and propagation of the rules."[186] For Harley, however, the future of understanding maps lies not in pursuing "better delineations of reality," but in starting "to read our maps for alternative and sometime competing discourses."[187]

Virtual reality similarly refutes the assumed superiority of an absolute and measured representation of space and place. As Ken Hillis explains, digitally realized virtual environments suggest "that the 'structure' of space might not be as constant or universal as absolute space traditionally might be taken to imply." For Hillis, absolute space "suggests macro-level or 'big picture' realities" that do not accord with the individual meanings of relative space, and the relational space of VR fosters "an ability to imagine a continuum or at least linkages between the meanings of absolute and relative space."[188] The Cotton Map has suffered long neglect due to a potent amalgam of unreconstructable lineage and cartographic disdain for the inaccurate and irrational. But in its representative function, the Cotton Map indeed performs such linkages between perceptions of absolute and relative space, and does so through a synthesis of Harley's "alternative and competing discourses." The various textual, historical, cultural, spiritual, and political expressions this study has found encoded within the Cotton Map make the map, in the words of Franco Moretti, "a field of narrative forces, whose reiterated interplay defines the nation as the sum of all possible stories."[189]

The synthetic, illogical character of the Cotton Map presents the world not as one of order and linear progression but as a matrix of many and conflicting meanings that resist clean and orderly analysis. In considering computer simulations of reality, Manuel De Landa argues that such virtual environments provide an alternative to the historically linear process of scientific analysis.[190] For De Landa, the traditional modes of hypothesis and evidence espouse the ideology of "reductionism," whereby all phenomena can in principle be reduced to a series of proven rules. [→73] In contrast, the technologies of simulation allow for the creation of a network of variables whose effect and influence on each other cannot be presupposed, but only studied and understood. By "nonlinear interaction," the limiting approach of "top-down" reasoning is replaced by one of "connectionism," which seeks to understand reality not through purely syntactic or formal relations, but rather as a variable set of "flexible behaviors" whose interactions generate a constantly changing set of synchronic patterns. [197] Through the understanding and development of simulated reality, De Landa argues, "these abstract worlds can also be used to synthesize the intuitions needed to dislodge other ideas blocking the way to a better understanding of the dynamics of reality."[191]

For too long cartography has sought to avoid "slogging into messy reality—hoping to no longer need a world for its own confirmation."[192] The "reality" of the Cotton Map is frustratingly messy. The process through which it was made is lost to us, and the lines of inquiry and influence that constructed it can only be reconstructed in the most tentative and hypothetical fashion. But the scientific and linear approach to the Cotton Map ignores the way to a better understanding of the reality of this Anglo-Saxon view of the world.

We can no longer study—or, rather, fail to study—this map as a set of untraceable sources. Instead, the Cotton Map must be understood as a synthetic response to Anglo-Saxon reality, a virtual representation of a world chaotically crammed full of disparate variables that bind together inside the framed world of folio 56v, and then inside the larger spatiotemporal context of the contents of MS Cotton Tiberius B.V. The reflected "world" of the Cotton Map is not one of logical order, but one of the conflict of perceived past and desired future, of classical and scriptural narratives struggling to occupy the same physical space, and of shifting yet simultaneous notions of what defines the center and the edge of a world. Though itself a material document, the Cotton Map is also a virtual landscape that defies the limits of absolute space by containing more than a one-to-one relation of represented object to represented space. This Anglo-Saxon map of the world, like other medieval *mappaemundi*, is not real, but *hyperreal*. Manifestly artificed in its construction, its synthetic, virtual construction of the world nevertheless works to reveal *and* fashion the messy reality of the eleventh-century Anglo-Saxon world.

Cyberspace, Sculpture, and the Revision of Medieval Space

The production of space, having attained the conceptual and linguistic level, acts retroactively upon the past, disclosing aspects and moments of it hitherto uncomprehended. The past appears in a different light, and hence the process whereby that past becomes the present also takes on another aspect.

—Henri Lefebvre

There was no such thing as "space" for medieval people.

—Michael Camille

Generally, and in spite of what we might have learned theoretically about the nature of space, we tend to regard it from a default mode that assumes a simple physical framework that in turn subsumes the objects within it. In everyday consideration, we do not give space much thought; space is always there, unrecognized but present. And while we can perhaps change what goes on inside space, by shuffling around the materials that fill it, and while we can learn more about space, for the most part we regard space as a physical constant, the x-, y-, and z-axes of the universe we inhabit.

But in both the medieval and the modern world, as Harald Kleinschmidt points out, "not only is space itself multidimensional, but also the concept of space."[1] By this, Kleinschmidt does not mean the recent explosion of academic applications of space as hermeneutic tool—literary space, gendered space, utopian space, legal space.[2] [→97] Rather, he proposes that space depends upon its reception by its subjects. In other words, space is always-already being reconstructed, reproduced, and redefined by its inhabitants. Similarly, the title of Henri Lefebvre's seminal materialist work *The Production of Space*, from which this chapter's opening quotation comes, also produces his thesis: all space must be understood not as natural, but as manufactured.

For such spatial theorists, space consists of two primary aspects, *object space* and *subject space*. Object space (or *place*) is the space we conceive in our everyday lives: the synchronic network of material objects organized in the physical world, with which we can interact tangibly and transparently. Subject space, on the other hand, derives from our perceptions of space, physical and otherwise. Subject space stands as the diachronic process by which we formulate and *practice* space—a process that includes continuous historical reconditioning and reproduction, and one capable of producing different spaces, dependent on historical and cultural contingencies. This epistemology has been significantly explored by Michel de Certeau, who argues for the constant shift of relationships (passages) between the "organized" space and the "practiced" place of a culture's social discourse, whether it be walking down a city street or reading a book.[3]

The "passages" between these different spaces are important as the spaces we produce today, in the twenty-first century, necessarily differ from those of the past. The opening quotation from Lefebvre reminds us that how we produce space today acts upon our production of the past. As we study the medieval period, we also re-produce medieval space, often unthinkingly, in modes instinctively derived from our modernity. But spaces existed for medieval subjects that do not operate as clearly today, if at all. For instance, as Jacques Le Goff has amply illustrated, the emergence of purgatory in the high Middle Ages was the beginning of a spiritual, yet culturally very real, space that linked the spiritual and physical realms.[4] For medieval subjects, Margaret Wertheim notes, purgatory emerged as "a new space of being," theorized by theologians, described by writers, and understood by the faithful as a vital link between physical space and "soul space."[5]

Wertheim argues that as a result of the physicalist cant of subsequent notions of space, begun in the late Middle Ages and maturing through the Enlightenment, other kinds of spaces, equally real to a medieval mind, devolved and rapidly disappeared. For Wertheim, the prime example of lost medieval space is spiritual space—the very real, if immaterial, space medievally "known" to exist beyond the spheres and under the earth. Medieval thinking did not subscribe to the homogeneity of space that is presumed in modern views, which allow only one type of "real" space to exist.[6] In other words, in medieval Europe, the City of God could be every bit as real as a city of man.

The *telos* of Wertheim's spatial study is the claim that the recent development of cyberspace heralds a return to the cultural production of "multiform space" that operated in medieval ontologies.[7] Far from being a "virtual" reality, cyberspace increasingly functions as a real space in our everyday lives—though we tend to resist this notion because we are conditioned to consider as real space only that which is mathematically reducible and measurable. Indeed, cyberspace does not differ greatly from Descartes' *res cogitans*, the poorer cousin of his now famous *res extensa*, the foundation for the infinite but absolute world of quantifiable space. Descartes placed the *res cogitans*, the projected spaces of thought, on a par with the physical world—a spatial equivalence soon overturned by the march of science.[8] Fundamentally, we do not understand space as medieval subjects understood space. As print rose to prominence in the early modern age, so too did the notion of a mensurable space and of a single-point perspective to represent it. As medieval *mappae-mundi* gave way to calculated measurements of the world, the conception of space also changed. [→153] Today, the homologies that arise between medieval conceptions of space and new dimensions of cyberspace frame for us the effect of modern space upon its medieval counterpart; these homologies also help us chart aspects of medieval space now marginalized, if not forgotten about entirely.

THE NUNBURNHOLME CROSS AND THE RESISTANCE OF SPACE

During a recent series of talks on the Ruthwell Cross, Fred Orton reviewed the particular problems the physical state of this famous Anglo-Saxon monument imposed upon interpretation.[9] [→20] In summing up its complicated reconstruction history, its gaps of content, the debate over the character of its plinth and pedestaling, and the reversed mounting of the cross's uppermost section, Orton commented in passing that Ruthwell stands today as a sculpture remarkably "resistant to space." In short, any reading of Ruthwell's form and content remains necessarily occluded by the physical nature and *in situ* context of the piece.

The phrase *resistant to space* also applies to a much more obscure monument from the period, the Anglo-Scandinavian Nunburnholme Cross. The Nunburnholme Cross remains one of those recalcitrant sculptures of which we can say we know more about what we do not know than anything else.[10] Extant sections of the Viking-era cross were rediscovered built into the walls of St. James Church in Nunburnholme, East Yorkshire, during nineteenth-century renovations.[11] The church at Nunburnholme was built in the late twelfth or early thirteenth century; during this time or later, the top and bottom fragments of the monument, each continuing a panel of figures on each side, were incorporated into the south porch of the building.[12] A head for the cross has never been found, though a mortise socket exists at the stone's top, and some debate continues over whether there might originally have been a middle section containing a third panel.[13]

The shaft is carved from ashlar, a limestone not typically found in the East Riding of Yorkshire. Most likely the stone is recycled, quarried from Tadcaster by the Romans and originally used in building at York or in a regional Roman settlement.[14] The limestone was then presumably reexcavated during Scandinavian settlement in the late ninth or early tenth century and transported to Nunburnholme for carving. Since James Lang, critics have generally agreed that two distinct sculptors worked on the stone during the Viking period. The First Sculptor, distinguished in the view of modern critics by a more sophisticated sense of modeling and inclined cutting, worked in late Anglian mode with "Carolingian echoes," and in a wholly Christian idiom.[15] However, the First Sculptor completed only perhaps one and one-quarter sides. The Second Sculptor, whose technique is generally characterized as less accomplished, finished the piece in a style markedly different from the First Sculptor's and, notably, introduced more explicitly secular and Scandinavian iconography to the work.[16]

The surviving sections of the cross reveal variations of the same design on all four faces. Each side consists of two main panels, roughly equal in size, edged by molding, with a small figural design at the top (see figures 18 and 19). In its "restored" state, the top and bottom sections of the monument have been reversed. The following description presents the cross in its earlier form before restoration; the original sides have been aligned.

Side D reveals what the First Sculptor intended to be the design scheme for all of the sides.[17] A frieze of two angels adorns the top, their heads centered on the corners, with arms reaching down to grasp an arch framing a beast in profile, with its head thrown back. Below the upper design, a pelleted arch and border frames the lower two panels, which each contain a figure dressed in ecclesiastical garments—a haloed saint above, and a figure holding a cup-like vessel (likely indicating a mass celebration) below. On their chests both figures wear square devices of indeterminate function, though the lower one might be a bishop's rational or perhaps a book satchel.[18] The lower half of the bottom figure has been overcarved with a scene of two seated figures. The First Sculptor also likely carved the angel frieze at the top of side B and began the angels and borders of side A.[19] The Second Sculptor, however, executed most if not all of the remaining original work, at times substantially altering the First Sculptor's scheme.

Figure 18. Nunburnholme Cross, sides D (top left and bottom right) and B (top right and bottom left).

Figure 19. Nunburnholme Cross, sides A (top left and bottom right) and C (top right and bottom left).

Side A contains a gripping angels motif at the top but, along with side B, lacks the small beast figure the First Sculptor included on Side D. The left border of the upper section also shows the outline of First Sculptor's border design, but remains unexecuted, most obviously lacking the pelleting of the adjoining side. The upper right border does not as clearly follow the original design. The upper panel of Side A shows a secular figure in half profile, seated on a chair and holding a large, pommeled, Viking-type sword, bearing a hat, helm, or possibly a halo terminating in volutes. The lower figure lacks its head (perhaps obscured by the modern concrete join) but also consists of a seated figure in half profile, holding a staff of some sort in the right hand and grasping a rectangular object, possibly a book, in the left. Though the feet of this figure largely remain, a later sculptor has overcarved the bottom of this scene with an intrusive scene of a centaur and a smaller, human figure.

Side B possesses the same layout as side A, preserving the gripping angels motif at the top but entirely lacking the First Sculptor's border design. The upper panel contains a front-facing ecclesiastical figure, who wears a double cowl that transforms into a stole grasped in both hands. On top of the stole, the figure displays a large rectangular device; as with the lower figure on side D, this could possibly represent a book satchel or a rational. Some question remains whether this figure is the work of the Second Sculptor, the First Sculptor, or even an additional sculptor.[20] In the lower panel, the Second Sculptor departs from the overall design by carving not a portrait but a beast chain instead.[21]

On Side C the Second Sculptor has abandoned the gripping angels design entirely, replacing it with two small facing dragons, bound at their necks by a narrow band that loops around the body of the left beast. The upper panel displays a Virgin Mary and Child, facing front. Mary has a deep, dished halo, and the Christ Child holds a rectangular object, possibly a book. As on side A, the head of the lower-panel figure is missing; two large birds perch on the shoulders of a figure, who reaches down and places his hands on the heads of two lower figures, who in turn reach out and touch his lower body. The scene is probably a crucifixion, though some critics have read it as a scene of benediction.[22]

The Second Sculptor also saw fit to overcarve the bottom section of the First Sculptor's mass priest in the lower panel of side D, adding a scene of two figures seated, facing each other. Though a reading of this scene cannot be definitively proven, Lang has presented a compelling argument that it represents part of the pagan Sigurd myth, where Sigurd cooks the heart of the dragon.[23] In a turn of plastic justice, a third sculptor, probably working more than 150 years later after the Conquest, then overcarved another pagan element onto a seated Second Sculptor figure (side A), adding the decidedly Romanesque figure of a centaur and child, an addition that has been described as a "Norman doodle."[24]

Nunburnholme, an Anglo-Scandinavian sculpture worked during a 150-year period by three or four or even five different sculptors with several iconographic and stylistic agendas, would be a difficult material discourse to unpack even if it survived wholly intact and in pristine condition. The First Sculptor's original, explicitly Christian, Anglian-derived design (side D) was substantially revised and, in one section, recarved by the Second Sculptor to admit more emphatically Scandinavian elements (sides A, B, C), perhaps with additional work by another contemporary sculptor (side B, top); this work in turn was overcarved by an Anglo-Norman artist, perhaps during the construction of the church building.[25] Further, at any point after the work of the first three/four sculptors, another sculptor could have drilled the eye holes for the corner angels, cowled figure, and centaur.[26]

And though Lang and I. R. Pattison have provided thorough, if not wholly conclusive, investigations into the iconography and stylistic steps of the cross's carving, we know little if anything about the purpose, design, or even specific content of the cross. Its intended location—its literal space—remains anybody's guess, while the very form of the object remains open to debate. Because of missing sections, most notably the head, it is not definite that the Nunburnholme Cross is even a cross at all.

The late medieval and modern history of the monument distorts the spatial issues even further. As noted, when the surviving sections were excavated in the late nineteenth century, they were reassembled reversed, so that the top half is now turned 180 degrees around from the bottom. Additionally, the cement used to join the surviving fragments may be understood as yet another instance of "overcarving," adding yet another layer (this time in both an interpretative and a literal sense) to be assessed.

The present status of the Nunburnholme shaft indeed resists space. Viewing the object *in situ* taxes the viewer, who must coordinate the actual physical presence of the object in space with a reconstructed imagining of its proper or "original" configuration. Viewing Nunburnholme for the first time—standing in the bell tower and looking at one side of the shaft while mentally replacing half of it with its opposite side, all the while trying to balance which sculptor carved what, and when—can be more than a little disorienting. One must work to connect the spatial dots, to navigate the space between the physically immediate object and the former, twisted, and now imaginary medieval monument.

These literal ways in which the Nunburnholme Cross resists space tie into the larger issues of how we need to understand the space of such early medieval objects. At this point, the easiest way to make sense of the Nunburnholme Cross is *not* to examine the actual object, but rather to study printed or digital reconstructions of it that restore the sides to their original order. Such remediation of the physical by the representational provides a particularly apt summary of how we subsume medieval space under both later technologies of representation *and* modern notions of how space functions. [→ 6] It further invites us to revise our modern *ordo* of medieval space, and to posit modes in which we may reclaim aspects of such space that have become largely lost— lost in translation—by our modern analyses.

THE PERSPECTIVE OF MODERN RESISTANCE

Whereas our notion of representation is grounded in the Aristotelian process of imitation of nature or in Platonic doubling of the "one" that becomes "two," both modified by Leon Battista Alberti's rules of perspective (1435), I believe that the medieval concept of representation had little to do with the prevailing tradition in Western culture that considers representation in terms of optical geometry (and its ideological, cultural, political and social consequences). . . . Rather, it embraced the ever-shifting relationship between theological, historical, and spiritual formulations that defined the conditions of existence in a place and in a space.[27]

With the significant exception of the mathematicians and scientists who actually understand and can apply Einstein's theory of relativity, our modern, quotidian understanding of the ways objects interact with space has changed very little since the Enlightenment.[28] The early modern period witnessed a shift from previous notions of space as a category used to classify sensory experiences to another kind of category—the mathematical attempt to precisely calculate and classify space.[29] Today, the physicalist manner in which we understand space derives from Newton's and Descartes's theories of classical physics, where space and objects in space are mathematically quantifiable, and where that space, though potentially infinite, is also uniform and absolute in its physical integrity—a measurable void that holds objects within it.[30]

As historians of space note, representation conditions cognition, and the revolutionary ideas of Descartes' *res extensa* and Newton's spatial absolutism did not spring into existence *ex nihilo*, but rather built upon new perceptions of space engendered by the late medieval and Renaissance pioneers of perspective.[31] Perspective dominates the ways in which we re-produce space, and its rise is generally understood to have provided a more accurate way of representing objects within space. Perspective did not inform the production of medieval art the way it does most modern forms of visual expression, yet it usually governs the ways in which modern audiences interpret and value early medieval objects. With Nunburnholme, for instance, perspectival skill dominates the critical estimation of the sculptors. Critics concur that the Second Sculptor practiced the craft less expertly than his predecessor. Lang, for instance, describes his work as "flat and crude," composed of "linear scratchings of an artless kind," and in particular singles out the "deformity" of the Viking warrior, whose hand appears to stick straight out of his chest, as a failed attempt at half-profile perspective.[32] All reasonably accurate, certainly, but these almost instinctive judgments also reveal, as subtext, how we have come to more or less blindly equate perspectival representation with both nature and accuracy, and how such physicalist assumptions station our own critical perspectives, and ultimately restrict our view of medieval representation.

The rise of Renaissance perspectivalism distilled the variegated "nows" of medieval art down to a single frozen moment of representation, a snapshot of an instant, what modern physicists now call a "zero-time" representation of space.[33] The emptying of time out of space allows for a comfortingly fixed and unchanging view of an object; the singularity of perspective, guided by the pure linearity of Neoplatonism, provided (and still provides) the illusion of a material reality that only, really, exists in its representation.[34] [→8] In his theories of relativity, Einstein took the revolutionary step of putting time back into space, and (to give a reductive summary) time became understood as a function of space, a fourth dimension as important as the three we can see.[35]

In contrast, medieval art often chose to define space not in terms of time but in spite of it. While time was generally conceived as a linear process in early medieval thought, "time's shape was no more than approximate."[36] Early medieval representations of actions and objects in space did not operate under the obligation of temporal fidelity; images often conflated separate times within the same space, and the representation of visual narrative often dispensed with the notion of chronology and sequence altogether. [→96] Medieval time with regard to representations of actions in space was porous; it seeped into, out of, and around events that (for us) should be sequential. Since such atemporal qualities are particularly marked in Scandinavian and Anglo-Saxon art of the period, this art is well suited to the purposes of our study.[37]

Perspectival representation, and the absolute Newtonian space that followed, created a wholly different brand of atemporality for modern consideration of medieval objects.[38] For modern scholars, artifacts such as early medieval stone sculpture became objects from the past to be reimagined in a singular snapshot of an "original" condition. In modern representation, the power of print culture joins with that of perspective to re-render medieval objects as singular, static, and unified. Specifically, in Lang's *Corpus of Anglo-Saxon Stone Sculpture*, the flagship treatment of Anglo-Saxon sculpture, the unintended effect of the format is to reconstruct the *essential* objects, frozen in some sort of imaginary zero-time. The *Corpus*—an incredibly valuable project, it must be noted—presents each entry through small black-and-white photographs, relying on extensive written commentary to reconstruct the object for the reader. [→103] The overall effect is also one of remediation, where the medieval three-dimensional object is re-rendered as words and two-dimensional images. [→20] As with Nunburnholme, we know almost nothing about the origin, "author," and purpose of most Anglo-Saxon monuments. The *Corpus*, in many ways, attempts to "fix" unknowns such as dates and, as Orton puts it, desires

> to provide [a monument] with an "author-function," a name and description of its origin, a locus of meaning for its complex signification, a value and mode of existence for its place in the history of Anglo-Saxon England and the discourse of Anglo-Saxon stone sculpture.[39]

While the *Corpus* presents evaluative information of great consequence, its approach to its subject does not make much allowance for a sculpture's "*historia* of several possible moments of production and use."[40] Orton, as he explores the Foucaultian limitations and potential pitfalls of the *Corpus*, argues against overreliance on such classificatory schema, which belong "to the Classical Age when to know was to tabulate . . . based in the ways and means of late-seventeenth-century–eighteenth-century natural history."[41] Such approaches, like perspectival representation, are, of course, most useful. But they also hauntingly recall Alfred Crosby's assessment of how the Renaissance urge toward *pantometry*—the measure of everything—now affects the way we conceptualize reality:

Reduce what you are trying to think about to the minimum required by its definition; visualize it on paper . . . and divide it, either in fact or in imagination, into equal quanta. Then you can measure it . . . then you possess a [precise] quantitative representation of your subject. . . . Visualization and quantification: together they snap the padlock—reality is fettered.[42]

With its three (or more) sculptors, its unknown purpose, and its complicated *historia*, the Nunburnholme Cross resists fettering or benign reduction to "the minimum required by its definition." The spatial disorientation that results from experiencing the monument *in situ* indicates a more substantial resistance in our current modes of trying to understand it. In the zero-time *eidos* of traditional space, the Nunburnholme Cross *qua* object quite simply does not exist. The artifact as it survives does not match any of its "original" states, and the heterogeneity of its contextual past denies *an* object that can be recovered through the hermeneutic equivalent of perspectival production. In other words, the cross resists reduction to a symmetrical or mensurable node in a synchronic field; traditional attempts—in print, in photographs, in the *Corpus*—to represent it as a function of a singular vanishing point can only, as it were, capture part of the picture, and inaccurately at that.

NUNBURNHOLME IN MEDIEVAL SPACE

Notions of absolute space existed before the Middle Ages, in Greek and Roman culture, and then rose to prominence again in the early modern period.[43] But the view that the Renaissance development of absolute space represented some sort of return to a spatial status quo denies medieval space meaning on its own terms.[44] As Lefebvre observes,

> during the supposed emptiness of the late imperial or early medieval period a new space was established which supplanted the absolute space, and secularized the religious and political space of Rome. These changes were necessary though not sufficient conditions for the subsequent development of historical space, a space of accumulation. The "villa," now either a lordly domain or a village, had durably defined a *place* as an establishment bound to the soil.[45]

Lefebvre locates the break from imperial space in the early medieval period as a tabula rasa of sorts, one that like, say, the Great Fire of Chicago cleared the way for all sorts of new ways to "build" or to reconfigure space. Lefebvre's assessment also acknowledges that after this spatial reconfiguration begins a process of new accumulation—a new economy. Likewise, Kleinschmidt notes that social organization in the early medieval period

> was based on the relations among persons in groups as well as among groups and not a homogeneous space of limited extension, to which we may refer as territory. In other words, groups constituted space more frequently than space constituted groups.[46]

In England, the transition from groups-constituting-space to space-constituting-groups was particularly pronounced in the Anglo-Saxon period.[47] As Della Hooke reports, the patterns and quality of settlements in mid-to-late Anglo-Saxon England spurred "such massive change that the characteristics they acquired have left an imprint on the landscape that has lasted to the present day, despite subsequent changes."[48] During the Anglo-Saxon age, the smooth space of Germanic migration began to nucleate, and developed into the striated English space of fixed, public, and group-centered locales: village and city, fort and castle, church and cathedral; the space of England became defined and connected by point-to-point networks of communication and community.[49] The result of this process of nucleation was, however, not stasis but a kind of planned motility, as the nomadic line became redrawn as a planned line, designed to move a subject through Anglo-Saxon space along roads and routes that reinforced the nucleation that developed as England began to coalesce into a unified national identity.

Consider, as one brief example, the itinerancy of Anglo-Saxon royal courts and their attendant bureaucratic apparatus. Early English rule was a shifting mode of governance sharply distinguished from the high and late medieval models that followed, which more firmly anchored government in one or two centers of rule.[50] By the end of the Anglo-Saxon period, communities no longer constructed space, as they did at its beginning; rather, by then, long-standing and fabricated spaces of living produced communities and shaped their existence. But during Anglo-Saxon settlement and growth, the physical space of England was liminal, not quite wild and yet not quite routed and settled. As Heinrich Härke observes,

> The introduction of open fields and nucleated villages created a broad division within England: an "ancient countryside" of hamlets and single farmsteads located in irregular fields, with considerable woodland; and

a "planned countryside" of large villages in large regular fields, with straight roads and only small clumps of trees. These "two Anglo-Saxon landscapes" survive in the landscape to the present day.[51]

The landscape of settlement in Anglo-Saxon England, then, represented a developing hybridity of space. Though modern England, to a degree, now lives within both, during the Anglo-Saxon period the combination of these competing versions of medieval space was still a new and ongoing process.

Inside this historical process of settlement, the arc of the Danelaw of Anglo-Scandinavian, which began in the last third of the ninth century and was integrated, albeit not smoothly, into the national identity by the time of (and perhaps through) the Norman Conquest, stands as a compressed version of such spatial reformulation.[52] As products of cultural interpretation, the stone sculpture surviving from this period, such as Nunburnholme, often resists the modern spaces into which we attempt to place it. Emile Durkheim's studies of tribal culture led him to propose a distinct correlation between the organization of a local community and its inhabitants' epistemology and representation of macrocosmic space.[53] [→ 138] The Nunburnholme Cross functioned as a monument that, ultimately, marked the space of Scandinavian settlement in East Yorkshire, and likewise articulates the larger issues of how the communities living in the decades after Viking incursions understood and represented the physical and cultural shifts that produced the place and space of their lives.

As with many Anglo-Saxon and Anglo-Scandinavian sculptures, no sure evidence exists for the intended purpose of the Nunburnholme Cross, or that that purpose even remained constant through the time of its manufacture. In early critical assessments, funerary monument for the unnamed Viking jarl led the conjectural pack, with the possibilities of preaching stone, village cross, and territorial marker trailing at respective distances.[54] Definition as some sort of sacral marker remains the default assumption about monuments such as Nunburnholme, and most modern critics do not even bother to raise such issues, as specific evidence for individual objects seldom exists. We do not and, short of a windfall literary or archaeological discovery, likely cannot know definitively the particular location and concomitant social purpose of Nunburnholme. However, due (or perhaps overdue) consideration of the more general role this sculpture played in the *production* of Anglo-Scandinavian space can still recover more of this object's social definition, and provide a surer sense of the space it helped shape.

At the time of the original carving of Nunburnholme, Anglo-Scandinavian settlements had existed for only a few decades. The Great Army took York in 867, and by 876, the *Anglo-Saxon Chronicle* notes, the Viking king Halfdan "shared out" the land in Northumbria and settlers began to "plough and make a living for themselves" [¬ þy geare Healfdene Norðanhymbra lond gedelde ¬ ergende wæron ¬ hiera tilgende].[55] The Vikings who relocated to East Yorkshire apparently embraced the agrarian lifestyle readily, settling and enculturating at a much quicker rate than their Scandinavian peers to the south in the Five Boroughs, or to the west in Dublin.[56]

A. L. Binns argues that the settlers of Yorkshire "ceased to be Vikings" when they abandoned the peripatetic lifestyle that defined Viking identity in England.[57] The shift from Viking motility to Anglo-Scandinavian settlement also marked the beginning of the shift Kleinschmidt identifies in the medieval production of the space around centered communities. In the last third of the ninth century, Scandinavian settlers began to work to define and mark their space of living. In other words, the group began to constitute the place. This definition of space occurs at the end of a "nomadic" movement, and anticipates the next phase of medieval space, where place begins to constitute group.

The transformation of Viking harrier into Scandinavian settler concurrently contributed much to the ongoing transformation of the landscape of northern England. The influence of Scandinavian emigration literally rewrote the topography of the area; Yorkshire today still has well over seven hundred place-names of Scandinavian derivation, while in the East Riding a full half of the names from the Anglo-Saxon period are Scandinavian in origin.[58] Though, as D. M. Hadley has recently shown, much remains to be proven about the specific scope and character of the Scandinavian settlement, it is safe to assert that such settlement played a significant role in the evolution of the living space of early medieval Yorkshire.[59] Härke summarizes one influence of the Danelaw upon the organization and use of territory:

> by the tenth century, Scandinavians were active participants in landscape reorganization and urbanization in England, and they may have even been initiators of both processes. . . . the main Scandinavian impact on the landscape was, in fact, in the more densely settled areas of central and eastern England: in the Scandinavian contributions to the ongoing processes of urbanization, nucleation of rural settlement, and creation of open field systems. . . . The earliest evidence of nucleated villages and

open fields, probably of ninth-century date, has been found in the Scandinavian-controlled Midlands where the reorganization of the landscape would have been easier to achieve for the new foreign lords than for the established Anglo-Saxon aristocracy. Even the mouldboard plough has been claimed as a Scandinavian introduction into Britain.[60]

Suffice it to say, at the very least, that Scandinavian settlers were active participants in the production of Danelaw space.

Unfortunately, as little is currently known about the actual space of late-ninth- and tenth-century Nunburnholme as about the sculpture itself.[61] The earliest reference to "Brunham" (the "Nun" was not added until after the founding of the post-Conquest nunnery) occurs in the Domesday Book, as a berewick of the manor of Warter, held previously by Morcar, the earl of Northumbria who was defeated in 1066 by Harald Hardrada's forces at the Battle of Fulford Gate, shortly before Harold Godwinson's victory at Stamford Bridge.[62] Though the name reveals an Anglo-Saxon, not Scandinavian, origin, the presence of the nearby town of Burnby with its distinguishing Old Norse ending "-by" suggests, along with the monument, a significant Scandinavian presence in the area.[63] At this point, the most that can be stated, tentatively, about Brunham is that its name does not indicate the establishment of a Scandinavian community in uninhabited wilderness, but rather an assumption of control of a preexisting Anglo-Saxon habitation.

Though recent critics have advocated such cultural fusion as an important, if not dominant, result of Halfdan's mid-ninth-century "sharing out of the land," the process of social synthesis would not have been an easy one.[64] The Anglo-Scandinavian control of York and its surrounding territory was, to say the least, tumultuous and tenuous; in eighty-seven years, settlers of the area saw royal rule change at least twenty times between Danish, English, and Norwegian hands, with some periods apparently lacking any clear leader at all.[65]

Further, the sharing out of Anglo-Saxon land to settling Scandinavians could be read as other than integration. In one version of the *Anglo-Saxon Chronicle*'s 876 entry on the Viking settlement of Northumbria ("¬ þy geare Healfdene Norðanhymbra lond gedelde ¬ ergende wæron ¬ hiera tilgende"), a scribal slip neatly betrays the violence underwriting Halfdan's agrarian scheme. Instead of reporting that the Vikings were *ergende* (plowing), the English compiler of the Peterborough version (manuscript E) writes *hergende* (harrying); what from one perspective was settling was, from another, profoundly unsettling.[66] What transpired to turn an Anglo-Saxon region into an Anglo-Scandinavian one likely fell somewhere in between *ergende* and *hergende*. [→ 94]

Michal Kobialka writes that in the instability of such medieval cultural crises "the interplay between representational places and spaces became visible before its traces [were] washed away by the mechanism of a classificatory grid." [→ 129] For Kobialka, the modern "grid" that now reproduces medieval space erases the residue of how medieval subjects represented and produced space (place) with the recorded "facts . . . shaped from conflicting imaginations, at once past and present."[67] The competing terms *ergende* and *hergende* in versions of the *Anglo-Saxon Chronicle* record one such trace of the discursive interplay of cultural instability; Anglo-Scandinavian stone sculpture has the capacity to preserve others. In the shift from *hergende* to *ergende*, Scandinavian settlers and their immediate descendants would have desired stability within the potentially explosive framework of a newly integrating society. Whatever their specific purposes, monuments like the Nunburnholme Cross both represented and contributed to the attempt to impose permanence on the settlement of territory. In effect, such objects worked to turn the *space* of northern England into the *place* of the Danelaw, a place that in turn would center and define the cultural groups that lived within it.

The history of Anglo-Saxon space was one of inherited lands, and the Anglo-Saxon "story of place had always to deal with the intertwined acts of possession and dispossession, both as historical fact and as future possibility."[68] Viewed as an active participant in this process, the Nunburnholme Cross becomes a cross of another kind, a cross between Anglo-Saxon and Anglo-Scandinavian cultures, as well as a cross between the desire for social stability and the tumultuous reality that marked the formation of the Danelaw. Scholarship on the cross has thus far only considered the stages of carving as part of the teleology of the finished monument—Kobialka's classificatory grid. But as Lefebvre explains, the representational space of a monument like the cross "overlays physical space, making symbolic use of its objects" and uncovers "space as directly *lived* through its associated images and symbols, and hence the space of 'inhabitants' and 'users.'"[69] In other words, the process of the carving of the Nunburnholme Cross can also reveal much about the struggle to produce the space and place of the Nunburnholme community.

The very source of the monument's limestone signals the distinctive nature of the cross. Roman ashlar originally mined thirty miles to the west at Tadcaster, and likely brought more than fifteen miles from York to Nunburnholme, falls far outside Richard Bailey's normative range for a source of sculpture stone.[70] The recycling of an ashlar column from Roman York suggests, at the very least, a connection between Nunburnholme and the current capital of the Danelaw. It also demonstrates a desire to produce new Anglo-Scandinavian space out of materials recycled from earlier Roman space. As Anglo-Saxon literature such as *The Ruin* and *Maxims II* reveals, contemporary English culture remained fascinated with the masonry construction of Rome that survived amid their timbered communities.[71] [→144]

The multi-staged sculptural process of the Nunburnholme Cross and its layers of stylistic and iconographic materials also project many of the cultural issues of the new space of Anglo-Scandinavian England. The work of the First Sculptor reveals nothing of a Scandinavian context for production, and if the monument survived with only the work of the First Sculptor, scholars could arguably date the stone as pre-Viking. The cross's early figures all derive from late Anglian modes, and therefore ultimately descend from a Continental, Carolingian style. Because the Scandinavian incursions and settlement fragmented the political unity of the north of England, the styles and motifs of most Anglo-Scandinavian sculpture can be mapped inside small circles of regional influence. However, the execution of the figures and design of side D, the most complete side of the First Sculptor, all point to an aesthetic range well "beyond the confines of Yorkshire" and perhaps suggest a pre-Viking context linked to "the cultural unity [previously] fostered by monastic contact."[72]

The execution and iconography of side D operate within a predominantly ecclesiastical context. The First Sculptor designed the gripping angels that frame the top corners of the monument, providing a heavenly context for the monument that symbolically pulls its content upward, away from the earthly. The two figures the First Sculptor carved, the saint in clerical garb and the priest celebrating mass, also suggest a wholly religious and specifically Christian milieu for the monument. The first stage of the cross's carving thus appears more at home in the realm of the monastic sculptural houses that dominated the production of stone monuments before the Viking incursions.[73] In short, the First Sculptor's cross reads more like an Anglo-Saxon monument than anything else.

The reason the First Sculptor did not finish his design cannot be known, and the possible reasons are manifold. Given the discrepancies between the style and content of the two sculptors, however, it is tempting to entertain the thesis that the cross is not the product of two sculptors working consecutively on the same commission. Instead, the monument may well have started as a project far removed in distance, patron, and perhaps time from its final form—itself being "conquered" by Viking invasion and settlement. Richard Bailey outlines the shift from monastic to lay production of stone sculpture that occurred across the late Anglian monastic decline and the beginning of Scandinavian settlement. In this process, the local "village vernacular" replaced more unified monastic models, and native English lay craftsmen had to adapt material primarily derived from wood carving to the less pliable medium of stone.[74] But whatever the specific *historia* of the sculpture's origin, the manifest incongruities of its three-stage style and its shift of content inscribe on one object the representational space of three different cultures. The revisions and additions of the Second Sculptor, even while including scenes of the Virgin and Child and the Crucifixion, easily read as a substantive redirection of the original upward-looking, Christian transcendence of the Anglian design. The Second Sculptor injects into the monument a healthy dose of the secular through the sword-wielding lord, and of the Scandinavian through the Jellinge style of the beast chain, and of the pagan through the overcarved Sigurd scene. The Third Sculptor, post-Conquest, reshapes the monument again, this time as a Romanesque practice piece, "trashing" its prior form and function, as well as the subjugated cultures that produced and preceded it.

The inclusion of the Viking-styled jarl on side A announces a personal, not institutional, affiliation for the monument, and provides a secular context for interpreting all of the Christian iconography. On a stylistic basis, the Second Sculptor distinguishes the warrior (and the likewise seated, possibly secular figure beneath him, which might, in an Alfredian mode, represent the "learned" side of him) from all the ecclesiastical figures by attempting to render him in a three-quarter profile. The figure represents an aristocrat, Scandinavian or of close Scandinavian descent, who in all probability was the ranking authority in the community and the patron of the stone. As D. M. Hadley notes, such aristocrats could retain explicit ties to Scandinavia far longer than poorer settlers, who might more rapidly gain an "English" identity.[75]

The beast chain on side B also pointedly disrupts the original scheme by filling a panel with overtly Scandinavian ornament instead of portraiture. Lang argues for the continuity and synthesis between the Christian elements of the First Sculptor and the secular elements of the Second Sculptor, maintaining that Mercian designs were likely the immediate source for the Nunburnholme beast chain.[76] It is true that beast chains from the Derbyshire St. Alkmund's Cross and elsewhere contain similarities to Nunburnholme's, and David Wilson considers side B's design a fusion of Jellinge (double-contour ribbon interlace) and Mercian (beast stance).[77] However, Mercian-influenced or no, the inclusion of a beast chain on Nunburnholme still reflects an affinity for iconography strongly reminiscent of Scandinavian art, shares much with the developing Scandinavian style of Jellinge beast chains, and supports the substantial movement from an Anglo-Saxon to a Scandinavian-derived aesthetic evidenced in Danelaw sculpture.[78]

The so-called Sigurd scene on side D remains the most explicit and invasive revision of the original design, as in the midst of the First Sculptor's mass figure the Second Sculptor carves an episode from a pagan myth. As Lang identifies it, in this scene Sigurd roasts the heart of the dragon he has killed and tastes its juices, an action that will give him the power to understand birds.[79] If this is the scene represented, the over carving of the pagan *onto* the Christian ironically reverses the general historical sense of Germanic spiritual progression—first pagan, *then* Christian.[80] Whatever the content of the scene, it does mark the intention to depart from the First Sculptor's strictly ecclesiastical design. At the same time, however, an interpolated pagan episode would create syncretic connections that conflate this mythic ritual of supernatural ingestion with the Christian celebration of the Eucharist.[81]

Side C is the only side that does not contain the gripping angels motif. In all possibility, when the First Sculptor mapped out the frieze of his design, side C rested on the ground and so was inaccessible.[82] While retaining the gripping angels motif on the other sides, the Second Sculptor replaces them here with two facing dragons. Yet a simple elision of explicitly Christian content cannot be the goal here; on this same side, the sculptor carves scenes of the Virgin and Child and the Crucifixion. Side C, in a fashion, sums up the social import of this monument. The iconography of the figures, along with the apparent attempt of the Second Sculptor to copy the First Sculptor's saint from side D, down to the Anglian-derived dished haloes, points to the influence of the Anglo-Saxon past upon the design.[83] Still, the monument's hybrid form disrupts the proposed harmony of an angel on every corner. While the Second Sculptor substantially revises the content of the First Sculptor, the final form of the monument does not efface but preserves the presence of the Anglo-Saxon discourse. As with other Anglo-Scandinavian sculpture, Nunburnholme includes both Anglo-Saxon and Scandinavian expression, but here the process of revision and intrusion more overtly records the tendentious, reciprocal relationship between two cultures sharing space and place within the representational confines of this monumental, territorial marker.

In its confusing construction and intricate, multicultural content, the Nun-burnholme Cross still helps define the space of the Anglo-Scandinavian settlement it once marked, and represents the shift from monastic to secular production of such cultural monuments. It encodes the desire for an integrated and stable community, and yet reveals the imperfect nature and disruption inherent in such a process. Through its differences of formal elements and design, the monument also suggests, perhaps, how the leaders of the settlement that eventually became Nunburnholme struggled in the process of ideologically producing their own space of living.

MEDIEVAL SPACE: SMOOTH AND STRIATED

Like Lefebvre, Gilles Deleuze argues that societies—or, more specifically, social ideologies of power—produce space. Deleuze also develops a spatial epistemology with an eye to how premodern space provides the transition to modern space and its economies—initially by considering the artistic representations of objects across the boundaries of prehistory and history.[84] For Deleuze, historical space arises out of a constant negotiation of two subsets of space, smooth and striated. Striated space is the sense of space that has dominated modern representation. It depends on optical distance and the qualities such distance engenders: "constancy of orientation, invariance of distance through an interchange of inertial points of reference, interlinkage by immersion in an ambient milieu, constitution of a central perspective."[85] In essence, striated space is the homogeneous space we now generally assume natural and real: Euclidean, Cartesian, and Newtonian space, geometrically constructed and anchored in the rise of modern perspective. Striation also describes the mechanics of modern criticism that approaches the world of medieval art as a network of point-to-point connections. In its extensive system of cross-references and visual indexing, the *Corpus of Anglo-Saxon Stone Sculpture*, for example, seeks to understand its objects of study through a network of scholarly and photographic striation.

Striation, though can be medieval as well. On the Nunburnholme Cross, the work of the First Sculptor supports striation. As critics have noted, the First Sculptor skillfully carves his side D portraits, shaping these figures with an accomplished performance of perspective, depth, and modeling. His design arises out of a careful network of interlinking points, panels, diagonals, and semicircles. In the surviving piece, we can still see the First Sculptor's adumbration of a scheme to connect all sides through a series of cleanly and clearly linked shapes. The border design for Side D is pelleted—lines explicitly constructed out of points—and the unfinished carving on the upper right border of side B reveals the plan to turn the lines of such pelleting into diamonds across the corners, part of a plan to emphasize a three-dimensional perspective across the flat planes of each face. Such a perspectival vision is most startlingly realized in the First Sculptor's innovative and emulated design of the gripping angels.[86] The angels do not clearly exist when one views the faces of the cross straight on—one sees instead two disembodied arms coming out of the top corners. Only when viewing the monument from its corners are the angels apparent, as the round faces become visible and the right and left arms are seen to link two separate, winged sides. The overall effect of the angels and the pelleting provides the monument with strong senses of linearity, interlinkage, and three-dimensional perspective.

The Second Sculptor imitates and continues many aspects of such striation, but also introduces its Deleuzian counterpart: smooth space. In what he terms the "nomad art" of prehistory, Deleuze discovers a space marked not by precise, stable systems of punctation and linearity but by their lack. Smooth space is precedent space, and less grounded in materialist and political production. It is haptic, more immediate, and characterized by instability, fluidity, and a variability or abstraction of line that does not reduce space to plane but instead "has no background, plane, or contour, but rather changes in direction and local linkages between parts."[87] [→19]

What Deleuze describes as the "nomadic line" of smooth space has been called by others the "Gothic line" of premodern representations of space.[88] The abstract nature of smooth space and its representation originates in an alternative perception of world-space, one connected to "nomadic" aspects of migratory culture that only slowly receded over the course of the Middle Ages, and usefully informs how the space of living in England changed during the Anglo-Saxon period. Smooth space occurs in much early English medieval art, of course. The "free and swirling, inorganic, yet alive . . . streaming, spiraling, zig-zagging, snaking, feverish line of variation" typifies much Anglo-Saxon and Hiberno-Saxon illumination sculpture and engraving.[89] The smooth lines of Anglo-Saxon and Celtic interlace also reflect and refract the spaces that contain them. "Woven" designs, whether on vellum or metal or stone, themselves become "curving lights which catch the light."[90]

Working, ultimately, from a Carolingian revision of classical traditions, the First Sculptor in his later Anglo-Saxon style does not promote such Insular smoothness. The Second Sculptor, however, discontinues most of Nunburnholme's original framing devices of pelleting and borders, and adds panels that either fail at the modeled perspective of the First Sculptor or ignore it alto-gether. The most obvious example, the poorly rendered perspective of the jarl's hand, has already been noted. And over the clean, orderly arrangement of the First Sculptor's figures, the Second Sculptor's invasively carved Sigurd scene is a jumble of figures and setting, a chaotic counterpoint to the earlier design. Finally, the Second Sculptor's beast chain on side B emphasizes smoothness, and embodies Deleuze's "snaking, feverish line of variation." Whether Scandi-navian or English in origin, these twisting lines define a stylistic shift toward smooth space that *counterpoints* the representational force of the sculpture and attenuates the striated unities of lines, points, planes, contours, and per-spectival orientation carefully orchestrated in the First Sculptor's original scheme.

Socially, Deleuze notes, smooth space can reemerge when the striated space of culture is disrupted through "catastrophe."[91] The circumstances of the artis-tic change that occurred in the carving of the Nunburnholme Cross remain hidden, as does the exact nature of the social and spatial disruption that must have occurred as the region around Nunburnholme changed from Anglo-Saxon to Anglo-Scandinavian. But the monument's conflation of smooth and striated space provides traces of this transition and integration *and* of the con-tinuous, potentially catastrophic volatility that inhered in the Scandinavian settlements of the late ninth and early tenth centuries.

Striation is the eventual outcome and agent of settlement; it "transforms territory into 'land,' which awaits allocation as property/proper place."[92] In settlement, society becomes rooted in locales that form points in the lines of communication and traffic, and the location of Nunburnholme itself points to the gradual striation of Anglo-Scandinavian culture. At the time of the Danelaw, Nunburnholme occupied a location of relative importance, lying between two converging Roman roads, as well as two Viking routes connect-ing the central point of Anglo-Scandinavian York to both the North Sea and the Humber River.[93]

Anglo-Scandinavian sculpture likewise participates in such social stria-tion. Without terming it as such, Richard Bailey developed a striated reading of Anglo-Scandinavian stonework, starting with a classificatory model that identifies iconographic and stylistic groups across sculptures, similar to the *Corpus* model. Bailey argues that "if we then plot out the distribution of these groups, it is often possible to get some notion of the economic and cultural links between particular villages and districts."[94]

In a related mode, David Stocker has recently adduced evidence for a strong connection between later tenth-century Hiberno-Norse funerary sculpture in Yorkshire and the rise of successful public markets for Viking traders and Anglo-Scandinavian merchants.[95] Even in the pre-Hiberno-Norse period, the majority of early Anglo-Scandinavian stone sculpture in the East Riding occurs along the primary trade and travel routes of the area.[96] Such placement points first to the privileged status of the settlers who occupied such routes. Second, the marriage of sculpture and status reinforces the relationship between stone sculpture and the gradual striation of Anglo-Scandinavian space as it turns into Anglo-Scandinavian place. The union of sacred and secular within such representational spaces as the Nunburnholme Cross confirms Lefebvre's claim that medieval space slowly became the "space of accumulation—its birthplace and cradle," first in the accumulation of knowledge (sacred space) and then in the accumulation of riches (market space).[97] In the developing Danelaw, these monuments literally demarcated the developing network of this settled space—the "inertial points" on the Anglo-Scandinavian socioeconomic grid.[98] Taken together, such sculptures and the places they helped define chart the rise of group-centered spaces that inculcate worldviews (and views of the world) increasingly striated in nature—an early, medieval part of the process of social definition that changed the representation and then the nature of "real" space, and moved it into modernity. [→154]

NUNBURNHOLME IN DIGITAL SPACE

In his assessment of how Old English texts portray landscape, Nicholas Howe classifies the Anglo-Saxon notion of landscape as "inherited, invented, and imagined." Howe concludes his study by wondering if any Old English text combines all three of these notions.[99] Strictly speaking, the Nunburnholme Cross is not a text about topography. But as we have seen, the monument does play a part in reflecting and shaping the forces that transform Anglo-Saxon space, place, and culture. The visual discourse of the cross embodies all of Howe's categories: the sculpture inherits and recycles the material of both Roman and Anglian representational space, and its hybrid style and content fashion a new representational space. While encoding the tumult of cultural fusion, the cross's styles, form, content, and purpose imagine desire and promote a stable and permanent Anglo-Scandinavian community, balanced between its ethnic components, integrated in both sacred and economic spaces, and ruled by a Viking aristocrat.

The overcarvings also lend an air of the palimpsest to the cross's final form. The Second Sculptor overwrites, but does not eradicate, the work that comes before him. The Anglo-Norman sculptor who intrudes again with the centaur on Side C provides a historical coda to the process of inheritance, invention, and imagination. That centaur, and the sculpture's subsequent destruction, pronounce the material end of this sculpture, destined to be recycled and assimilated itself in the construction of a new representational space in England: the Anglo-Norman church.

In "reading stone" of Anglo-Saxon sculpture, modern scholars are forced to deal with a frustrating set of unknowns, and their objects of study remain intersections of multivalent and often ambiguous narratives and meanings.[100] Early medieval objects like the Nunburnholme Cross now confound us, because they do not have a monolithic, monologic, and recoverable form. This cross was first a Roman column, then a Christian monument, then a Scandinavian marker of social desire, then an Anglo-Norman practice piece, then a medieval church wall stone, and finally a modern, reconstructed historical artifact. All of this *historia* is not generally considered in the modern study of this sculpture because it does not fit the modern desire for the zero-time singularity of an essential, unchanging, and recoverable object. Or, as Simon Biggs views the difference,

> modern pictorial space can be seen as objective and democratic, stripped of symbolic motility, whilst Medieval space is subjective and hermetic; where the meanings of the individual elements shift in relationship to one another and the overall frame of reference.[101]

The "symbolic motility" of medieval representational space may also be understood in Deleuzian terms as a kind of hermeneutic smoothness, and challenges our generally striated attempts to understand it. The medieval space of the Nunburnholme Cross, like the liminal period between migration and group-centered spaces, is both smooth *and* striated in nature. To better study and comprehend its variegated meaning, a discourse capable of containing smooth and striated notions of space is vital. As we have seen throughout this book, the technology of print excels at striated analyses. But with regard to stone sculpture, the practice of print scholarship also regresses the space of study from three dimensions to largely two dimensions, flattening the discourse and, in the case of most academic assessments, reducing the object of study to a series of low-resolution black-and-white drawings and/or line drawings. Inside the overwhelmingly linear and planar format of the printed page, smooth analysis is difficult, if not impossible.

The Nunburnholme Cross of medieval space no longer exists in the physical reality of the sculpture. Sections are missing—at least the head, if not a middle panel—and the modern reassembling of what survives has literally twisted the medieval space 180 degrees around. But if physical space now fails the medieval monument, digital space can help reclaim it. In the past few decades, cyberspace has become a virtual location for real experience; inside the realm of the representational, digital space trumps printed space, increasing "in number or level of dimensions as compared to the scroll, codex, printed book, and other traditional forms of communication."[102] With such extradimensionality comes the potential for smooth discourse. Cyberspace is an inherently fluid medium, with the ability to change or manipulate the represented object across a range of contexts or user inputs. In cyberspace, the studied object is no longer a static object, but becomes alive and responsive to interpretative possibilities. If the space of print is fixed, linear, and hierarchical, digital space is *rhizomic*, a foundational concept in the theories of Deleuze and Félix Guattari and one that in recent years digital theorists have seized upon to explain the function and operation of cyberspace.[103] Rhizomic space, an evolution of spatial conception, collapses smooth and striated space. It is a space, in the words of Deleuze and Guattari, of

> acentered systems, finite networks of automata in which communication runs from any neighbor to any other, the stems or channels do not preexist, and all individuals are interchangeable, defined by their state at a given moment.[104]

The rhizomic framework of digital space also encourages the reconstitution of objects such as the Nunburnholme Cross in multiple forms, as well as the combination of traditional and emergent modes of studying them. Cyberspace creates a new practice of space, one that embodies both Euclidean forms and alternatives to them.[105] In cyberspace, space and virtual space constantly form relationships, allowing for not only a single zero-time perspective of an object in space—that is, placing the object—but many, theoretically limitless in number and constitution.[106] The rhizomic network of cyberspace can contain both the striated approaches of older forms of source-and-analogue scholarship and smooth analyses that enact a more fluid and plural range of "perspectives," from the important striations of formal studies such as *Corpus* scholarship to the equally vital smoothness of medieval spaces that operate beyond physicalist assumptions of what constitutes "real" space.

In a digital edition of the Nunburnholme Cross, one can conceivably reproduce any or all of the *historia* of the monument, updating and adapting the physical space of the object of study as context demands. Certainly (with our physicalist concerns) the reproduction of the material object within a three-dimensional virtuality remains a paramount goal. With the current advances in the high-resolution digital scanning of three-dimensional art, the reproduction of a navigable virtual object is now within the realm of the possible for technologically aware academics.[107] Once a high-resolution model is rendered, the user can work within a fluid (or smooth) mode of magnification, choosing from not one or two static resolutions (as is common in print), but a dynamic spectrum that ranges from the entire object to individual chisel marks. [→193]

In a sense, digitizing the Nunburnholme Cross re-creates its representational space as one of multiple places of meaning (*subject spaces*) in a manner impossible within its current physical state. Once the material object is digitized, its physical nature becomes malleable, and rerenderable into any of a number of forms.[108] In the case of Nunburnholme, the most obvious advantage is the ability to return a three-dimensional representation of the object to its original layouts and designs, thus countering the spatial disorientation of the monument's current, misrestored state. Additionally, a digital form would allow the cross to be easily "edited" in reproduction to highlight and isolate the work of individual sculptors, and to re-create various stages of construction and even test hypotheses of reconstruction. A digital edition could also provide contextual reproductions, placing the object in any or all of its historical milieus, or virtually "repainting" the cross to give a sense of its original polychroming. Ultimately, a virtual model could allow the user to interactively "mix and match" possible sculptural scenarios. Given the fluid manipulation of digital data now possible, reconstructions could even be produced by "cloning" the work of the original sculptors and then modifying it to fit a reconstructive scheme.

As the image of a digitally rebuilt side A shows (see figure 20), such reconstructions can be seamless even up to a close magnification—and perhaps too alluring and convincing virtually real. As we have seen, the *historia* of Nunburnholme is confused and complicated enough already, and in such productions of lost medieval space, due care must be taken to distinguish extant materials from projected materials, as the line between the two can easily be blurred. Despite the potential power of a digital edition of the Nunburnholme Cross, most of the features described still only remediate older technologies of reproduction, and only improve upon approaches to medieval discourse already established in print. Though technology allows great advances in the processing and presentation of data, we have yet, at least in most approaches to medieval

Figure 20. Nunburnholme Cross, side A, digitally reconstructed.

materials, to see a corresponding *conceptual* shift in the way such discourse may be virtually realized. [→192]

As we have seen, medieval representational space uses time differently than the "zero-time" function of modern space. In cyberspace, the fixed quality of time much more readily becomes "unbound."[109] With specific regard to Anglo-Saxon sculpture, Orton's call that scholarly study not "fix the date" of such monuments but instead construct "a *historia* of several possible moments of production and use" makes the same case as software designer Brenda Laurel's critique of the way computer programs unnecessarily spatialize and striate the process by which users create their files. Laurel charges that she does not

> want to *page* back through versions of my work; I want to turn back the clock. The dimension of change is best represented through time, not fixed states. A simple chronobar would suffice. Yes, the implementation is hard, but the hardest part is probably visualizing the appropriate representation in the first place.[110]

Likewise, in "Liquid Architectures in Cyberspace," Marcos Novak argues that the representational potential of digital space can produce a "dematerialized architecture . . . no longer satisfied with only space and form and light and all the aspects of the real world."[111] [→76] As the capability of digital technology continues to progress (at meteoric rates), a similar application of "dematerialization" to the study of medieval objects such as Nunburnholme should soon be feasible.

The digital production of space and time will play a big role in the development of such new programs, and in reconfiguring our older appreciation of time, space, and place within New Media. Lance Strate observes a remediated "bias toward spatialization characteristic of computer software and contemporary culture in general," and argues in response for the development of alternative interfaces that do more than "simply store and access data."[112] For Nunburnholme, one might design a "chronobar" for a sliding scale of construction, one that begins with a Roman column and ends with a church wall, and factors in the gradations of change performed on this object throughout its complicated two-thousand-year history. Such an approach would not limit the cultural meaning of this object to one "fixed" time—for example, Anglo-Scandinavian monument—but instead reconfigure the signifying space of this stone to display all of its possible meanings within the same digital space.

Such representational moments along this scale could still be contextualized within the striated interpretative places of the monument—the regional connections of Anglo-Scandinavian or Anglian style, for instance, or an archaeological survey of pre-Conquest Nunburnholme, or the trading routes of the emergent Danelaw. These "contextual places" provide as much supporting material as possible to understand a particular aspect, a particular moment, or a particular interpretation of the monument. Such places function in smooth space as well, flexibly revising the material in response to adjustments in context, such as dates, locations, cultural emphases. These smooth spaces could in turn operate within a rhizomic docuverse of cyberspace, connecting to virtual editions of other objects across a range of times, styles, cultures, and theoretical approaches, extensible and modifiable as needed.

In his 1967 essay "Of Other Spaces," Foucault writes that modern space has now also come to encompass "the storage of data, the intermediate results of a calculation in the memory of a machine"—a position that presaged cyberspace's rise as a real space.[113] Digital space now has become the data living in the memory of the machine realized for human users. In the same essay, Foucault theorizes the rise of *heterotopias*, or "placeless places" that have a very real effect on the production of modern space. For Foucault, heterotopias are "virtual places" that intersect the imagined idealism of utopia and the experience of space, physical or otherwise.[114] The medieval space of the Nunburnholme Cross fuses these senses of utopian and real as it contributes to the marking, and re-marking, of the Anglo-Scandinavian space and place of settlement, containing both smooth and striated discourses of space in the process. Inside the immaterial and malleable realm of the digital, smooth and striated can also coexist, and the heterotopia of cyberspace permits an object not only to be represented but, theoretically, to be representable through any number of spatial modes.[115] This discussion has been a first, tentative step toward such visualization. It began as a consideration of the hybridity of the medieval space of an Anglo-Scandinavian cross shaft. It ends with an outline for the production of a heterotopia: an imagined intersection of the classical, medieval, modern, and postmodern spaces of the Nunburnholme Cross, within the full discursive and scholarly potential of the virtual space of the digital. This study serves to remind us that not all space is physical, and that not all meaning, while produced, is necessarily "material."

Epilogue

For All Practical Purposes: Medieval Studies in a New Media Age

If the aggregate time spent writing scholarly works and in reading them could be evaluated, the ratio between these amounts of time might well be startling.... The difficulty seems to be, not so much that we publish unduly in view of the extent and variety of present-day interests, but rather that the publication has been extended beyond our present ability to make real use of the record. The summation of human experience is being expanded at a prodigious rate, and the means we use for threading through the consequent maze to the momentarily important item is the same as was used in the days of square-rigged ships.

—Vannevar Bush

The goal of this book has been to some extent cannibalistic, as it seeks to show, through case examples in the academic subspecialty of Anglo-Saxon studies, that in fact the printed book "has been extended beyond our present ability to make real use of the record." At the same time, this book, with more than seven hundred footnotes, almost five hundred cited sources, and a neat, closure-inducing epilogue, is an exercise in striation and structural unity, enacting in print much of what it critiques about print. This exploration and exploitation has focused primarily on theoretical aspects of how New Media can make us aware of the particular mandates and limits print culture has placed upon early medieval studies, as well as of post-print frameworks for interpretation that are just beginning to emerge.

Vannevar Bush, though, was less concerned with interpretation than with practical application. The Memex apparatus (utilizing combinatory and annotative microfilm) that he envisioned in a 1945 precursor to the desktop computer was a mechanical aid for the scholar in response to the information overload that print could no longer handle efficiently.[1] [→14] In medieval studies, generally, the digital programs and applications developed for scholarly studies have not conceptualized new modes of study, but instead have reacted to new technologies with an eye to improving older methodologies. But just as this book has assessed technological change in more abstract terms of critical approaches to Anglo-Saxon culture and expression, the New Media theory studied here holds equally for more practical applications—the development of new electronic editions, software, and environments for research and interpretation of medieval discourse of all kinds.

TOLSTOY IN HYPERTEXT

Poised on the cusp of a new technological age, we still for the most part do not know exactly where we stand. Exactly how difficult our position is with respect to the potential of New Media crystallized for me recently during a seminar on digital literature I was teaching. In an online discussion of Robert Coover's essay titled (playfully, not prophetically) "The End of Books," one graduate student posted that while he understood the potential of hypertext fiction, he did not see how it applied to "preserving the classics," concluding "I hardly see the point (or possibility) of reading Tolstoy in hypertext." [→40]

Such a statement should not be viewed as a failure of imagination, but rather as a ratification of how strongly print conditions our approach to literary and artistic studies, both in interpretation and in the development of scholarly apparatus for interpretation. I certainly saw where my student was coming from: Tolstoy was an author who wrote for print, and his works, like most modern literature, are linear, sequential, and designed to have physical beginnings and ends. But in framing my subsequent contribution to the online discussion, I pondered what it meant to imagine Tolstoy in hypertext, and I realized that, as a medievalist, I was more prepared than I had thought to consider the effect of new technologies upon older literary forms.

All of medieval literature existed before print, but except at the highest level of study, all medieval literature is now experienced *as* print. When we read *The Canterbury Tales* today, for example, we do not read them in their original chirographic medium. Instead we read a technologically transformed text that preserves some of the early form and quality, but that also loses other aspects and adds still other characteristics. Medieval readers of Chaucer would have never read the work in a standardized, unified form, in an orthographically fixed language and with an editorially agreed-upon order of the tales.[2] [→19] Given the considerable differences between the phenomena of literature in medieval and modern contexts, the very notion of "the" text of *The Canterbury Tales* would have carried a much different meaning to a medieval reader, if any meaning at all. Substantive differences between media are perhaps even more apparent when considering the shift from oral to written forms of the same text. When *Beowulf* was written down, the act preserved much of what modern readers value in a piece of literature. At the same time, the translation of this poem to the newer, more singularly disposed representational technology of writing closed off the text from alternative modes of content that the dynamic medium of oral performance and transmission allowed and encouraged. [→26]

Sitting on the other side of the print/manuscript divide, while we as scholars and students might acknowledge such media gaps in the texts we study, our critical work remains, necessarily, a function of print culture. Consider, then, a day in the future when digital media will have more or less replaced print as the dominant mode of literary and scholarly expression, much as print has today replaced prior media. In this future, readers will indeed read Tolstoy—and Chaucer and *Beowulf*—as hypertext, or hypermedia, or whatever digital texts come to be called. And in the same way that writing *Beowulf* down changed it forever (even as it preserved it), and that printed editions of Chaucer's corpus changed it forever (even as they disseminated it), so too will the form and text of Tolstoy's novels change. We just cannot yet tell for certain or even imagine the full extent or nature of that change. What we can realize right now, however, is that currently we are trying to adapt new forms of digital technology to our older forms of study, when we should be thinking about doing the reverse.

Since the late 1980s Anglo-Saxonists have formed the vanguard, even the avant-garde sometimes, in integrating digital technology into the discipline. ANSAXNET, the electronic discussion group for Anglo-Saxonists set up in 1987, was one of the first academic listservs, while Patrick Conner's 1990 *Beowulf Workstation* and Allen Frantzen's 1992 *Seafarer* program, both implemented as HyperCard stacks, were two of the earliest hypertext programs in higher education.[3] More recently, Kevin Kiernan's *Electronic Beowulf* and many subsequent projects too numerous to catalogue here have set new precedents for how digital technology may be applied to both scholarship and pedagogy.[4] We have, in the past decade, reached a kind of tipping point with respect to the presence of digital technology in Anglo-Saxon studies. Medieval studies in general have witnessed an explosion of digital initiatives, and many projects in the works for years have finally been published and/or gained recognition in the field. As Peter Robinson notes in his 2003 assessment of digital media and medieval scholarship, "it is now nearly impossible to find a single large-scale editorial project in western Europe or America which does not already have, or is not actively preparing, a digital dimension."[5]

But in his 1999 review of the current state of Anglo-Saxon scholarship for *A Companion to Anglo-Saxon Literature*, Frantzen recognizes the tendency of the discipline to continue to read through tradition, not innovation, and often not to recognize its own subjective view as it does so.[6] After half a millennium of use, print, once an innovation, has long since become a silent partner in the tradition of Anglo-Saxon studies. Print has in turn imprinted scholarship with its dominant qualities: the fixity and homogenization of its display, its linear nature, and the general privileging of the written word over other forms of discourse. In Nicholas Howe's essay for the same volume, he considers the potential power of new digital database projects such as the *Dictionary of Old English* or *Fontes Anglo-Saxonici* to transform the future of scholarship, observing:

> The challenge facing us as Anglo-Saxonists will be *not* to treat them as databases, as more complete or user-friendly or accurate versions of older resources in the field. . . . As the quantity of our knowledge increases in more codified and ordered forms, we will have to learn ways of using this knowledge so that it does not paralyse or bury us. . . . I suspect that the first effect these large projects will have on the field, when they become available in final form, will be to collapse some of our long-standing linguistic and historical models: for instance, that denotation is fixed across a range of texts (especially when they are datable in close proximity to each other) and is also consistent within a given text; or that tradition works in explicit, linear ways as manifested through direct and acknowledged citations. As more and more evidence is gathered meticulously and presented imaginatively, Anglo-Saxonists will need to recognize that they will be faced with a set of complex theoretical questions they had not foreseen [and that] our usual ways of working were often simply matters of convenience.[7]

Howe recognizes both that print is not *the* way to do scholarly work (but so far the convenient way), and that the leap into "level four" (digital) information management should have massive consequences for Anglo-Saxon scholarship. [→34] The formal structure and qualities of these new digital initiatives will eventually impress themselves on the method and meaning of interpretation in the same way the printing press did. The "linear ways" in which denotation and citation in Anglo-Saxon texts have been read—whose collapse Howe here foretells—derive ultimately from the now convenient nature and operation of print. Accordingly, Howe cautions against treating recent Anglo-Saxon electronic database projects as simple upgrades to their printed ancestors because, in many ways, that is exactly what their directors have designed them to be.

The goal must not be to do old work more efficiently, but to do new work differently.

REMEDIATION AND THE FUTURE

The double logic of remediation, the recursive influence of new media upon old and old media upon new, is always in operation. [→6] Howe's consideration of recent electronic resources in Anglo-Saxon studies shows that we are still in the earliest stages of understanding the power of digital media, and that in some ways not much has changed since Computers and Medieval Data Processing (CAMDAP) began cataloguing such resources in 1971.[8] As the opening sentence of "Computers and the Medievalist," *Speculum*'s first-ever report on the subject from 1974, notes, "Computers imply quantification, and quantification is nothing new to medievalists, who have [always] been interested in word counts, in manuscript collation, and in various kinds of demographic and economic data."[9] The earliest applications of computers to medieval studies drew inspiration from the potential to continue at a heightened pace forms of study founded on the mensurable and fixed-text quality of modern scholarship. [→169]

In the first few decades of our efforts to develop electronic resources for medieval studies, we have more or less followed in the remediating footsteps of the first modern printers, who mass-produced incunabula. It took centuries for the "printed manuscript" to evolve to the printed book, and for print culture to develop, realize, and then capitalize fully upon its own new and unique power. Likewise, the strategies of even our most recent digital efforts still remediate more than innovate. [→4] The design of the *Digital Edition of the Bayeux Tapestry*, which I began in 1994, provides a number of unintended remediations of which I could only have become aware (and embarrassed) long after it was published.

For example, print culture demands that an image be of fixed resolution. On most web pages today, images reproduced digitally retain this static quality. At best, users might have the option of enlarging a picture and then toggling back and forth between two fixed resolutions of the same image. Completely fluid magnification of a digital image, though quite feasible, remains relatively rare on web pages (though it is obviously now a *sine qua non* of video games). In designing a digital version of the Bayeux Tapestry, I provided three levels of magnification, including one that attempted to show details of individual threads, but never even considered that I could or should offer the ability to examine images of the tapestry along a graduated scale, though such capability could easily have been implemented. Further, though I had come to understand that the tapestry was a spatial document, likely meant to be viewed as a cyclical narrative as well as a linear one, I never thought to display the tapestry in any format other than strictly linear, with a set beginning and an end. [→97] In the linear scrolling of the digital tapestry display, one cannot return to the beginning of the work by scrolling past its end, or vice versa. For all of its posturing, my digital design emulated the form and structure of the printed versions to which it sought to be a bold new alternative.

As my own growing awareness that our current digital work looks back as it strives to move forward indicates, these functional remediations will change. But tradition holds on tight, and in the face of innovation it resists in ways we might not even recognize as tradition. The allure of the physical remains a chief concern of scholars and publishers: a book can last (theoretically) a thousand years, but CD-ROMs are thought to have a physical lifespan of around fifteen. The 1986 Domesday Project, which cost millions of pounds to produce, is often held up as an important, impotent, and cautionary lesson.[10] Containing thousands of images, maps, texts, and video of life in Great Britain, the Domesday Project was designed to provide a twentieth-century analogue to William the Conqueror's Domesday Book. Fifteen years later, it was considered all but unusable, as the laser-disk technology and the specialized machines designed to play the project had become obsolete. In 2003 an article in the *Observer* proclaimed the project "unreadable," and snarkily observed, "We're lucky Shakespeare didn't write on an old PC." So much, apparently, for the New Media.[11]

In the early digital age, forms of electronic scholarship still cannot compete against the massive economic, cultural, and perhaps even cognitive apparatuses of print culture. Anxieties of the physical still inform the very production of scholarship, as many publishers are loath to publish digital scholarship or to include CD-ROMs of data as accompaniment to printed books, given that the CD is unlikely to last as long as the book. When Johns Hopkins first published George Landow's seminal study *Hypertext*, it did so both on disk and in print. The disk never gained scholarly approval for citation, and Landow's second and third editions—ironically titled *Hypertext 2.0* and *Hypertext 3.0* after the nomenclature of software upgrades—subsequently came out only in print.[12]

While unavoidable at present, the attitudes and practices surrounding digital scholarship simply signal the first, instinctive sputterings that accompany the early stages of major technological remediation. The content of the

Domesday Project was ultimately recovered, and the project has now continued on to a happy afterlife, available in one version at the National Archives and online for constant public access in another.[13] It is always possible, of course, that the physical fragility of any medium could result in the loss of information, but with the nature of digital media, in many ways that possibility is not increased but reduced. As the printing press superseded monastic copyists with its relative ease of mass production, so digital media surpass print in that their variability and modularity allow for a longevity that transcends the physical form. [→7] Libraries, themselves traditional bastions of print culture, and yet also straining under problems of physical capacity, are eagerly embracing the shift from material texts to digital ones.[14] As libraries are beginning to understand, though with constant use a physical CD-ROM might last only one percent as long as a medieval manuscript, the ease with which its contents can be transferred, copied, and updated ensures the multiplication and survival of its content long after its printed counterpart has crumbled.

As we still tend to privilege the atom over the byte in our academic practices, even when focused on the digital, so too do we continue to elevate the word above other forms of signification in digital practice. TEI (Text Encoding Initiative), for instance, logically began in the 1980s as a markup standard by which literary texts might be encoded, or tagged, in digital form for more precise stylistic and structural reproduction, and for quick and efficient searching.[15] Though already an extraordinarily useful development for electronic editions, TEI still has a number of issues to be worked through, most notably that its encoding format operates on the basis of nested hierarchies, whereas texts often need overlapping tags of different values that do not work easily within a hierarchical format.[16] More recently, in a burgeoning number of initiatives, TEI and other markup languages such as XML have begun to be applied as a standard for encoding medieval manuscripts and other pre-print materials as well.[17] Such projects, of course, can greatly aid the study of the materials of medieval expression, as codifying particular locations and descriptions of them in the fluid form of New Media means that one can quickly locate, parse, and combine data in ways unimaginable a few decades ago. But such initiatives also continue the textualization of medieval materials formerly (re)produced in print. [→103] Markup encoding of a manuscript essentially renders a physical object into words, inserting another level of textual signification between the visual object of medieval text and its study. In some way, codifying and quantifying the visual material of a medieval manuscript by means of encoded tags, while providing a more flexible mode of study, recursively promotes the typographic goal of earlier scholarship, rendering all nonprint material into forms of the mechanical word.

However, alternatives to logocentric technology already have begun to emerge. Recent work at Keio University, for example, has explored a purely visual computer analysis of medieval and early modern letter forms, suggesting that the critical apparatus for manuscript reproduction and analysis might someday be able to dispense with the intermediate (and interfering) step of textual description and representation altogether.[18] Based on comparing the visual data of scribal or typographic letter forms, such software avoids the step of first developing a textual system to describe all possible variations in letter forms, a system still drives most current digital projects concerned with manuscript study. Purely image-based analysis that never translates data into words allows for a much smoother scheme of study, wherein letter forms can be compared and contrasted through a massively more sensitive set of variables and gradations of similarity or difference.

This discussion of remediation in early attempts to marry digital technology to scholarly resources is only the briefest and most undeveloped sketch of issues that deserve an entire study in their own right.[19] A new vocabulary is gradually emerging from the technological discourse of New Media development—terms like recursion, extensibility, topology, interoperability, transiency, interactivity, traversal functions, oscillation, maneuverability, and lexial fragmentation, to mention just a few, are defining an alternative horizon of scholarship.[20] Most immediately and obviously, digital space has in turn already started to remediate the striated architecture of traditional studies of medieval objects with more flexibility and efficiency than print technology has ever realized, and has begun to explore how to fix the bulky problems now engendered by late-age-of-print scholarship.

Digital editions permit textual commentary and graphic object to coexist in layers inside the same display, so the critical apparatus does not dominate the reproduction of the object, but serves it as needed, and is accessible in a transparent fashion. Future digital editions also could allow students and scholars to always begin with a virtual facsimile of the physical medieval artifact—in three dimensions, or at a specific temporal moment of its existence, if necessary—as opposed to a textually translated one.

So, for example, by rolling over a certain section of text or objects like the manuscripts of Anselm's devotional writings, the Nunburnholme Cross, the Cotton Map, or the Bayeux Tapestry, at any level of magnification, one could call up all the relevant information available, with links to other texts, objects, or commentary that might further the exploration of a particular aspect of study. As New Media develops, this ability to present information in layers or "thick data" on the same surface of display could result not only in interactivity (the user manipulating the media for specific exploration) but in what has been termed *oscillation*. In oscillation, the layers of available information themselves interact dynamically, at various depths of display, in response to user input, to combine in endless ways on the surface; more radically, the content of specific text or image can also oscillate between different functions or meanings inside the same signifier, endowing a text or image with variable/multiple significations, not in the act of interpretation, but in act of representation.[21] Such an architecture of smooth study will separate future scholarship from our own at a remove analogous to how we view the antiquarian efforts of Matthew Parker and his circle today. [→ 10]

On a more immediately practical level, digital editions and scholarship can house high-resolution images of recognized analogues to be called up inside a dynamic environment, along with immediate comparisons along a sliding scale of resolution. As technology progresses, it will be possible to have such editions become *extensible*—to have each analogue rendered and accessible as its physical nature demands, with accompanying and updatable scholarly apparatus, and "plugged in" to other objects of study through an architecture of modules. At this point, scholarship will begin to realize the rhizomic nature of Ted Nelson's imagined *docuverse*, an information universe where no one text or object is centered but all are equally and transparently connected through the fluid—or, better, smooth—space of digital discourse. [→40]

Likewise, the *interoperability* of digital media—the enabling of several users to dynamically interact with discourse in collaboration and with immediate effect—can change the very way scholarship is produced and published. A recent technology, RSS (Really Simple Syndication), allows Web sites to be constantly and automatically updated with content-specific syndication feeds, while wiki software (as in *Wikipedia*) now allows continuous and collaborative editing of documents online. New community-based digital initiatives such as the *Digital Medievalist Project* are taking early advantage of RSS, wiki, and other new electronic tools and programs, and point the way, in essence, to the new mechanics of future scholarship. In 2007, the *Middle English Dictionary* was made freely available online, and scholars were invited to link words from electronic editions of medieval texts to entries in the dictionary. In another approach, two theologians have recently used videogame technology to create an virtual tour of the Assisi Basilica, integrating interactive gaming software with academic commentary.[22] The evolution of such efforts should revolutionize the way one gathers, archives, and assembles research, and lead to the establishment of "living editions" of medieval texts or objects, constantly updated and revised, thereby dispensing with the finite capacity and fixed form of the printed edition.

Finally, in scholarship, New Media has begun to produce a new kind of fragmented, hypertextual form of reading and research, one that recursively promotes a practice that slowly evolved out of the written word. Walter Benjamin's prescient view that in scholarship "the book is already . . . an outdated mediation between two different filing systems" reminds us that academic work has long functioned through, as Gregory Ulmer terms it, "disengagement and citational graft."[23] [→16] The process of disengagement and creation of discrete units of information has, according to Derrida, existed since language began.[24] But spoken language is also naturally linear in its formulation, rolling off the tongue in time, each utterance physically and temporally linked to the one before it. Early writing in scrolls mimicked this quality of linearity; only with the development of the codex did the material fragmentation of writing begin in earnest.[25] The development and refinement of the index furthered the process, and now in their work students and scholars (myself included) make liberal use of "index-trolling," where a book is consulted only for specific content, which is often then used with little or no reference to the rest of the book that contains it.

Even then, though, the reader still has a reminder in the physical presence of the book that the material consulted lives within a larger tangible framework for which it was written as a component. In hypermedia, no such materiality exists, and individuated lexia, like Anselm's *paragraph* is, are often designed to exist outside traditional textual linearity. In the process of reading hypertextually, readers often forge nonce lines of inquiry that by their nature operate outside the unity and form of any single text. Such practices will continue to grow as we more and more read digitally for our meaning.

As the influence and effect of New Media slowly grow, the long, linear, and logical form of scholarship—a pedigree of typography—will begin to change as well. Certainly, to return to the notion of Tolstoy in hypertext, traditional forms of printed scholarship have begun to be remediated in essential ways through their digitization. Electronic text archives such as JSTOR have digitized entire print runs of academic journals and entered every word of these texts into a searchable database.[26] Such resources greatly refine and expedite the means by which tens of thousands of pages may be considered for relevant material, as JSTOR search results give you the option of going right to the pages of an article that contain one or more of your search terms. But JSTOR does not simply store journals for ease of access; through its intermediality it also reconfigures how one accesses and uses the academic content it holds, shifting the perusal of scholarly materials closer to a lexia-driven format, where one jumps from semantic link to semantic link, eschewing the traditional linearity of scholarly production.

Google's recent endeavor, Google Book (earlier known, ironically, as Google Print), continues the remediation of the printed form on a much vaster scale. Partnered with libraries of such universities as Harvard, Stanford, and Oxford, Google is in the process of digitizing millions of printed volumes. In Google Book one can perform keyword searches across this digital collection and call up quotations ("snippets") of sections of texts containing the desired terms, or the page (with two or three surrounding pages for context) of a book with the term or terms highlighted for ease of location. In the words of its creators, Google Book is (of course!) meant to be "a book-finding tool, not a book-reading tool," which allows you to "search the full text of books to find ones that interest you and learn where to buy or borrow them."[27] The effect of such a resource, though, will inevitably be much different from the stated intent, pointing the way to the ultimate remediation of the older printed form into a fragmented, fluid network that breaks down the previous monolithic linearity of print and translates it into a version of Nelson's hypertextual docuverse.

This is, of course, only the earliest phase of such a shift, as we are just now beginning to translate and read older scholarship hypertextually, and understand what that means. The real shift will come when we begin to *produce* scholarship hypertextually, in ways that fundamentally differ from the older practices of print. The above examples of technological change and their implications for medieval studies and scholarship are in their infancy. Doubtless as this book is read (in whatever fashion) in the future, they will also have been superseded by far more powerful and convincing evidence of the new academic age we are only just entering. But while such structures point the way to exciting and fundamental transformations in how we can study medieval culture and discourse, the question of when and how such transformations will occur remains. As Simon Biggs muses,

Is it therefore surprising that as the camera and such mechanical means of representation are lost in history, and replaced by the fictions of digital imaging techniques, that visual paradigms will enter a similar shift away from the continuities of Cartesian space? What is surprising, perhaps, is not this expectation but that virtually all the computer graphics produced to date seek to function within, or exploit, these established but now irrelevant conventions. When will applications of other approaches to the dimensioning of space, as facilitated through the computer, occur? There is no doubt that the envelope of a symbolic world is as important as the symbols it contains and, as those symbolic values shift, the nature of the envelope shall shift as well.[28]

The elasticity of the digital form can easily accommodate systems of meaning and scholarship based not only on striation but on smoothness as well—a realization of Foucault's heterotopian architecture. [→188] Granted, such a dematerialized infrastructure of scholarly "placeless places" for digital treatments of the objects and texts studied in the chapters above would at present entail a Herculean amount of work, and for the near future will likely remain outside the realm of possibility. For starters, the current complexity and cost of digital technology impose serious limitations on what academicians can feasibly accomplish. This will change. The more daunting obstacle to realizing fully the potential of virtual editions is, as Biggs implies, the fact that our cognitive assessment and organization of information remain closely tied to a modern, physicalist perception of space and, in conjunction, the fixed space of the printed text. Only when we can conceive of methods of discourse that reproduce information, data, and knowledge in forms not wholly dependent on the striated, static, fragmented, and ultimately obsolete mechanics of the written word as we currently use it can we develop the virtual to its fullest promise. If new modes of discourse develop that organically encode the hyperlinks that we now laboriously produce between words and images, a heterotopian model of a truly virtual edition will arise as a matter of course.

All this, of course, is a long way off. As I stated in the introduction to this book, the late age of print looks to be a very long age. And inside the scholarly world, we continue to remain uncomfortable with fluid, nonlinear "texts" of smooth immateriality. In considering how critics review and discuss digital fiction, Espen Aarseth asks, "how can reviewers of cybertexts face the fact they probably missed large numbers of scriptons [i.e., lexia]?"[29] But we are in some ways like Anglo-Saxons after the Conquest, who lived in what should be considered the "late age of Anglo-Saxon." Striated views of history aside, Anglo-Saxon England never actually ended, it just slowly transformed into something else entirely, as the culture of medieval and then modern England gradually divested itself of qualities and aspects that no longer functioned under a series of new social orders. Similarly, in the cleaved evolution of media and scholarship, some aspects and forms of print will never disappear, much as we still have Old English words in our language today. But certainly, to presume as long a view of print and New Media as we now can of Anglo-Saxon England, we can begin to imagine and in our own work anticipate what will come next. Such innovation is hard to conceive, but as Brenda Laurel states, "the hardest part is probably visualizing the appropriate representation in the first place."[30] New Media is not going away anytime soon, much like the printing press five hundred years ago. And in the end we will not adapt New Media to suit our scholarly work and desires—New Media will adapt and transform the nature of our work, the medieval past we produce, and eventually even ourselves.

Notes

The main epigraph is from McLuhan, *The Gutenberg Galaxy*, 275, 278.

Introduction: "Nothing Like a CD-ROM"

1. National Endowment, "Guidelines," accessed September 10, 2004.

2. Stipends@neh.gov, "RE: Summer Stipend application query," September 21, 2004 (personal e-mail); emphasis added.

3. Bolter, *Writing Space*, 1–3.

4. Abbott, *The Annotated Flatland*.

5. Cf. Andersen, *Digital Scholarship*.

6. Bush, "As We May Think," 106.

7. McLuhan, *Understanding Media*, iv.

Chapter 1. Print and Post-Print Realities in Anglo-Saxon Studies

1. Bolter and Grusin, *Remediation*, 273.

2. Ibid., 53–62.

3. See, for instance, Clanchy, "Looking Back"; Blake, "Manuscript to Print."

4. Eisenstein, *Printing Revolution*. See Robertson, *The New Renaissance*, for a concise distillation of Eisenstein's arguments. See, to cite just a few of the studies that followed, Chartier, *Cultural Uses of Print* and *The Culture of Print*; Steinberg, *Five Hundred Years of Printing*; McKitterick, *Search for Order*; Kleinman, "The Gutenberg Promise"; Bland, "Appearance of the Text"; Clegg, "History of the Book." Earlier important treatments include Febvre and Martin, *Coming of the Book*; McLuhan, *The Gutenberg Galaxy*.

5. For arguments attenuating the "revolutionary" aspects of print culture, see Clanchy, "Looking Back"; Voights, "Scientific and Medical Books."

6. Hobart and Schiffman, *Information Ages*, 90.

7. Ibid., 101–2.

8. Foxe, *Actes and Monuments* (1583), 2D5v, cited in B. Robinson, "Dark Speech," 1063.

9. Kleinman, "The Gutenberg Promise," 81. Cf. McLuhan, *The Gutenberg Galaxy*; Deibert, *Parchment, Printing, and Hypermedia*, 45–110; Crosby, *The Measure of Reality*; Ong, *Orality and Literacy*, 117–38; Bland, "Appearance of the Text," 126; Landow, *Hypertext 2.0*, 49–89.

10. Ong, *Orality and Literacy*, 78–138.

11. Ibid., 81.

12. Camille, "Philological Iconoclasm." See also his "Sensations of the Page."

13. See Ivins, *Prints and Visual Communication*, for his groundbreaking survey of how the printed image affected learning, knowledge, and thought.

14. Eisenstein, *Printing Revolution*, 192.

15. McLuhan, *The Gutenberg Galaxy*, 185.

16. Kleinman, "The Gutenberg Promise," 66.

17. Ibid., 85.

18. Bolter and Grusin, *Remediation*, 20–31.

19. Febvre and Martin, *Coming of the Book*, 29. Cf. Clanchy, "Looking Back," 8: "the sixteenth and seventeenth centuries saw more of the Middle Ages than had ever been available to anyone in the Middle Ages." For a discussion of the text selection of early printers, see Goldschmidt, *Medieval Texts*. See also Blake, "Manuscript to Print"; Crick, "Art of the Unprinted."

20. Goldschmidt, *Medieval Texts*, 74.

21. For an introduction to the first Anglo-Saxon scholars, see Graham, "Anglo-Saxon Studies." For more specific studies, see the various essays collected in Graham, *Recovery of Old English*; Frantzen, *Desire for Origins*, 35–50; Clement, "Printing in Anglo-Saxon"; Lucas, "From Politics to Practicalities"; B. Robinson, "Dark Speech."

22. B. Robinson, "Dark Speech," 1064, 1080. See also Christie, "Image of the Letter," 137–40; Frantzen, *Desire for Origins*, 39–40; Lucas, "Testimonye," 163–65, and "From Politics to Practicalities," 28–29; Lutz, "Study," 1–6; Clement, "Printing in Anglo-Saxon," 206–8.

23. L'Isle, *Treatise*, qtd. in Pulsiano, "William L'Isle," 182.

24. Christie, "Image of the Letter," 138. For a similar argument concerning the work of the eighteenth-century Anglo-Saxonist Elizabeth Elbstob, see Sutherland, "Editing for a New Century," 228.

25. "Quorum sane lectio & veteris tibi linguae, ac quondam domesticae memoriam renouabit," cited and translated in Lucas, "Testimonye," 28 and n2.

26. Clement, "Printing in Anglo-Saxon," 206.

27. Ibid., 207–8; cf. Bland, "Appearance of the Text," 100.

28. See Bland, "Appearance of the Text," for a detailed discussion of such strategies. Cf. Lucas, "From Politics to Practicalities," 34–42; Kleinman, "The Gutenberg Promise," 81–82.

29. Lucas, "From Politics to Practicalities," 37–38.

30. Cf. McGillivray, "Post-Critical Edition," 180–81.

31. Frantzen, *Desire for Origins*, 45; Graham, "Anglo-Saxon Studies," 421–25; B. Robinson, "Dark Speech," 1062–64, 1075.

32. Lee, "Oxford, Bodleian Library, MS Laud Misc. 381"; Pulsiano, "William L'Isle," 188–91.

33. Graham, "Anglo-Saxon Studies," 421.

34. Galbraith, *St. Alban's Chronicle*, xi. See also B. Robinson, "Dark Speech," 1077 and n74. Robinson notes, "The seemingly haphazard inclusiveness of the Parkerian editions, the willingness to fill all textual gaps with material pirated from other texts and even other chroniclers, has confused or infuriated those [modern] editors who have run up against Parker's assertion . . . that he has placed his manuscript exemplars in Corpus Christi to be seen by anyone who wants proof that nothing has been added or removed from the original" (1079).

35. Cf. Crick, "Art of the Unprinted," which studies the "script-print interface" and examines the continuation of scribal practices in antiquarians' work into the seventeenth century, as well as Blake, "Manuscript to Print," 411–18, and Chartier, *The Culture of Print*, 2–3. For a case study of the scribal practices of one early Anglo-Saxonist, see Graham, "John Joscelyn."

36. Christie, "Image of the Letter," 129.

37. Clement, "Printing in Anglo-Saxon," 193–95; Lutz, "Study"; Graham, "Anglo-Saxon Studies," 423.

38. Lowe, "William Somner"; Lerer, "The Anglo-Saxon Pindar"; Lutz, "Study," 40–72; Graham, "Anglo-Saxon Studies," 426; Frantzen, *Desire for Origins*, 50–57.

39. See Frantzen, *Desire for Origins*, 50–95, for a sustained study of the origin and then far-reaching influence of Germanic philology and the later philological studies in modern Anglo-Saxon studies.

40. Bland, "Appearance of the Text," 126; see also Plumer, "Construction of Structure," 244. See also Frantzen, *Desire for Origins*, 45–46, and Christie, "Image of the Letter," 136–37, for discussions of the early forces toward standardization and regularity of Old English in movable type, and Rider, "Shaping Information," 43, for a more general discussion of such standardization in print technology.

41. Gibson, "Literacy, Paradigm, and Paradox," 6.

42. See Bland, "Appearance of the Text," esp. 101, 117, 126. For an analogous discussion of the modern typography of Middle English, see A. Edwards, "Representing the Middle English Manuscript."

43. Lerer, "The Anglo-Saxon Pindar," 37.

44. For a similar case, see Kees Dekker's catalogue of printed sources used by Francis Junius for his Old English dictionary, in "That Most Elaborate One," 323–36.

45. Lerer, "The Anglo-Saxon Pindar," 29, 59–61; Graham, "Anglo-Saxon Studies," 429.

46. Kemble, *Beowulf*, 1:xxiv, qtd. in Prescott, "Electronic Beowulf," 185, and in Frantzen, *Desire for Origins*, 63.

47. See Frantzen, *Desire for Origins*, 57–58, for similar, more recent examples of Kemble's sentiment.

48. Franzten, *Desire for Origins*, 198.

49. F. Robinson, *Editing*, 37; McGann, "The Rationale of Hypertext," 20.

50. See F. Robinson, *Editing*, 3–24; Kiernan, "Alfred the Great's Burnt Boethius," 20–21. Kiernan's comments are especially pointed: "Although they do provide punctuation, glossaries, explanatory notes, and the like, the existing modern editions are remarkably unhelpful guides to reading this particular manuscript."

51. Baudrillard, *Simulacra and Simulation*.

52. Kiernan, "Alfred the Great's Burnt Boethius," 20.

53. Bush, "As We May Think," 101.

54. Lerer, "The Anglo-Saxon Pindar," 38n34.

55. Kleinman, "The Gutenberg Promise," 81, emphasis added.

56. Discussed in Moulthrop, "You Want a Revolution?" 93. For McLuhan on hot and cool media, see *Understanding Media*, 22.

57. Benjamin, *Reflections*, 78.

58. Bolter and Grusin, *Remediation*, 33–34.

59. The terminology is Jerome McGann's; see his "What Is Critical Editing?"

60. On medieval and early modern punctuation, see Parkes, *Pause and Effect*. See Plumer's contrasting of the considerably different forms of the first three lines of *Beowulf* from Frederick Klaeber's nineteenth-century edition and Laurence Nowell's sixteenth-century transcription for a brief but cogent example of such "shock of the new" ("Construction of Structure," 244–45), and then her careful charting of the evolving editorial drift of seventeenth- and eighteenth-century scholarship toward such modern conventions, with especial attention paid to lineation and capitalization (245).

61. L. P. Harvey, qtd. in B. Mitchell, "The Dangers of Disguise," 387.

62. B. Mitchell, "The Dangers of Disguise"; Stanley, "A3 Lines in *Beowulf*"; Godden, "Old English."

63. B. Mitchell, "The Dangers of Disguise," 399.

64. Ibid., 402–12.

65. Szarmach and Scragg, *Editing of Old English*, 3. Szarmach takes the notion of conjectural emendation from "On the Emendation of Texts," an essay in the same volume by Michael Lapidge, who does not apply it to editorial punctuation but rather to the necessary correction of scribal error; as Lapidge states, "medieval scribes were human and therefore fallible, and the texts which they transmitted could, when in obvious error and probably on other occasions also, scarcely represent what the author had written" (53–54). Putting aside the weary debate of authorial intention, I would like to suggest that such practices as modern punctuation may also be classified as "conjectural emendation," as they too often count as best guesses with regard to syntax and grammar; cf. Scragg's comments, "Quo Vadis, Editio?" 300–301. For the continuation of debates surrounding the editing of Old English in the 1980s and 1990s, see the wide range of essays in Szarmach and Scragg, *Editing of Old English*, especially Lees, "Whose Text Is It Anyway?"; Doane, "Editing Old English Oral/Written Texts"; Scragg, "Quo Vadis, Editio?"

66. F. Robinson, *Editing*, 42. See Robinson, 7–8, for a discussion of the bodily labor involved in Old English writing; see also Ong, *Orality and Literacy*, 94–96.

67. F. Robinson, *Editing*, 3. See also O'Keeffe, "Editing and the Material Text."

68. Camille, "Sensations of the Page," 44. See also Nichols, "Philology and Its Discontents" and "Philology in a Manuscript Culture," for similar materialist concerns in what has been termed the New Philology.

69. Indeed, in my reading of *The Dream of the Rood* presented below, as well as in the readings of many of the critics I cite, no need was felt to consult the Vercelli Book or facsimiles thereof. See also Rumble, "Paleography," 39–43.

70. F. Robinson, *Editing*, 25.

71. McGillivray, "Post-Critical Edition," 175.

72. Cf. Frantzen, *Desire for Origins*, 66–68; see also Patterson, *Negotiating the Past*, 77–113, for a detailed discussion of how various schools of textual editing of medieval texts all, in the end, contribute to a distinctively modern and subjective construction of the medieval expression.

73. Parallel editions in print remain an option, of course, but print still severely limits such efforts. Two parallel texts is one thing; a dozen or more is another. See McGillivray, "Post-Critical Edition," 184 and n18.

74. F. Robinson, *Editing*, 41.

75. Cf. F. Robinson: "To expect a medieval copyist (or head of a scriptorium) to submit himself mindlessly to his exemplar and refrain from introducing anything of himself into his performance would have seemed as unreasonable as to expect that a minstrel should suppress his creative talents when giving an oral rendition of a ballad or romance" (*Editing*, 38), and Pasternack: "Because of the natures of books and libraries in Anglo-Saxon England, readers would not have compared versions as we might today. . . . the whole mentality of using vernacular and reading verse calls for each text to be taken as its own expression" (*Textuality*, 27).

76. McGillivray, "Post-Critical Edition," 181.

77. B. Mitchell, "The Dangers of Disguise" 413.

78. Irvine, "Anglo-Saxon Literary Theory," 32.

79. Though debate continues as to whether all of the Ruthwell Cross was carved at a single time, the monument is generally dated to the first half of the eighth century; see MacLean, "Date"; Orton, "Rethinking," 88–89. For overviews of the monument, see Orton, "Rethinking"; the essays in Cassidy, *The Ruthwell Cross*; Wood, "Ruthwell: Contextual Searches"; Ó Carragáin, "Ruthwell Crucifixion Poem." For the Brussels Cross, see Lefèvre, "Un reliquaire." Since the completion of this chapter, Ó Carragáin's *Ritual and Rood* has been published, which considers liturgical contexts for the poem and both objects.

80. See Swanton, *Dream of the Rood*, 9–42 and plates I–II. In this edition, the Brussels Cross, which only potentially shares two lines of text with the Old English poem, is not treated in any detail.

81. Ó Carragáin, "Ruthwell Crucifixion Poem." As recent Ruthwell scholars (e.g., Karkov, "Naming and Renaming," 35) have noted, it remains impossible to prove that some parts of the monument, and possibly the runic inscriptions, could not have been added sometime later to the original early-eighth-century carving. Nevertheless, given the relatively late date of the Vercelli manuscript, in all probability the Ruthwell text predates the Vercelli text.

82. Swanton, *Dream of the Rood*, 41–42.

83. Ibid., 41.

84. Ibid., 9. The same implicit textual bias may be found in the full title of Ó Carragáin's recent book on these objects and poems; *Ritual and the Rood: Liturgical Images and the Old English Poems of the Dream of the Rood Tradition*.

85. Landow, *Hypertext 2.0*, 49–89, esp. 76–77.

86. Krapp, *The Vercelli Book*, 61; translation is my own. For a standard edition of the

poem, see Swanton, *Dream of the Rood*. See also Cook, *Dream of the Rood*; Krapp, *The Vercelli Book*, 130–32.

87. Cook, *Dream of the Rood*, lii.

88. Pope, *Eight Old English Poems*, 61; Huppé, *The Web of Words*, 78; Swanton, *Dream of the Rood*, 65, 110, 114–15; Pasternack, "Stylistic Disjunctions," 171; Johnson, "Old English Religious Poetry," 181–84. See Pasternack, "Stylistic Disjunctions," 168–69, for a discussion of other critics who have "worked on defining the poem's formal unity."

89. Irvine, "Anglo-Saxon Literary Theory," 52.

90. Pasternack, *Textuality*, 103.

91. T. Hall, "Prophetic Vision," n.p. I am grateful to Tom Hall for making an early draft of this essay available to me.

92. Ibid. See Irvine, "Anglo-Saxon Literary Theory," 53–54, for another discussion of simultaneity in this episode.

93. Langer, *Philosophy in a New Key*, 79–102.

94. Cf. T. Hall, "Prophetic Vision," n.p.

95. For translation and commentary, see Wallis, *Reckoning*.

96. Flegg, *Numbers: Their History and Meaning*, 17.

97. Williams, "Finger Numbers," 590–93.

98. "De computo vel loquela digitorum," lines 21–32. All citations of *De temporum ratione* are from Jones's edition, all translations from Wallis, *Reckoning*.

99. Lines 49–50.

100. Wallis, *Reckoning*, 254–61. For a detailed overview of systems of finger counting through history, see Ifrah, *From One to Zero*, 55–80.

101. Flegg, *Numbers Through the Ages*, 31–37.

102. See Flegg, *Numbers: Their History and Meaning*, 39–80, 150–71, for general overviews of the impact of writing and of mechanical devices on the evolution of calculation. See Martin, *Calculating Machines*, for a detailed chronology of the development of mechanical calculators.

103. Wallis, *Reckoning*, 254–55.

104. Ong, *Orality and Literacy*, 81–83.

105. Wallis, *Reckoning*, 260, suggests this locutionary figure here indicates an instruction to say the number aloud in order to help fix the figure in the memory. Even accepting this interpretation, the notion of orality is still firmly connected to Bede's description.

106. Lines 65–71.

107. Lines 6–8: "Neque enim contemnenda parvive pendenda est regula cuius omnes pene sacrae expositores scripturae, non minus quam literarum figuras, monstrantur amplexi." Wallis, *Reckoning*, 9, curiously translates "literarum figuras" as "verbal expressions," further blurring the relationship between writing, speech, and finger calculation.

108. Lines 8–21. Cf. Jerome, *Adversus Joviniamum* 1 (PL 23.213B–214A). See Wallis, *Reckoning*, 10n2, for additional citations.

109. Leupold, *Theatrum arithmetico-geometricum*, reproduced in Eisenstein, *Printing Revolution*, 39. Leupold's caption reads "Rechen Taffel vermittelst der Finger und Hände wie solche beÿ dem Beda entlehnet" [Table of calculation using fingers and hands, like the one employed by Bede]. Flegg, *Numbers: Their History and Meaning*, 15, also reproduces this engraving, under the caption "Bede's finger counting," as does Ifrah, *From One to Zero*, 58.

110. On Leupold, see Ferguson, "Leupold's 'Theatrum Machinarum'"; Lockett, "Jacob Leupold."

111. Eisenstein, *Printing Revolution*, 38.

112. Compare Leupold's engraving with both the text presented in Wallis, *Reckoning*, 10, and the visual chart adapted from a twelfth-century manuscript she provides, 256. Flegg, *Numbers: Their History and Meaning*, 15–17, notes a similar confusion in the 1494 description from Luca Pacioli's *Summa*.

113. See Flegg, *Numbers: Their History and Meaning*, 15–18, for some other surviving accounts of finger counting in the Middle Ages. Ifrah, *From One to Zero*, 58–59, prints three representations of this system of finger counting, two printed engravings—Leupold's (1727) and Pacioli's (1494)—and one Spanish manuscript from 1210. Notably, only the version in the medieval manuscript remains accurate to Bede's system.

114. For examples, see Ifrah, *From One to Zero*, 58–59.

115. Wallis, *Reckoning*, lxxxv; on pp. xcvii–xcix she surveys the relative popularity of this chapter as an *excerptum* in early print publications.

116. Manovich, "New Media as Faster Execution of Algorithms Previously Executed Manually or through Other Technologies," sec. 6 of "New Media from Borges to HTML," 20–22.

117. Robertson, *The New Renaissance*, 19–22.

118. Ibid., 22–24.

119. Bolter, *Writing Space*, 40. Cf. Provenzo, *Beyond the Gutenberg Galaxy*, 260–61; Brody, "The Medium Is the Memory," 146; Robertson, *The New Renaissance*, 112–13.

120. For introductions to the fluidity and variability of digital media, see Manovich, *Language of New Media*, 36–48; Landow, *Hypertext 2.0*, 33–48.

121. Cf. Ong, *Orality and Literacy*, 135; Duggan, "Unrevolutionary Aspects"; McKitterick, *Search for Order*, 9, 21.

122. P. Robinson, "Where We Are," par. 6. See Johnson, "Digitizing the Middle Ages," for a representative (if understandable) call for standardization.

123. P. Robinson, "Where We Are," par. 6 and par. 21.

124. Cf. McGann, "The Rationale for Hypertext," 21–22.

125. For representative discussions, see Conner, "Beyond the ASPR"; Deegan and Robinson, "The Electronic Edition."

126. Howe, "The New Millennium," 502.

127. McLuhan, *The Gutenberg Galaxy*, 141; Ong, *Orality and Literacy*, 135–38; Bolter, *Writing Space*, 72–74. See also Provenzo, *Beyond the Gutenberg Galaxy*, 51–59.

128. See, among a number of others, McGillivray, "Post-Critical Edition"; Sperberg-McQueen, "Text in the Electronic Age"; Feinstein, "Hypertextuality and Chaucer"; Machan, "Chaucer's Poetry, Versioning, and Hypertext"; Brown and Valentine, "Networking in Medieval and Postmodern Cultures"; Driver, "Medieval Manuscripts and Electronic Media"; Dickey, "Poem Descending a Staircase," 148–49; Bolter and Grusin, *Remediation*, 12.

129. Camille, "Sensations of the Page," 37–38, 45. Cf. F. Robinson, *Editing*, 7–8.

130. Christie, "Image of the Letter," 146.

131. For rehearsals of this thesis, see the essays collected in Swan and Treharne, *Rewriting Old English in the Twelfth Century*.

Chapter 2. Anselm's Hypertext

The epigraph is from Bolter, *Writing Space*, ix.

1. Bolter, *Writing Space*, x.

2. The corpus of *Orationes sive Meditationes* (*OsM*) is in Anselm, *Opera Omnia*, 3:1–91. See Ward, *Prayers and Meditations*, which provides context for their composition and a loose translation. For additional background, see Southern, *Saint Anselm*, 91–117; Wilmart, "Le recueil."

3. Anselm, *OsM*, 3. All translations are my own, unless otherwise noted.

4. See Landow, *Hypertext 2.0*, 3–25, for a basic introduction to hypertext and hypermedia.

5. Ibid., 34. On Theodore Nelson's seminal notion of the docuverse, first expressed in 1965, wherein all documents are seamlessly interconnected with all other documents in a giant electronic network, see his *Literary Machines 93.1*.

6. Bolter, *Writing Space*, 22.

7. On Anselm's basic biography, see Southern, *Saint Anselm*, xxvii–xxix. It should be noted that Southern raises the possibility that Anselm composed *De grammatico* before the *OsM*. For other discussions of dating the bulk of Anselm's prayers to the early period, see Wilmart, "Le recueil," xix–xxxiii; Bestul, "Private Prayers," 356.

8. For this letter, Epistola 10, see *Opera Omnia*, 4:121. Cf. Southern, *Saint Anselm*, 92–93.

9. Southern, *Saint Anselm*, 106–9.

10. Ibid., 109–12.

11. Ibid., 111–12. Cf. Wilmart, *Auteurs spirituels*, 162–72, and "Les prières"; Pächt, "Illustrations," 70–71.

12. Wilmart, "Les prières."

13. For lists of surviving medieval manuscripts, see Wilmart, "Le recueil," lvi–lxi, and "La tradition"; Pächt, "Illustrations," 83; Bestul, "Verdun Anselm," 386–88, and *Durham Book*, 11–12.

14. Ward, *Prayers and Meditations*, 18; Migne, *Patrologia Latina*, vol. 158.

15. Wilmart, *Auteurs spirituels*, 162–201.

16. Cf. Southern, *Saint Anselm*, 99–106.

17. Bestul, "Private Prayers."

18. For a sense of the volume of literature devoted to the ontological proof, see Hopkins, *Companion*, 261–65, or more recently Kienzler, *International Bibliography*, 178, 180–93.

19. The work of Bestul in the late 1970s and the 1980s remains the singular exception to this assertion. Bestul focuses primarily on stemmatic studies of manuscript variants, discernment of apocrypha, and patristic and cultural precedents for Anselm's devotional models. See "Devotional Traditions"; "Verdun Anselm"; "Anselm's Prayers"; "Monastic Community"; "Private Prayers"; "St. Augustine." Additionally, see Roques, "Structure et caractères"; Evans, "Mens Devota"; Ward, "Inward Feeling."

20. The structure of Southern's analysis in *Saint Anselm*, which describes the "great meditations" of the *Monologion* and the *Proslogion* as Anselm's "first peak" (113) and *Cur Deus homo* as "the greatest of his later works" (197), may be taken as emblematic. For a canonical collection of Anselmian writing, see Deane, *St. Anselm: Basic Writings*, which contains translations of the *Proslogion*, *Monologion*, and *Cur Deus homo*.

21. See, for instance, Ward, "Inward Feeling," 177, which notes the prayers "are at best early and minor compositions of Anselm, somewhat apart from the main body of his works." Cf. Evans, "Mens Devota," 109; Southern, *St. Anselm*, 112; Schufreider, *Rational Mystic*, 19–21.

22. Schufreider, *Rational Mystic*, 1–17, esp. 3–4.

23. Anselm, Epistola 28, *Opera Omnia*, 3:136.

24. Bestul, "Private Prayers," 360. Anselm himself contributed to ensuring that his prefaces remained attached to his works of meditation. In his preface to the *Monologion* he beseeches, "Precor autem et obsecro vehementer, si quis hoc opusculum voluerit transcribere, ut hanc praefationem in capite libelli ante ipsa capitula studeat praeponere" (8) [But it is my prayer and earnest entreaty that, if any shall wish to copy this work, he shall be careful to place this preface at the beginning of the book, before the body of the meditation itself] (*Basic Writings*, 83).

25. M. Grabmann, cited in Stock, *The Implications of Literacy*, 329. For an extensive bibliography of scholarship related to Anselm's influence on the formation of scholastic theology, see Stock, 329n7. Cf. Henry, *Logic of Saint Anselm*, 12–30.

26. Bestul, *Durham Book*, 2–3.

27. Rule of St. Benedict, chaps. 9–19; see Fry, *RB 1980*; see also Daly, *Benedictine Monasticism*.

28. Cf. Southern, *St. Anselm*, 448.

29. Ibid., 93–95; Ward, *Prayers and Meditations*, 27–28.

30. Evans, *New Generation*, 1–33, esp. 28–30. See also Southern, *St. Anselm*, 122–23.

31. Ward, *Prayers and Meditations*, 27–28. For scriptural allusions in the *OsM*, see Ward's appendix, 268–74.

32. "quatenus auctoritate scripturae penitus nihil in ea persuaderetur, sed quidquid per singulas investigationes finis assereret, id ita esse plano stilo et vulgaribus argumentis, simplicique disputatione et rationis necessitas breviter cogeret et veritatis claritas patenter ostenderet" (Anselm, *Monologion*, 7) [in order that nothing in Scripture should be urged on the authority of Scripture itself, but that whatever the conclusion

of independent investigation should declare to be true, should, in an unadorned style, with common proofs and with a simple argument, be briefly enforced by the cogency of reason, and plainly expounded in the light of truth] (*Basic Writings*, 81). For further discussion of Anselm's suspension of Scripture, see Schufreider, *Rational Mystic*, 20–21.

33. Ward, *Prayers and Meditations*, 48–49. For another mutual discussion of the prayers of Anselm and Fécamp, see Evans, "Mens Devota," passim.

34. Gellrich, *Idea of the Book*, 66.

35. See, for example, Hopkins's discussion in *Companion*, 97, of Anselm's belief in the limits of reason in regard to the truth of Scripture.

36. "considerans illud esse multorum concatenatione contextum argumentorum, co-epi mecum quaerere, si forte posset inveniri unum argumentum, quod nullo alio ad se probandum" (Anselm, *Proslogion*, 93), translated in Schufreider, *Rational Mystic*, 101; cf. Schufreider's subsequent discussion, 101.

37. Schufreider, *Rational Mystic*, 97.

38. Cf. Southern, *St. Anselm*, 123–27; Evans, *Anselm and Talking*, 121–22.

39. For these discussions from Alan of Lille's *Summa quoniam homines* and Abelard's *Dialecta*, see Evans, *New Generation*, 83–91, esp. 88–89.

40. Anselm, *Proslogion*, chaps. 2–4; *Basic Writings*, 53–56.

41. Southern, *St. Anselm*, 129–32, see especially 130; Schufreider, *Rational Mystic*, 250. For other examples of this type of grammatical reasoning, see Colish, "Anselm's Philosophy of Language," 117–19.

42. The term is Schufreider's; see *Rational Mystic*, 251 and n9. See also 270–71 and n22; Henry, "Linguistic Disciplines," 328–29; Gellrich, *Idea of the Book*, 94, esp 103–4.

43. For Hugh, see Southern, *St. Anselm*, 122–23, which compares Hugh of St. Victor's theory of meditation to Anselm's, and notes as a prime difference between them the idea that Hugh requires that meditation begin with the specific reading of an authoritative text, whereas Anselm is less concerned with the text than with the reading mind itself. On Fécamp, see above and note 34.

44. "ad excitandam legentis mentem ad dei amorem vel timorem" and "ad accendendum affectum orandi" (Anselm, *OsM*, 3); "compunctio scilicet contritionis vel dilectionis, in eis per supernum respectum inveniatur" (Anselm, Epistola 28 "ad Gondulfum," *Opera Omnia*, 3:136).

45. Bolter and Grusin, *Remediation*, 53–56.

46. For discussions of writing as an unnatural and difficult technology in the Middle Ages, see Ong, *Orality and Literacy*, 81–83; Clanchy, *From Memory to Written Record*, 88–115.

47. Eadmer, *Life of St. Anselm*, 15.

48. Ibid., 14–15.

49. Anselm, Oratio 6, *Opera Omnia*, 3:14, lines 31–35; translation from Ward, *Prayers and Meditations*, 108, lines 53–60.

50. See *Opera Omnia*, 2:201–6. Cf. Colish, "Anselm's Philosophy of Language," 118; Heron, "Problem of the *Filioque*" and "Anselm and the *Filioque*."

51. For a concise discussion of Anselm's conception of the divine *Verbum*, and necessary differences from human language, see Evans, *Anselm and Talking*, 17–38.

52. E.g., Stock, *The Implications of Literacy*, 338; Schufreider, *Rational Mystic*, 41–63, esp. 43–51.

53. Stock, *The Implications of Literacy*, 341. Cf. Schufreider, *Rational Mystic*, 44–45, 51.

54. Evans, *Anselm and Talking*, 117.

55. Anselm, *OsM*, 74. Translation in Ward, *Prayers and Meditations*.

56. Gellrich, *Idea of the Book*, 34–35.

57. Ibid., 66 and n27.

58. Bolter, *Writing Space*, 9.

59. Negroponte, *Being Digital*, 11–20, 68–70.

60. E.g., Slatin, "Reading Hypertext"; Birkerts, *The Gutenberg Elegies*; Landow, "The Rhetoric of Hypermedia"; Bolter, "Topographic Writing."

61. Ward, *Prayers and Meditations*, 49.

62. Bolter and Grusin, *Remediation*, 58–59.

63. Ibid., 191–92.

64. Schufreider, *Rational Mystic*, 54. See also his discussion of existence in reality, 130–31.

65. Ibid., 67.

66. See, for instance, Poole, *Trigger Happy*, 128–36; Herz, *Joystick Nation*; Douglas and Hargadon, "Immersion and Interaction"; Bolter and Grusin, *Remediation*, 89–103.

67. Bolter and Grusin, *Remediation*, 161–62.

68. On New Media as an aesthetic and intellectual stage that accompanies all technological shifts, see Manovich, "New Media from Borges to HTML," 19–20. In 1936 Walter Benjamin criticized the illusory efforts of film: "in the studio the mechanical equipment has penetrated so deeply into reality that . . . the equipment free aspect of reality here has become the height of artifice; the sight of immediate reality has become an orchid in the land of technology" (*Illuminations*, 233). On perspective, see Andrews, *Story and Space*; Gaggi, *From Text to Hypertext*, 1–15. See also Bolter and Grusin's discussion of early modern perspectival art in *Remediation*, 24–25, and their use, among others, of Panofsky, Dürer, and Leon Battista Alberti.

69. *Myst* and *Riven: The Sequel to Myst*.

70. *Riven*, "User's Manual," 3.

71. Anselm, *Basic Writings*, 49.

72. Cf. Ward, *Prayers and Meditations*, 51–52. For a contrary view, see Evans, "Mens Devota," 110.

73. "Ne ergo sine immani rugitu cordis tui toleres horrorem interioris vultus tui. . . . Malum hinc, peius inde, malum undique" (*OsM*, 28); "porrige animae pauperis servi dilectoris tui dei de illa opulenta cella mentis" (*OsM*, 45); e.g., "aeneo carcere clauditur. . . . Caecus non videt foveam in quam cadit, insanus putat se debere facere quod facit.

Qui autem sponte peccat, videns et sciens praecipitio se tradit" (*OsM*, 58–59); "O 'abyssus abyyssum invocat'! Peccata mea, tormenta quoque quibus me servatis abyssus sunt" (*OsM*, 59).

74. Satô Ikuya, qtd. in Poole, *Trigger Happy*, 168. See also Poole, 168–76; Douglas and Hargadon, "Immersion and Interaction," 203–4; Gaggi, *From Text to Hypertext*, xiii–xiv, 106–15; Bolter and Grusin, *Remediation*, 162; J. Walker, "How I Was Played."

75. Translation from Southern, *Life*, 12–13.

76. Southern, *Life*, 35–36.

77. Cf. Bolter and Grusin, *Remediation*, 162.

78. For comparative discussions of the operations of image and text in medieval manuscripts or printed texts, see Weitzmann, *Roll and Codex*; Alexander, *The Decorated Letter*; Tufte, *Visual Display*.

79. Pächt, "Illustrations." Pächt also lists a number of early MSS of the *OsM* that are illuminated.

80. Landow, *Hypertext 2.0*, 80.

81. Pächt, "Illustrations," fig. 18b.

82. Anselm, *OsM*, 30.

83. Ibid.

84. Soc. Ant. London (SAL) MS Rawlinson 392, MS Bodley 271, MS Auct. D.2.6, and Soc. Ant. London (SAL). MS 7. Cf. Ward, *Prayers and Meditations*, 19–20; Bestul, *Durham Book*, 1.

85. This written summation of Stock's argument is itself a rather extreme reduction. For his full treatment of Anselm's assertion of the superiority of the oral mode to the written, see *The Implications of Literacy*, 335.

86. Anselm, *Monologion*, 7; translation from Schufreider, *Rational Mystic*, 20.

87. Stock, *The Implications of Literacy*, 336. Cf. Southern, *St. Anselm*, 118–19.

88. Schufreider, *Rational Mystic*, 61. See also Stock, *The Implications of Literacy*, 338–40.

89. See Southern, *St. Anselm*, 77–80, for an extended discussion of Anselm's meditative progression from images to cogitation to meditation to contemplation.

90. Bolter, *Writing Space*, 22.

91. Ong, *Orality and Literacy*, 136–37.

92. "Excitatio mentis ad contemplandum deum" (Anselm, *Proslogion*, 97); see also Ward, *Prayers and Meditations*, 239.

93. Southern, *St. Anselm*, 78. On the characteristic nature of such imagery and sensory appeal in the bulk of the writings of Anselm, see Evans, *Anselm and Talking*, 120.

94. Anselm, *OsM*, 53; translation modified from Ward, *Prayers and Meditations*, 180, lines 202–10.

95. Anselm, *OsM*, 48; translation modified from Ward, *Prayers and Meditations*, 169, lines 193–98.

96. Anselm, *OsM*, 48; translation from Ward, *Prayers and Meditations*, 169, lines 199–203. Cf. 1 John 3:17.

97. 2 John 1:12 and 3 John 1:13–14.

98. "Indignum profecto sese judicans, cujus laudem secutura posteritas ex litterarum monimentis pretii cujusvis haberet"; see Southern, *Life*, 150. Cf. Southern, *St. Anselm*, 410, for an account of Eadmer's biographic project and Anselm's opposition to it.

99. "Et quoniam nec istud nec illud cuius supra memini dignum libri nomine aut cui auctoris praeponeretur nomen iudicabam, nec tamen eadem sine aliquo titulo, quo aliquem in cuius manus venirent quodam modo ad se legendum invitarent, dimittenda putabam" (Anselm, *Proslogion*, 94); trans. *Basic Writings*, 48.

100. Cf. Evans, *Anselm and Talking*, 116–20.

101. Cf. Bolter, *Writing Space*, 30: "In general, the reader of an electronic text is made aware of the author's simultaneous presence in and absence from the text, because the reader is constantly confronting structural choices established by the author."

102. Cf. Southern, *St. Anselm*, 91; Bestul, "Private Prayers," 360–61; Ward, "Inward Feeling," 177. On the relative lack of Anselm's direct influence upon theological scholars who followed him, see Evans, *New Generation*, 7–12.

103. Bestul, "Private Prayers," 359.

104. On Eadmer's prayers and meditations, see Southern, *St. Anselm*, 430–36. For Ralph of Battle, see Bestul, "Verdun Anselm."

105. Wilmart, "La tradition."

106. Ward, *Prayers and Meditations*, 18; Bestul, *Durham Book*, 5–6.

107. Bestul, "Private Prayers," 356.

108. Comments on the diluted or inferior nature of most Anselmian apocrypha have been made by a number of critics, e.g., Southern, *St. Anselm*, 91; Ward, "Inward Feeling," 177.

109. The following discussion is considerably indebted to Wogan-Browne et al., *The Idea of the Vernacular*, whose invaluable survey of late Middle English adaptations (see parts 3.1–3.5, 212–38) of the Anselmian devotional model serves as the basis for much of this analysis.

110. Edited by Westra, in *Talkyng*.

111. Preface adapted from Wogan-Browne et al., *Vernacular*, 223.

112. Cf. Ward, "Inward Feeling," 178–79, comparing the two prefaces.

113. Ibid., 179–82.

114. Ibid., 181.

115. See Pearsall, *Vernon Manuscript*; Wogan-Browne et al., *Vernacular*, 214.

116. Hodgson and Liegey, *The Orcherd of Syon*. Cf. Wogan-Browne et al., *Vernacular*, 236–38; Hodgson, "English Mystical Tradition." For a recent discussion of *Orcherd*'s use at Syon, see Despres, "Ecstatic Reading and Missionary Mysticism."

117. Wogan-Browne et al., *Vernacular*, 236.

118. Ibid., 224–29.

119. E.g., Wogan-Browne et al., *Vernacular*, 231. For discussions of both this prologue and Julian of Norwich's reversal of the Anselmian model of devotional reading, see 213–15, 230–35.

120. See Deane, *St. Anselm: Basic Writings*, 23–45, for summations of these thinkers' discussions of Anselm's proof.

121. Kienzler, *International Bibliography*, 188–92.

122. This is from the second sentence of Schufreider's *Confessions of a Rational Mystic*. See also Hopkins, *Companion*, 89: "The history of Anselm's *Proslogion* argument testifies amply to its subtle richness. Except for Zeno's Achilles' paradox, perhaps no philosophical argument has been so fertile in engendering sustained and vigorous controversy. Rejected by Aquinas, it was revived in one form or another by Descartes, Spinoza and Leibniz. Kant dealt it a crippling blow; but in recent times Kant's own criticism has come under attack."

123. Schufreider, *Rational Mystic*, 2.

124. McArthur, *Clay Tablet to the Computer*, 69.

125. See Anselm, *OsM*, 2, for the highly variable contents and order of eleven manuscripts of the *OsM*. Cf. Bestul, "Private Prayers," 359.

126. Ward, *Prayers and Meditations*, 56–80, esp. 61–64, 67–68, 72–75.

127. Ibid., 65.

128. Ibid., 57.

129. Jameson, *Postmodernism*, 67.

130. Ibid., 68.

131. Ibid., 1–67, esp. 44–45.

132. Gaggi, *From Text to Hypertext*, 98.

133. E.g., Gaggi, *From Text to Hypertext*, 98–101; Bolter and Grusin, *Remediation*, 56–57.

134. Jameson, *Postmodernism*, 54.

Chapter 3. Closure and the Missing End of the Bayeux Tapestry

The epigraph is from Joyce, *Afternoon: A Story*, "work in progress."

1. In this discussion, the terms *ending* and *closure* are used with a general, if often blurry, distinction: *ending* usually denotes either the material or expressed cessation of a narrative, while *closure* relates more closely to issues of interpretative reception and the resolution of expectation of this ending. See Hult, *Concepts of Closure*, iii–vii.

2. Panels 169–73 and plates 71–73. All citations of the tapestry will be dual, with panel numbers referencing Foys, *Digital Edition*, followed by plate numbers referencing Wilson, *The Bayeux Tapestry*.

3. Panels 171–73, plate 73.

4. Foys, *Digital Edition*, contains full facsimiles of both the Montfaucon and Stothard reproductions. See also Montfaucon, *Les monumens*, vol. 2, plate IX (also reproduced as fig. 1 in F. Wormald, "Style and Design"), and C. Stothard, *Vetusta Monumenta*, vol. 6, plate XVI. On Stothard's reconstruction, see his "Some Observations." On all pre-photographic reproductions, see Hill, "Establishment."

5. For a thorough summary of the early history of the Bayeux Tapestry, see S. Brown, *History and Bibliography*, 1.

6. Wace, as canon of Bayeux, likely consulted the tapestry during the composition of the *Roman de Rou* in the 1150s; see Bennett, "Poetry as History?" 23.

7. S. Brown, *History and Bibliography*, 3.

8. Bertrand, "History," 78.

9. Gurney, "Observations," 359; Turner, *Normandy*, vol. 2, cited in Dawson, "Restorers," 254. For an image of the storage winch, see Foys, *Digital Edition* (Museum), or Dibdin, *Tour*, vol. 1, 247.

10. See Bertrand, "History," 83; Dawson, "Restorers," 288; Digby, "Technique and Production," 52–53. For the recent dating of the restoration to the 1860s, see Oger, "Results," 121.

11. Gibbs-Smith, "Notes on the Plates," 176.

12. Bertrand, *Tapisserie de Bayeux*, 24.

13. Only Geffrei Gaimar omits the coronation, but he has almost nothing after the battle except that William then reigned for nearly twenty-two years; see Bell, *L'estoire des Engleis*. For other literary accounts of the events found within the tapestry, produced within one hundred years of the Battle of Hastings, see Whitelock, *Anglo-Saxon Chronicle*; van Houts, *Gesta Normannorum Ducum* and "Brevis Relatio"; Davis and Chibnall, *Gesta Guillelmi*; Bosanquet, *Eadmer's History*; Mynors et al., *Gesta Regum Anglorum*; Henry of Huntingdon, *Historia Anglorum*; E. Edwards, *Liber Monasterii de Hyda*; Searle, *Chronicle of Battle Abbey*; Holden, *Roman de Rou*, translated in E. Taylor, *Master Wace*; Chibnall, *Ecclesiastical History of Orderic*; Barlow, *Carmen de Hastingae Proelio*; Brown and Herren, "Adelae Comitissae"; Darlington and McGurk, *Chronicle of John of Worcester*.

14. See, among the chronicles listed in note 13, *Anglo-Saxon Chronicle* (ed. Whitelock), "Brevis Relatio" and William of Jumièges (van Houts), Eadmer of Canterbury (Bosanquet), William of Malmesbury (Mynors et al.), Henry of Huntingdon (Greenway), *Hyde Chronicle* (E. Edwards), Geffrei Gaimar (Bell), and *Chronicle of Battle Abbey* (Searle).

15. All but Eadmer of Canterbury, Geffrei Gaimar, and the *Hyde Chronicle* contain this detail.

16. See panel 47/plate 21, panel 49/plate 22, panel 52/plate 23, panel 116/plates 49–50.

17. See panels 52–53/plate 23.

18. Davis and Chibnall, *Gesta Guillemi*, 70–77.

19. See Gillingham, "Bastard at War," 109–10; Keats-Rohan, "Breton Contingent," 163–66; D. Douglas, *William the Conqueror*, 178–79.

20. See S. Brown, "History or Propaganda?" 19; Lewis, *Rhetoric of Power*, 93.

21. See panel 1/plate 1. For Edward's seal, see Foys, *Digital Edition* (Museum), or Barlow, *Edward the Confessor*, plate 6.

22. Edward: panel 1/plate 1, panel 65/plate 28; Guy: panel 20/plate 10; Harold: panel 72/plate 31, panel 75/plate 32.

23. William: panel 27/plate 13, panel 37/plate 16, panel 58/plate 25, panel 80/plate 35, panel 113/plate 48, panel 117/plate 50.

24. The term is Messent's, from *Embroiderers' Story*, 72–77.

25. Messent, *Embroiderers' Story*, 72. See Whitelock, *Anglo-Saxon Chronicle*, 144–45, for *Chronicle* entry.

26. Kermode, *Ending*, 18, argues that though relations between the beginning, middle, and end may evolve and become more sophisticated, "radical fictions" disconfirming as well as confirming narrative predictions of endings, still, because of transcendental concerns such as the eschatological, rely on older, more naive and "simpler" fictions. See also B. Smith, *Poetic Closure*, 33–37. For a few of the many other studies that follow Kermode's and Smith's early work, see Brooks, *Reading for the Plot*; Gerlach, *Toward the End*; Stanzel, "Consonant and Dissonant Closure." See also D. Miller, *Narrative and Its Discontent*, esp. xii, n3.

27. B. Smith, *Poetic Closure*, 33–34.

28. See Strohm, *Theory and the Premodern Text*, 61–62; Carr, *Time, Narrative, and History*.

29. Doss, "Traditional Theory and Innovative Practice," 213–15. In both *The Gutenberg Galaxy* and *Understanding Media*, McLuhan also formulated the operation of print culture as a closed system of meaning, conducting all sensory experiences through the single sense of vision.

30. Ong, *Orality and Literacy*, 132.

31. J. Y. Douglas, *End of Books*, 92.

32. Panels 1–59/plates 1–26, panels 60–103/plates 26–44, and panels 104–end/plates 44–73. Critics commonly view the events of the tapestry along such structural lines—witness the schematizing of the tapestry as a "play" with a prologue, two acts, and an epilogue by David Bernstein in *The Mystery of the Bayeux Tapestry*, 16–26, and the attempts of others to locate the narrative center of the tapestry in Harold's oath to William (e.g., Stenton, "Historical Background," 15, which calls it the "climax of the story" and "the turning-point of the whole action displayed in the Tapestry") or in William's Channel crossing (e.g., Cetto, *The Bayeux Tapestry*, 7).

33. E.g., William of Poitiers's account of William's response to Harold's envoys before the battle (Davis and Chibnall, *Gesta Guillelmi*, 120–23).

34. Panel 55/plate 24 and panel 59/plate 25.

35. Werckmeister, "Political Ideology," 567–76. See also Lewis, *Rhetoric of Power*, 93–97; Brooks and Walker, "Authority and Interpretation," 10–12.

36. See Werckmeister, "Political Ideology," 563–79; Cowdrey, "Interpretation," 97–98; Bernstein, *Mystery*, 116–17; D. Douglas, *William the Conqueror*, 176–77, 540–45; Lewis, *Rhetoric of Power*, 103–4.

37. Panel 59/plate 25.

38. Panels 60–62/plates 26–27.

39. Lewis, *Rhetoric of Power*, 103.

40. Panels 72–75/plates 31–33.

41. On this semantic distinction, see Stenton, "The Historical Background," 17.

42. See Garnett, "Coronation and Propaganda," for a discussion of how Norman claims for a legal succession from Edward to William were hindered by Harold's coronation, and the Norman strategies by which this coronation could then be legally invalidated.

43. On Stigand, see M. Smith, "Eye of the Needle." English literary sources claim

Ealdred of York presided at the coronation. On this debate see Garnett, "Coronation and Propaganda," 96; Stenton, "Historical Background," 18; Chibnall, *Ecclesiastical History of Orderic*, 138n1; J. Nelson, "Rites of the Conqueror," 393.

44. "Quod sermone nequit, innuit et manibus" (Barlow, *Carmen de Hastingae Proelio*, 48–49, line 16).

45. On the comet, see Mynors, *Gesta Regum Anglorum*, 2:211–12; Freeman, *Norman Conquest*, 3:645–50.

46. This is not to deny that the gestural language of the Bayeux Tapestry often pulls the viewer both backward and forward at the same time, or that moments of semantic connection between the upper and lower borders and the central narrative create vertical progressions of meaning. Such alternative linear movements are, however, generally momentary and in addition to the dominant narrative mode.

47. Panels 134–144/plates 57–61.

48. T. E. Hulme, *Speculations*, 224, cited in Doss, "Traditional Theory and Innovative Practice," 213.

49. See, for instance, Donato, "Ending/Closure"; Zumthor, "Impossible Closure"; J. H. Miller, "Problematic of Ending"; D. Miller, *Narrative and Its Discontents*, esp. xii–xv, 188–90, 265–68.

50. Barthes, *S/Z*, 15–16.

51. Fish, *Is There a Text in This Class?*

52. See Lesieur, "Lisible et visible"; Brilliant, "Stripped Narrative"; Wissolik, "Code," 69–71; Lewis, *Rhetoric of Power*, 132–34.

53. McGerr, "Medieval Concepts of Literary Closure," 159, 169. On scribal anxiety see McGerr, 162–63; Hult, "Scribal Closure in the Oxford Roland." On lack of closure in medieval narrative, see Sklute, *Virtue of Necessity*; Allen and Moritz, *A Distinction of Stories*, 77n3; Strohm, *Theory and the Premodern Text*, 51–64.

54. McGerr, "Medieval Concepts of Literary Closure," 154.

55. Bernstein, *Mystery*, 25, and Maclagan, *The Bayeux Tapestry*, 14, are rare exceptions.

56. Gurney, "Observations," 361. Gurney also states that the tapestry is "not complete in its ornamental work, but I think complete in its history" (370).

57. Lethaby, "The Perjury at Bayeux," 137.

58. Lewis, *Rhetoric of Power*, 132–34.

59. For critiques of the accuracy and artistry of the restorations, see Dawson, "Restorers"; Lejard, *The Bayeux Tapestry*, 22; S. Brown, "Why Eustace, Odo and William?" 11–12.

60. See Foys, *Digital Edition* (Facsimiles), or Montfaucon, *Les monumens*, plate IX, or F. Wormald, "Style and Design," fig. 1. For a full overview of all surviving and recorded copies of the Tapestry into the nineteenth century, see Hill, "Establishment."

61. Panel 173/plate 73.

62. Panel 70/plate 30; panel 84/plate 36.

63. Messent, *Embroiderers' Story*, 74.

64. Cf. Wissolik, "Code"; and Bernstein, *Mystery of the Bayeux Tapestry*, 163–64.

65. Strohm, *Theory and the Premodern Text*, 64.

66. See Chibnall, *Anglo-Norman England*, 9–53; Williams, *The English and the Norman Conquest*, 7–70.

67. Davis and Chibnall, *Gesta Guillelmi*, 150–51.

68. Ibid.

69. Whitelock, *Anglo-Saxon Chronicle*, 136–38; for dating the meeting of Edward and Harold, see Cowdrey, "Interpretation," 101n26; D. Douglas, *William the Conqueror*, 177–79; I. Walker, *Harold*, 91.

70. Panel 65/plate 29. On Edward's appearance, see Owen-Crocker, "Telling a Tale," 50–52; Gibbs-Smith, *The Bayeux Tapestry*, plate 11. By all accounts Edward became ill, most likely from a series of strokes, only in late November of 1065, and died on January 4, 1066; see Barlow, *Edward the Confessor*, 233–40.

71. Panel 70/plate 30.

72. Panels 66–69/plates 29–30.

73. Stenton, "Historical Background," 16–17.

74. For theories of mistaken embroidering, see Verrier, *Queen Matilda's Tapestry*, 16; Bachrach, "Observations," 7; Koslin, "Turning Time," 37–42. For dramatic design, see, among others, Thompson, "Kingship-in-Death," 114; Gibbs-Smith, *The Bayeux Tapestry*, 9; Parisse, *The Bayeux Tapestry*, 75–76; Brooks and Walker, "Authority and Interpretation," 21–23. For narrative flashback, see Parisse, 76; Grape, *Norman Triumph*, 70; Bertrand, "Study," 31–32. For narrative ambiguity related to both Anglo-Saxon and Norman literary sources, see Lesieur, "Lisible et visible," 177–79.

75. The tapestry does earlier show another reversal of narrative order, where William's messengers arrive at Guy of Ponthieu's palace (panel 22/plate 10) before William dispatches them (panel 27/plate 13). However, as both Holmes, review, 181, and Brooks and Walker, "Authority and Interpretation," 23n71, argue, this scene is actually simply a reversal of directional display, not the confusion of temporality found at Edward's funeral.

76. Frank, *The Widening Gyre*; W. Mitchell, "Spatial Form in Literature." For an extensive bibliography of narrative uses of spatial form, see Smitten, "Space and Spatial Form," 245–63.

77. Smitten, "Space and Spatial Form," 17.

78. Langer, *Philosophy in a New Key*, 79–102.

79. For an alternative, but related, approach to how medieval images and text can operate together to form expressions outside linear narrative traditions, see Emmerson, "Visualizing Performance," 248–51. Emmerson employs the semiotic notions of "pre-text" and "cotext" to demonstrate how illuminations of a medieval play derive not from the literary text of the drama but from its performance. Further, he argues that the interplay of text and image in Besançon MS 579, like the tapestry's conflation of Langer's discursive modes, derive from cotexts that memorialize a performance of a dramatic piece, *Jour du Jugement*. As such, the images do not derive from the text; both together function to re-create the space of the performative, a space that exists outside the

linear sequence of the literary text and traditional hierarchies of image-text relationships.

80. For discussions of the spatial dynamic and display of the tapestry, see Brilliant, "Stripped Narrative"; Swanton, "Not Stichic, but Stitched."

81. For Orderic Vitalis, see Chibnall's edition, 184–85.

82. Translation adapted from E. Taylor, *Master Wace*, 269, lines 8997–9010.

83. Hult, *Concepts of Closure*, iv.

84. See, among others, Owen-Crocker, "Telling a Tale"; Dodwell, "French Secular Epic"; McCloud, *Understanding Comics*; Noxon, "The Bayeux Tapestry." See also Burt, "Re-embroidering the Bayeux Tapestry in Film and Media," for the most recent consideration of the BT through nonliterary media.

85. E.g., J. Y. Douglas, *End of Books*; Moulthrop, "Reading from the Map"; Harpold, "Conclusions"; Aarseth, "Nonlinearity and Literary Theory."

86. Brilliant, "Stripped Narrative," 111–19.

87. See Bernstein, *Mystery*, 107; Parisse, *The Bayeux Tapestry*, 51; Grape, *Norman Triumph*, 79–80; Gameson, "Origin, Art, and Message," 175; Cowdrey, "Interpretation," 110.

88. See Bolter, "Topographic Writing"; Landow, *Hypertext 2.0*, 115–77; Lanham, *The Electronic Word*, 55; Doss, "Traditional Theory and Innovative Practice."

89. See, for instance, George Landow's commentary on Adam Wenger's map of "Adam's Bookstore" in "What's a Critic to Do?" 25; Bolter, *Writing Space*, 136.

90. Bolter, *Writing Space*, 143.

91. See Landow, *Hypertext 2.0*, 189–92; J. Y. Douglas, *End of Books*, 39–42.

92. Bertrand, "Study," 38; Hill, "Establishment," 387.

93. J. Y. Douglas, *End of Books*, 88.

94. Ibid., 89–122.

95. Ibid., 106, 108.

96. Dibdin, *Tour*, 240.

97. Ibid.

98. Antiquariolus, "Tapestry," 18.

99. C. Stothard, "The Bayeux Tapestry," plates 1–17. Full plates also available in Foys, *Digital Edition* (Facsimiles). See also S. Brown, *History and Bibliography*, 13.

100. Gurney, "Observations," 359.

101. Dibdin, *Tour*, 249; see also Foys, *Digital Edition* (Museum).

102. See Antiquariolus, "Tapestry"; H. D., "Further Remarks."

103. E.g., H. D., "Further Remarks"; Lowell, "The Bayeux Tapestry"; Colby, "Bayeux and Its Marvels."

104. Mrs. Stothard, *Letters*, 121–22.

105. H. D., "Further Remarks," 313.

106. Fowke, *History and Description*.

107. Cf. Bishop, "1066"; Denny and Filmer-Sankey, *The Bayeux Tapestry*; Neveux, *The Bayeux Tapestry*; Setton, "900 Years Ago."

108. Gameson, *Study*. A notable exception is Lucien Musset's 1989 edition of the Tapestry, republished in French in 2002, and translated into English in 2005. Musset's edition lavishes long, overlapping strips of the Tapestry on every page, along with relevant close-ups.

109. See, for example, Lewis, *Rhetoric of Power*, which introduces an ambitious, but underdeveloped, poststructural program of reading, and by the end of the work returns to more traditional modes of formal analysis. For a full critique, see Foys, "Above the Word, Beyond the Page."

110. Gameson, *Study*, xii.

111. E.g., Landow, *Hypertext 2.0*, 68–69; Doss, "Traditional Theory and Innovative Practice"; Schillingsburg, "Principles."

112. Cf. Landow's "What's a Critic to Do?" where he considers the state of literary criticism in light of New Media textuality.

113. See Foys, "Hypertextile Scholarship," for a full description of the digital edition.

114. J. Y. Douglas, *End of Books*, 122.

Chapter 4. The Virtual Reality of the Anglo-Saxon *Mappamundi*

The epigraphs are from Langer, *Philosophy in a New Key*, 79–80; Bolter, *Writing Space*, 81; Stoppard, *Rosencrantz and Guildenstern Are Dead*, 84.

1. Harley and Woodward, *History of Cartography*, plate 22.

2. See, for instance, J.A.J. De Villiers's comment that in presenting "this square representation of the known world . . . it will therefore be more convenient in order to see the countries in our accustomed way, to have this [map] thrown sidewise on the screen" ("Famous Maps," 171).

3. Kimble, *Geography in the Middle Ages*, 187.

4. For an introduction to the precepts of critical cartography, see Harley, *New Nature of Maps*.

5. Harley and Woodward, "Concluding Remarks," 508.

6. See McGurk et al., *Cotton Tiberius B.V*, 79.

7. Ibid., 33–34; on paleographic evidence, the editors date the Cotton Tiberius B.V manuscript to the second quarter of the eleventh century, closer to 1050. However, they also consider, tentatively, the possibility that some script of the map is of a slightly later date, possibly as late as the early twelfth century. Conversely, McGurk and Dumville also consider that this script may be the work of the manuscript's main scribe (30). Ker, *Manuscripts Containing Anglo-Saxon*, 255–56, item 193, dates the manuscript to the first quarter of the eleventh century but notes that the composition of some of the material (e.g., an episcopal list and Sigeric's itinerary) dates from ca. 990.

8. See K. Miller, *Mappaemundi*, 3:29, where the map is called "berühmte und vielcitierte," and Edson, *Mapping Time and Space*, 76. McGurk et al., *Cotton Tiberius B.V*, 79n1, provides citations for the half dozen or so general histories of geography and cartography that briefly consider the map. Most recently, Englisch, *Ordo Orbis Terrae*, 245–58, provides a basic overview of the map.

9. K. Miller, *Mappaemundi*, 3:29–37; McGurk et al., *Cotton Tiberius B.V*, 79–87.

10. De Villiers, "Famous Maps," 171; Crone, Campbell, and Skelton, "Landmarks of British Cartography."

11. E.g., Malone, "King Alfred's North," plate III; Flint, *Imaginative Landscape*, 31 and plate 3; Westrem, "Against Gog and Magog," 60; E. Campbell, "History of Cartography," 97; Hodgkiss, *Understanding Maps*, 75–76. The brief treatments of the Cotton Map found in Howe, *Angle on This Earth*, 9–13, and Edson, "World Maps and Easter Tables," 32–35, stand out as notable exceptions.

12. The quotation is from the nineteenth-century cartographer Manuel Francisco Santarem, cited in Kimble, *Geography in the Middle Ages*, 189. See Kimble, 182; De Villiers, "Famous Maps," 168–73; Hodgkiss, *Understanding Maps*, 72; E. Campbell, "History of Cartography," passim; King, *Mapping Reality*, 20, for similar attitudes toward medieval maps.

13. De Villiers, "Famous Maps," 169–70.

14. See Flint, *Imaginative Landscape*, 3–41 and passim, for Columbus's use of medieval maps, and his rejection of Ptolemy.

15. Edson, *Mapping Time and Space*, 132.

16. McGurk et al., *Cotton Tiberius B.V*, 80–86.

17. Ibid., 7. For a full list of medieval *mappaemundi*, categorized by type and century (including the eleventh), see Destombes, *Mappemondes A.D. 1200–1500*.

18. For examples of the T-O map, see Woodward, "Medieval *Mappaemundi*," 343–47.

19. Hodgkiss, *Understanding Maps*, 75–76.

20. Harley and Woodward, *History of Cartography*, plate 22.

21. Woodward, "Medieval *Mappaemundi*," 347–48.

22. Ibid. For Orosius's description, see *Historiarum adversum paganos libri VII* I.2.9–40, translated in *Seven Books*, 34–47. All subsequent quotations of Orosius are from Zangemeister's edition.

23. K. Miller, *Mappaemundi*, 3:35, notes that only 75 of 146 inscriptions may be found in Orosius.

24. K. Miller, *Mappaemundi*, 3:31–35 cross-references all of the inscriptions of the Cotton Map with several possible sources, as well as later maps that he views as analogues.

25. De Villiers, "Famous Maps," 171.

26. S. Brown, *History and Bibliography* and her update "Bibliography of Bayeux Tapestry Studies: 1985–1999."

27. Lawton, "Surveying Subject," 9.

28. Kupfer, "Medieval World Maps," 262.

29. King, *Mapping Reality*, 18.

30. Winterson, *Sexing the Cherry*, 81.

31. Baudrillard, *Symbolic Exchange and Death*, 73 (Baudrillard's emphasis).

32. Cf. *Oxford English Dictionary*, which cites Chaucer's "To Rosemounde" as one such example: "Madame, ye ben of al beautè shrine, As fer as cercled is the mapamonde"

(2); on the medieval permeability of the term, see Woodward, "Medieval *Mappae-mundi*," 287.

33. Bolter and Grusin, *Remediation*, 244.

34. See, for example, Lévy, *Becoming Virtual*, 1–34.

35. Rothenberg, *Hand's End*, qtd. in Hillis, *Digital Sensations*, xiii.

36. Naimark, "Aspen Movie Map." See also Nielsen, *Hypertext and Hypermedia*, 36–38.

37. Cf. Heim, *Virtual Realism*, 47–48: "We no longer need to believe we are representing the real world of nature. Virtual worlds do not represent the primary world. . . . Each virtual world is a functional whole that can parallel, not re-present or absorb the primary world we inhabit." [→8]

38. Doel and Clarke, "Virtual Worlds," 263. Ironically, one early example of an immersive VR technology was named CAVE (Cave Automatic Virtual Environment) in reference to Plato's myth; see Heim, *Virtual Realism*, 26.

39. Doel and Clarke, "Virtual Worlds," 269, 271.

40. See Hillis, *Digital Sensations*, fig. 1, xix.

41. For related discussions of virtuality and information, see Heim, *Virtual Realism*, 125; Light, "City Space to Cyberspace," 109–10; Piper, *Cartographic Fictions*, 157; Imken, "Convergence."

42. Qtd. in Woodward, "Medieval *Mappaemundi*," 287.

43. Harley, "Iconology of Early Maps," 38.

44. Kline, *Maps of Medieval Thought*, 10. See also Kline's introduction to the Hereford *Mappamundi*, 2–5.

45. Hillis, *Digital Sensations*, xxvii–xxviii.

46. Cf. Light, "City Space to Cyberspace," 109; Starrs, "Sacred," 197.

47. E.g., Woodward, "Medieval *Mappaemundi*," 286: "The primary purpose of these *mappaemundi* . . . was to instruct the faithful about the significant events in Christian history rather than to record precise locations." For critical challenges to such a view, see Lawton, "Surveying Subject"; Kupfer, "Medieval World Maps."

48. Tomasch, "Medieval Geographical Desire," esp. 3–7.

49. Ibid., 5.

50. Cf. Kupfer, "Medieval World Maps," 279: "*Mappaemundi* more than showed the geographical organization of the terrestrial space; they were coordinated with other signs to position viewers—from princes to prelates, cloistered monks to lay public—within a political, social and spiritual order."

51. Harley, *New Nature of Maps*, 164.

52. Cf. Howe, *Angle on This Earth*, 13: "we need to question our practice of using maps as illustrations, as when we reproduce a *mappamundi* for a frontispiece of an encyclopedia of the Middle Ages." Woodward, "Medieval *Mappaemundi*," 287, speculates that the purpose of the maps can be separated from the text and be understood as "independently valuable."

53. K. Miller, *Mappaemundi*, 3:35.

54. Woodward, "Medieval *Mappaemundi*," 301.

55. J. Bately, *The Old English Orosius*. Curiously, Bately does not connect these two Anglo-Saxon representations of Orosian material, instead relying on the superficial identification of the Cotton Map with Priscian's *Periegesis*, the text in MS Tiberius B.V that the map may have been included to illustrate, though its content bears little resemblance to the map.

56. Gilles, "Territorial Interpolations," 84.

57. Orosius I.2.20, I.2.25 "montem Taurum"; I.2.37 "Tauri montis"; I.2.44 "mons Taurus."

58. I.2.25. Orosius also notes the Cimmerian Sea to the northeast, which the map represents but does not name.

59. I.2.20–22: "A flumine Tigri usque ad flumine Euphraten Mesopotamia est, incipiens a septentrione inter montem Taurum et Caucasum. Cui ad meridiem succedit Babylonia, deinde Chaldea, novissime Arabia Eudaemon, quae inter sinum Persicum et Arabicum angusto terrae tractu orientem versus extenditur."

60. Slightly to the east, and in the Orosian section immediately above the passage in question, the Cotton Map also reproduces, in order, four of the five territories Orosius lists as between the Indus and Tigris rivers: "quod est ad occasum regions sunt istae: Arachosia, Parthia, Assyria, Persidia et Media" (I.2.16–17). The Cotton Map lists, in southward order, "Aracusia, Siria, Persidea and Media" between two rivers that are unnamed but likely the Indus and the Euphrates. The other inscriptions contained in this area are "Arabia Eudemon" (see current discussion, below) and the non-Orosian, biblical city "Nineve." For a slightly later map that also reproduces this Orosian group and the one discussed above with an even more rigidly linear presentation, see the early-twelfth-century Jerome Map of the Holy Land (BL Add. ms 10049, f. 64) in K. Miller, *Mappaemundi*, 2:14.

61. J. Bately, *The Old English Orosius* I.i, p. 10, lines 14–15. On this departure from Orosius, and the interpolation of the Sabei, see 161 and lxv–lxvi. Elsewhere Bately notes that these changes to Orosius could have come from such texts as Isidore or Bede; see "Geographical Information," 49–50.

62. Westrem, *The Hereford Map*, no. 189.

63. Deuteronomy 1:1: "These are the words which Moses spoke to all Israel across the Jordan in the wilderness, in the Arabah against the Red Sea, between Paran and Tophel and Laban and Hazeroth and Dizahab." N.B.: The King James version of the Bible consistently translated the Hebrew *arabah* as "wilderness" or "plain," while earlier versions retained it as an actual name. For the connection to Deuteronomy 1, see K. Miller, *Mappaemundi*, 2:34.

64. Exodus 31:18.

65. Exodus 2:1–9.

66. On such itineraries, see Edson, *Mapping Time and Space*, 142, 153, 176–78, 183; Kline, *Maps of Medieval Thought*, 215; P. Harvey, *Mappa Mundi*, 42. K. Miller, *Mappaemundi*, 3:62, discusses a map of the Holy Land showing the passage of Exodus sketched in the margin of an eighth-century copy of Orosius (Orosius codex 621, St. Gall), along with two other maps—a three-continent *mappamundi* and a map of Italy marked with Rome. See also C. Smith, "Geography or Christianity?" 150.

67. Howe, *Migration and Mythmaking*; Foot, "The Making of *Angelcynn*," 31; P. Wormald, *Making of English Law*, 416–29; Frantzen, *King Alfred*, 11–21.

68. White, *Content of the Form*, 24–25.

69. Lienhard, qtd. in Starrs, "Sacred," 211.

70. Moretti, *Atlas of the European Novel*, 8.

71. Woodward, "Medieval *Mappaemundi*," 288, 292.

72. Howe, *Angle on This Earth*, 10.

73. Crone, *Maps and Their Makers*, 23.

74. Westrem, "Against Gog and Magog."

75. King, *Mapping Reality*, 45; K. Miller, *Mappaemundi*, 3:31.

76. Hillis, *Digital Sensations*, 72–77.

77. Ibid., xxix.

78. Howe, *Migration and Mythmaking*, 90.

79. K. Miller, *Mappaemundi*, 3:36. For other discussions of glosses on primary material as sources of geographic information, see Herren, "Graeco-Roman Mythology," 92–97; J. Bately, Geographical Information," 62.

80. McGurk et al., *Cotton Tiberius B.V*, 84.

81. Cf. Woodward, "Medieval *Mappaemundi*," 326.

82. Cf. Bede, *A Biblical Miscellany*, xxxi. See also Edson, *Mapping Time and Space*, 115, for a discussion of how such biblical geography may also portray the six ages of history.

83. McGurk et al., *Cotton Tiberius B.V*, 84. Three tribes, Zebulon, Neptalim, and Manasseh, occur twice.

84. Bridges, "Of Myths and Maps," 74–75.

85. Howe, *Migration and Mythmaking*, 92.

86. Ibid., 103.

87. Paul Starrs, for instance, finds an "omniscient quality" in cyberspace that "invokes the real with the surreal; the seen with the unseen; commerce with the artistic and the avant-garde . . . [and can] make the computer an extension of the all-seeing eye" ("Sacred," 207).

88. Take the dilemma during the second Gulf War of having the same tribe of Kurds split between Turkey, Iran, and Iraq. At the time of this writing, the United States is encouraging the Kurds of northern Iraq to play an active role in the new national government, but the Turkish government is reported to seek to suppress the tribe in their country, out of concern that the Kurds in Turkey may then also desire independence. Cf. the discussion of twentieth-century divisions of Arab and Soviet land in King, *Mapping Reality*, 49–56.

89. King, *Mapping Reality*, 51. For further discussion, see Said, *The Question of Palestine*, 57; Salem, "Archaeology of the Text."

90. Starrs, "Sacred," 193.

91. King, *Mapping Reality*, 16, argues about Disneyland, "when the ride is over . . . what is the world outside the simulator, the rest of the Disneyland enclave, other than another level of virtual reality?" Cf. Eco, *Travels in Hyperreality*, 3–58, esp. 39; Heim, *Virtual Realism*, 153.

92. Virilio, cited in J. Taylor, "Emerging Geographies," 183.

93. King, *Mapping Reality*, 17.

94. Cf. J. Taylor, "Emerging Geographies," 180.

95. Gellner, *Nations and Nationalism*, 21.

96. *Princeton Encyclopedia of Classical Sites*, 258–59.

97. S. Mitchell, *Anatolia*, 1:118–42, esp. 119 and map 9.

98. Orosius I.2.23.

99. Howe, *Angle on This Earth*, esp. 1–10.

100. Silberman, *Chorographie*, 82; cf. Bridges, "Of Myths and Maps," 70–71.

101. Silberman, *Chorographie*, 82.

102. Bridges, "Of Myths and Maps," 70–71.

103. Gildas, *Ruin of Britain*, 89; Colgrave and Mynors, *Bede's Ecclesiastical History*, 89.

104. Howe, "North Looking South," n.p.

105. Gildas, *Ruin of Britain*, 89, 91.

106. Bridges, "Of Myths and Maps," 71.

107. J. Bately, *The Old English Orosius*, 36. On the role of the east as origin and west as the end of the world in Christian historiography and geography, cf. Lawton, "Surveying Subject," 12; Kimble, *Geography in the Middle Ages*, 184.

108. On the general notion of the earthly corners, see Gordon, "Sacred Directions," 211–12; for this concept in Anglo-Saxon England, see Roy, "Shape of the World," 479. Variations of the Old English phrase *feowerum foldan sceatum* occur in *Christ III (Judgement Day)*: Krapp and Dobbie, *The Exeter Book*, 3–49, line 878; in "De Die Judicii'" ("The Apocalypse of Thomas"): Scragg, *Vercelli Homilies*, 253–61, line 129; in "In Die Iudicii": Napier, *Wulfstan*, no. 40, 182–90, line 25; and in "The Gospel of Nicodemus Homily" (Cambridge, Corpus Christi College MS. 41): Hulme, "Old English Gospel of Nicodemus," 579–614, line 62. Variations of *foldan sceatum*, which might in certain contexts also mean "the earth's surface," are too numerous to mention but include *Dream of the Rood*: Pope, *Eight Old English Poems*, 67–68, line 8.

109. Cf. Foot, "The Making of *Angelcynn*," 36; Howe, *Migration and Mythmaking*, 108–42.

110. Bridges, "Of Myths and Maps," 72.

111. M. Campbell, "Witness," 53.

112. On dating the origin of Anglo-Saxon identity, see Foot, "The Making of *Angelcynn*"; Harris, "Alfredian World History."

113. Harley, *New Nature of Maps*, 157.

114. However, *Brittania* could also serve as a more convenient name for all of the islands represented, as opposed to only the Anglo-Saxon state.

115. Cf. Bridges, "Of Myths and Maps," 71: "The classical heritage of the *literati* of Anglo-Saxon England included *mappaemundi* and cosmographical writings of various kinds that were 'centred' around Rome or Greece—if I may use the concept of centre here less in the graphical sense than in the sense of an authoritative vantage point."

116. E.g., Howe, *Angle on This Earth*, 9; M. Brown, *Anglo-Saxon Manuscripts*, 34.

117. The notion that Jerusalem was the exact center of the world ultimately derives from Psalms 74:2 and Ezekiel 5:5. For a full discussion, see Higgins, "Defining the Earth's Center"; cf. Woodward, "Medieval *Mappaemundi*," 340. For Bede's commentary, see "On Holy Places" in *A Biblical Miscellany*, 10. For convenient color illustrations of all the *mappaemundi* mentioned, see P. Harvey, *Mappa Mundi*, at 1, 20, 29, 31.

118. Higgins, "Defining the Earth's Center," 49; Woodward, "Medieval *Mappaemundi*," 340–42.

119. Cf. Henry of Mainz (or Sawley) Map in P. Harvey, *Mappa Mundi*, 23. See Woodward, "Medieval *Mappaemundi*," 318–21, for a full discussion of medieval conceptions of the shape of the earth and cartographic treatments of it. Woodward also notes the inversion of this convention—a square earth inside a circular outline—though this practice appears rarely, if at all, in English world maps.

120. E.g., the Sawley or Mainz Map (P. Harvey, *Mappa Mundi*, 23), the Hereford Map (Westrem, *Hereford Map*, map 9), the so-called Isidorian Mappamundi (Woodward, "Medieval *Mappaemundi*," 350 fig. 18.61), and the Psalter Map (Woodward, "Medieval *Mappaemundi*," 350 fig. 18.63).

121. McGurk et al., *Cotton Tiberius B.V*, 81–83.

122. Ibid., 81–82.

123. The twelfth-century Sawley Map, for instance, reproduces the cities of Rouen and Paris, among other features; see Edson, *Mapping Time and Space*, 114.

124. Lindsay, *Isidori Hispalensis Episcopi Etymologiarum Sive Originum*, XIV.vi.2. Similarly, Orosius writes that Britain and Ireland "in aversa Galliarum parte ad prospectum Hispaniae sitae sunt" (I.2.75).

125. Edson, "The Oldest World Maps," 182.

126. Other "th" inscriptions lack the eth character.

127. Cf. Edson, "The Oldest World Maps," 177–78, which discusses the inscription "Bret" in the early-ninth-century Orosian *mappamundi* Vat. Lat. 6018, concluding that it is both the latest (and only) post-Roman inscription and possibly the earliest cartographic reference to the success of the Anglo-Saxon invasions.

128. As noted above (note 7), the Cotton Map has not been dated more surely than the first half of the eleventh century, perhaps even slightly later. The elision of contemporary France may possibly derive from a combination of a Roman source and a Germanic emphasis on Scandinavian regions. If the map was drawn around 1050, this elision may also express the negative attitudes toward Normandy rapidly developing among some Anglo-Saxon factions. Even if the absence of France and Normandy is a product of early, ninth-or-tenth-century Anglo-Saxon cultural concerns, this omission certainly could have taken on new meaning after 1050. See R. Allen Brown's chapter "England, Normandy and Scandinavia" in *The Normans and the Norman Conquest*, 94–121, for the scale of and attitudes toward the Norman presence in pre-Conquest England.

129. Bhabha, "Of Mimicry and Man," 86, qtd. in Withers, "A Sense of Englishness," 331.

130. "Neronorroen" (Norway), "Scridefinnas" (Finland), "Island" (Iceland), "Sleswic," "Sclavi," and "Daria (Dacia), ubi et Gothia" (where are the Goths).

131. McGurk et al., *Cotton Tiberius B.V*, 82; Orosius I.2.53.

132. For discussion of these misidentifications, including the impossibility of identifying the Geats as an actual Scandinavian tribe, see Harris, "Alfredian World History," 485–89.

133. Harris, "Alfredian World History," 487, shows how the Thracian tribe came to be thought Nordic by association with the ancient Get[ae], and perhaps even explains why Bede thought the Picts came from Scythia.

134. J. Bately, *The Old English Orosius*, 13–18, lxxi–lxxii.

135. Gilles, "Territorial Interpolations," 90.

136. Cf. Gilles, "Territorial Interpolations," 83, which notes that the Old English adaptation of the Orosian opening across Anglo-Saxon history places Britain "at its center."

137. Harris, "Alfredian World History," 494.

138. Ibid., esp. 499–504.

139. Ibid., 504.

140. Ibid., 507–9.

141. Howe, *Migration and Mythmaking*, 108–42, esp. 108–20.

142. Lévy, *Becoming Virtual*, 16.

143. Ryan, *Narrative as Virtual Reality*, 36.

144. Hillis, *Digital Sensations*, 72–81.

145. Benedikt, "Cyberspace: Some Proposals," 125.

146. Langer, *Feeling and Form*, 72, argues that "the harmoniously organized space in a picture is not experiential space, known by sight and touch. . . . like the space 'behind' the surface of the mirror, it is what the physicists call 'virtual space'—an intangible image."

147. Ryan, *Narrative as Virtual Reality*, 42.

148. The Nile is represented in similar fashions in most of the detailed medieval *mappaemundi*. See Westrem's treatments of these fragments in the Hereford Map (*The Hereford Map*, nos. 69, 194, 427, 441). The Cotton Map may also simply be trying to follow Orosius's own complicated description of the river's route. Orosius notes the river rises near the Red Sea, runs west and then turns north to water Egypt. In the next sentence, though, Orosius admits that other writers believe the river originates in the west of Ethiopia, near Mount Atlas, and flows *eastward* "towards the ocean" until it turns and then flows down to Egypt. Orosius attempts to resolve this contradiction by theorizing that a subterranean channel might connect these two apparently different rivers. Confusion about mapping the Nile continued throughout the medieval period and into the early modern; see Crawford, "Medieval Theories."

149. Orosius 1.2.9 and 1.2.90, 92, respectively.

150. Exodus 7:15–25.

151. Woodward, "Medieval *Mappaemundi*," 336. On church orientation, see Gordon, "Sacred Directions," 215; Woodward, 340.

152. Woodward, "Medieval *Mappaemundi*," 336–37; Gordon, "Sacred Directions," 212–21; C. Brown, "Cardinal Direction Terms," 124. Gordon, 221, notes the longstanding tradition in England that suicides be buried to the north of the church. On Hugh St. Victor, see Edson, *Mapping Time and Space*, 160; Kupfer, "Medieval World Maps," 269–70. In his description of a pictorial cosmographical design in *Libellus de formatione arche*, Hugh marks Paradise in the east, and the Last Judgment in the west; through the north door of Noah's Ark, the chosen people are led into captivity, while through the south door they proceed into the Promised Land.

153. Edson, *Mapping Time and Space*, 121 and fig. 6.5.

154. Howe, "North Looking South," n.p.

155. Ibid.

156. Ortenberg, "Archbishop Sigeric's Journey to Rome."

157. Tooley, "Medieval Theory of Climate," 68; Friedman, *Monstrous Races*, 37. See also Woodward, "Medieval *Mappaemundi*," 330–33.

158. The description of the Turchi comes from the Hereford Map (see Westrem, *The Hereford Map*, no. 302); the information ultimately derives from Æthicus Ister. See also O'Keeffe, "Geographic List," 128–29, 137.

159. Friedman, *Monstrous Races*, 51–54.

160. The contrast to single-word inscriptions in the north is most marked in Africa, where one finds several inscriptions like "Gentes Aulolum pertingeates ussque ad oceanum" and "Hic oberrant gangines Ethiopes."

161. Pierpont Morgan MS 644, fol. 33–34. See Edson, "The Oldest World Maps," 178, for discussion. A late-eleventh-century copy of this map (BL Add. MS 11695, fols. 39v–40r) is reproduced in color in Edson, *Mapping Time and Space*, plate XI.

162. "Africa est enim fertilis sed ulterior bestiis et serpentibus plena" [Africa is in fact fertile, but also full of beasts and serpents]. Cf. K. Miller, *Mappaemundi*, 3:35, which cites Isidore as the nearest analogue, and Edson, "The Oldest World Maps," 180.

163. For an introduction to Beatus maps, see Edson, *Mapping Time and Space*, 149–59; Woodward, "Medieval *Mappaemundi*," 303–4.

164. For a discussion of medieval conceptions of the fourth continent, and the torrid equinoctial zone thought to separate it from the north, see Flint, *Imaginative Landscape*, 26–34.

165. Roy, "Shape of the World," 466.

166. See Woodward, "Medieval *Mappaemundi*," 353–55, for a concise overview of zonal *mappaemundi*.

167. On the zonal map, see McGurk et al., *Cotton Tiberius B.V*, 65, 107–8; Flint, *Imaginative Landscape*, 32–34; Edson, *Mapping Time and Space*, 3.

168. The text is a paraphrase of Macobius II.vi.2. As Edson notes, Eratosthenes' calculation may have been accurate to within fifty miles (*Mapping Time and Space*, 4).

169. Cf. Friedman, *Monstrous Races*, 47–48.

170. Flint, *Imaginative Landscape*, 32–33.

171. These figures are likely Peter and Paul—my thanks to Catherine Karkov for our discussion of this identification.

172. Kimble, *Geography in the Middle Ages*, 186.

173. Tooley, "Medieval Theory of Climate," 82; see Tooley's examination of Jean Bodin's arguments to privilege the northwest, 77–83. As King has argued in *Mapping Reality*, the cartographic bias of the north persists today, and in modern maps the north "remains physically above the south, in a position historically far from accidental" (38–39). Mercator's projection, for instance, greatly exaggerates extreme latitudes, with "almost all of the land affected . . . in the northern hemisphere, the far south containing relatively little land mass. Northern lands thus appear to account for a far greater proportion of the surface area of the world than is really the case" (37).

174. Flint, *Imaginative Landscape*, 23–41.

175. Qtd. in Piper, *Cartographic Fictions*, 183. Cf. King, *Mapping Reality*, 19.

176. Woodward, "Medieval *Mappaemundi*," 340.

177. Hodgkiss, *Understanding Maps*, 74.

178. For a good introduction to portolan charts, see Kimble, *Geography in the Middle Ages*, 191–93.

179. Cf. King, *Mapping Reality*, 44–47, especially the discussion of Samuel Edgerton's examples of pre- and postlinear representations of the city of Florence.

180. Hodgkiss, *Understanding Maps*, 80.

181. Harley and Woodward, "Concluding Remarks," 502–3. See also P. Harvey, *Mappa Mundi*, 285, on the role of scientific geographical theory in the development of cartography.

182. Excerpts from *De Nuptiis Philologiae et Mercurii* from Willis's edition, *Martianus Capella*, VI. 580–82 and 588–89. Translations are adapted from Stahl, *Seven Liberal Arts*, 2:281–91. See also Stahl's commentary in volume I, 125–28.

183. Tomasch, "Medieval Geographical Desire," 1.

184. Willis, *Martianus Capella*, VI. 579, and Stahl, *Seven Liberal Arts*, 217–18; emphasis added.

185. King, *Mapping Reality*, 31.

186. Harley, *New Nature of Maps*, 154.

187. Ibid., 168. See also Hillis, who considers the effect "contemporary science's assumption of a 'separate, quantifiable, objective world'" (*Digital Sensations*, 75) has had on perceptions of space, and Piper, for whom the discipline of cartography, in effect, is a struggle over narrative, and "the way in which colonial and developmental rhetoric has animated the history of cartography. Because cartography is based in the perpetual superseding of 'inaccurate' maps by 'accurate' maps, geographic knowledge is believed to be progressive in nature" (*Cartographic Fictions*, 179–80).

188. Hillis, *Digital Sensations*, 73.

189. Moretti, *Atlas of the European Novel*, 20.

190. De Landa, "Virtual Environments."

191. Ibid., 275–76.

192. Piper, *Cartographic Fictions*, 168.

Chapter 5. Cyberspace, Sculpture, and the Revision of Medieval Space

The epigraphs are from Lefebvre, *The Production of Space*, 65, and Camille, "Signs of the City," 9.

1. Kleinschmidt, *Understanding the Middle Ages*, 33.

2. Cf. Hanawalt and Kobialka, *Medieval Practices of Space*, ix. Likewise, my own discussion of spatial narrative in chapter 3 of this book must be considered a part of this school.

3. Certeau, *Everyday Life*, 117. Certeau writes that "space is a practiced place . . . thus the street geometrically defined by urban planning (a place) is transformed into a space by walkers. In the same way, and act of reading is the space produced by the practice of a particular place: a written text, that is, a place constituted by a system of signs."

4. Le Goff, *The Birth of Purgatory*.

5. Wertheim, *Pearly Gates*, 69, 64.

6. Ibid., 44–154.

7. Ibid., 224.

8. Ibid., 36–37; Lefebvre, *The Production of Space*, 1–2.

9. Orton, "Rethinking," n.p.

10. Outside Lang's *Corpus* summaries, at 3:38 and 3:189–93, the most recent substantive discussions of Nunburnholme were written in the 1970s: Pattison, "Anglo-Danish Sculpture"; Lang, "Sculptors."

11. For accounts of the discovery, see M. Morris, *Nunburnholme*, 82; J. Romilly Allen, "Pre-Norman Cross-Shaft," 99.

12. For the history of the Nunburnholme church, see M. Morris, *Nunburnholme*, 69–88.

13. Cf. Pattison, "Anglo-Danish Sculpture," 210; Lang, "Sculptors," 92.

14. Lang, *Corpus*, 3:189.

15. Lang, "Sculptors," 86, and *Corpus*, 3:192. See Side D, top, for the plan of the First Sculptor's unfinished design.

16. Lang, "Sculptors," provides a thorough stylistic analysis of each sculptor's work.

17. For the sake of consistency, Lang's lettered classification from the *Corpus* has been retained.

18. Lang, "Sculptors," 3:85; Bailey, *Viking Age Sculpture*, 232.

19. Lang, *Corpus*, 3:192.

20. Lang, "Sculptors," 80, and "Pre-Conquest Sculpture," 2.

21. Given that most beast chains occupy the entire side of a shaft, Lang, *Corpus*, 3:192, acknowledges the "slim case" that the fragments represent two different monuments, but favors the stylistic unity promoted by the iconography of the other sides.

22. Cf. Lang, *Corpus*, 3:193; Bailey, *Viking Age Sculpture*, 156–57.

23. Pattison, "Anglo-Danish Sculpture," 230; Lang, "Sigurd and Weland," 89–90. For a full account of the Sigurd myth, see Bailey, *Viking Age Sculpture*, 116–24.

24. Lang, "Pre-Conquest Sculpture," 2.

25. Lang, "Sculptors," 88, notes the stylistic congruency of the centaur face and the Romanesque faces carved on the church's chancel arch.

26. Lang, "Sculptors," 88.

27. Kobialka, "Staging Place/Space," 129.

28. Cf. Kleinschmidt, *Understanding the Middle Ages*, 33.

29. Lefebvre, *The Production of Space*, 1–3.

30. Davies, *Space and Time*, 11–19.

31. Edgerton, *Heritage of Giotto's Geometry*, 45; cf. Wertheim, *Pearly Gates*, 118; see also Lefebvre, *The Production of Space*, 38–39, on practitioners of representations of space "all of whom identify what is lived and what is perceived with what is conceived. . . . this is the dominant space in any society."

32. Lang, "Sculptors," 80, and "Pre-Conquest Sculpture," 3–4.

33. Crosby, *The Measure of Reality*; see also Andrews, *Story and Space*. For notions of timelessness and classical conceptions of space, see Strate, "Hypermedia, Space, and Dimensionality," esp. 281; Davies, *Space and Time*, 22.

34. Cf. Crosby, *The Measure of Reality*, 177–79.

35. For an accessible introduction to the basic concepts underlying Einstein's work, and theories of relativity, see Wertheim, *Pearly Gates*, 165–75.

36. Crosby, *The Measure of Reality*, 28.

37. See, for instance, David Wilson's discussion (*Viking Art*, 139 and plate LXI) of the Viking Rasmus rock and Gök Stone and other Scandinavian art, which fragment elements of the Sigurd myth to such a degree that, for Wilson, certain motifs of the narrative "become completely meaningless." In Anglo-Saxon art, the conflation of narrative sequences within a single image frequently occurs; see, for instance, David Bernstein's analyses of such depictions in the Anglo-Saxon Hexateuch and Junius 11 manuscripts in *Mystery*, 93–94. For an exploration of how medieval architecture and cultural practices within it also did not privilege optical geometry as modernity does, see Kobialka, "Staging Place/Space."

38. But see Andrews, in *Story and Space*, who argues that in the early stages of perspective art, at least in Italy, some painters experimented with simultaneous narrative through single-point perspective, and that our modern, photographic bias about perspective has ignored this early experimentation.

39. Orton, "Rethinking," 89. Orton continues his argument in "Northumbrian Identity," esp. at 105–8. For a conceptual and functional defense of the *Corpus*, see Bailey, "Great Offence."

40. Orton, "Rethinking," 91.

41. Ibid., 67.

42. Crosby, *The Measure of Reality*, 228–29.

43. Lefebvre, *The Production of Space*, 137–54.

44. As an example, at a recent reading of a conference paper on connections between classical and Renaissance notions of perspective, the presenter opened by describing the Middle Ages as a "cognitive wedge" that had interrupted the "progress" of perspectival development.

45. Lefebvre, *The Production of Space*, 256.

46. Kleinschmidt, *Understanding the Middle Ages*, 36.

47. Cf. Lefebvre, who considers the year 1000 "a truly pregnant moment" in which a new form of space is being prepared (*The Production of Space*, 253).

48. Hooke, "Mid-Late Anglo-Saxon Period," 95. Hooke's essay studies the shift to place-centered groups in Anglo-Saxon settlements.

49. Kleinschmidt, *Understanding the Middle Ages*, 47–48. For an introduction to the nucleation of Anglo-Saxon England, see Härke, "Kings and Warriors," especially the subsection "Intensification and Nucleation," 152–57.

50. On the peripatetic nature of the Anglo-Saxon royal household, see Loyn, *Governance of Anglo-Saxon England*, 95–106.

51. Härke, "Kings and Warriors," 155.

52. For reviews of the historical development of the Danelaw in Yorkshire, see Hadley, "In Search of the Vikings"; Binns, *Viking Century*; C. Morris, "Northumbria."

53. Kern, *Time and Space*, 138; cf. Wertheim, *Pearly Gates*, 307.

54. E.g., Collingwood, "Anglian and Danish Sculpture," 266; M. Morris, *Nunburnholme*, 185, 193.

55. J. Bately, *MS A*, 50. See discussion and other, similar reports in Sawyer, "Conquest and Colonization," 128. Hadley's "And They Proceeded to Plough and to Support Themselves" stands as one of the most recent and comprehensive overviews of the critical debate over the character and process of the Scandinavian settlement. For other discussions of the process of Viking settlement in northern England, see Bailey, *Viking Age Sculpture*, 30–44; C. Morris, "Northumbria"; Binns, *Viking Century*; Härke, "Kings and Warriors," 157–61.

56. Binns, *Viking Century*, 14, 23–25.

57. Ibid., 27.

58. Härke, "Kings and Warriors," 158.

59. Hadley, "And They Proceeded." Hadley argues against the monocausal and binary conclusions drawn from many later interpretations of the seminal studies of place-names by Gillian Fellows-Jensen and others; see 69–75, and Bailey, *Viking Age Sculpture*, 33–40. It is not the purpose of the current study to join this rather vigorous debate. Here it suffices to observe, as Hadley does, "on a very broad level that the large numbers of Scandinavian place-names and of Scandinavian words for landscape features are the result of a significant influx of Scandinavians" (74).

60. Härke, "Kings and Warriors," 157, 161. On the mouldboard plough, Härke cites Astill and Langdon, *Medieval Farming and Technology*.

61. For a material survey of the layout and types of building construction included in a Scandinavian settlement, albeit further north in the Tees Valley, see C. Bately, "Rural Settlement." For a social survey of such settlements, see Hadley, "And They Proceeded."

62. M. Morris, *Nunburnholme*, 21–23.

63. Additionally, but more tenuously, the area appears to have remained in the control of Scandinavian descendants until the Conquest. The Domesday Book records that one of the thanes holding Brunham during the mid-eleventh century was named Turchil, a name of Scandinavian derivation and related to the nearby place-name of

Thirkleby. Post-Conquest, William the Conqueror granted Brunham to Forne, son of Sigulf, another name of Scandinavian origin; see M. Morris, *Nunburnholme*, 23, 25–27.

64. For representative discussions, see Hadley, "And They Proceeded"; C. Morris, "Northumbria"; Sawyer, "Conquest and Colonization."

65. C. Morris, "Northumbria," 81–90. For a regnal list of York during the Danelaw, see Binns, *Viking Century*, 19–20.

66. Swanton, *The Anglo-Saxon Chronicle*, 75. In another version, "hergende" was originally written but the "h" was later erased; see Cubbin, *MS D*, 26.

67. Kobialka, "Staging Place/Space," 143.

68. Howe, "Landscape of Anglo-Saxon England," 93.

69. Lefebvre, *The Production of Space*, 39.

70. Bailey, *Viking Age Sculpture*, 238. "Frequently the distance involved is less than a mile; rarely is it more than ten miles."

71. Howe, "Landscape of Anglo-Saxon England," 92–98; for a detailed survey of Anglo-Saxon recycling of Roman materials, see Hunter, "Sense of the Past," esp. 35–45.

72. Lang, *Corpus*, 3:92. See also Bailey, *Viking Age Sculpture*, 82, and Bailey's discussion on 176–206 of the close regional groupings of Anglo-Scandinavian sculptural styles.

73. Bailey, *Viking Age Sculpture*, 81–84.

74. See Bailey, *Viking Age Sculpture*, 176–77; Wilson and Klindt-Jensen, *Viking Art*, 104–5.

75. Hadley, "And They Proceeded," 87.

76. Lang, *Corpus*, 3:38. "It would be wrong to see the Nunburnholme beast-chain as an intrusive Scandinavian feature or a part of a Viking impact on local taste."

77. Wilson and Klindt-Jensen, *Viking Art*, plate 38b, 103–5. For arguments for the purely Anglian, or even Mercian, origin of the Nunburnholme beast chain, see Lang, "Anglo-Scandinavian Sculpture," 13; Cramp, *Studies in Anglo-Saxon Sculpture*, 231.

78. For discussions of the origins of Jellinge beast chains and biting beasts as Scandinavian and not Insular, see Bailey, *Viking Age Sculpture*, 55–56; Wilson and Klindt-Jensen, *Viking Art*, 99.

79. Like most of this monument, the Sigurd scene cannot be authoritatively defined, but this discussion follows the lead of Lang, who provides compelling contextual evidence. The inclusion of other Scandinavian elements (jarl and beast chain) strengthens the case. See Bailey, *Viking Age Sculpture*, 116–17, 122; Lang, "Sigurd and Weland," 88–90.

80. Cf. Howe, *Migration and Mythmaking*, 108–42.

81. Lang, "Sigurd and Weland," 89.

82. Lang, "Sculptors," 77.

83. Cf. Bailey, *Viking Age Sculpture*, 77.

84. Deleuze, "Nomad Art: Space."

85. Ibid., 166–67.

86. The gripping angels motif from Nunburnholme was later copied by an artist at York on the Newgate 1 cross shaft; see Lang, "Sculptors," 86, 90, and *Corpus*, 3:105.

87. Deleuze, "Nomad Art: Space," 169.

88. Ibid., 171: "for us . . . the abstract line is fundamentally 'Gothic,' or rather nomadic, not rectilinear." Deleuze draws from the arguments of Wilhelm Worringer. See Worringer's *Form in Gothic*: "Actually, that which Gothic man could not transform into naturalness by means of clear-sighted knowledge, was overpowered by this intensified play of fantasy and transformed into a spectrally heightened and distorted actuality" (81).

89. Deleuze, "Nomad Art: Space," 171.

90. H. R. Ellis Davidson, cited in Dodwell, *Anglo-Saxon Art*, 39.

91. Deleuze, "Nomad Art: Space," 166.

92. Nunes, "Virtual Topographies," 69.

93. For a detailed description of Nunburnholme's position between Roman roads, see M. Morris, *Nunburnholme*, 14–15.

94. Bailey, *Viking Age Sculpture*, 176; see his subsequent analyses, 177–206.

95. Stocker, "Monuments and Merchants," 200–206.

96. Binns, *Viking Century*, 27.

97. Lefebvre, *The Production of Space*, 263.

98. Deleuze, "Nomad Art: Space," 167.

99. Howe, "Landscape of Anglo-Saxon England," 108–9.

100. Hawkes, "Reading Stone."

101. Biggs, "Hybrids, An Imaginary Ecology."

102. Nunes, "Virtual Topographies," 61; Strate, "Hypermedia, Space, and Dimensionality," 269.

103. Spiller, *Cyber Reader*, 96–97; Nunes, "Virtual Topographies," 64–65.

104. Deleuze and Guattari, *A Thousand Plateaus*, cited in Nunes, "Virtual Topographies," 65.

105. Tomas, "Old Rituals for New Space." Compare to Lefebvre, who earlier views computer technology as simply a more powerful way to create singular, striated spaces of meaning: "computer science [can] dominate space in such a fashion, that a computer—hooked up if need be to other image- and document-reproducing equipment— can assemble an indeterminate mass of information relating to a given physical or social space and process it at a single location, virtually at a single point" (*The Production of Space*, 355). Lefebvre's language is a throwback to perspective and vanishing point—but, importantly, not as a stable object but as a momentary focus in a shifting space. The "object" fashioned by perception in cyberspace is wholly a function of its representation, and then is gone.

106. Cf. Benedikt, "Cyberspace, Some Proposals," esp. 132.

107. See, for instance, the recent accomplishments of the Digital Michelangelo Project; for a summary of the project, see graphics.stanford.edu/papers/dmich-sig00/ dmich-sig00.html (a copy of the project paper that appears in the Proceedings from SIGGRAPH 2000, New Orleans, 2000).

108. Manovich, *Language of New Media*, 36–45. See also Foys, "New Media and the Nunburnholme Cross," n.p.

109. Joyce, "Lingering Errantness of Place," 160.

110. Laurel, *Computers as Theatre*, 114–15; see also Strate, "Hypermedia, Space, and Dimensionality," 274–77.

111. Novak, "Liquid Architectures in Cyberspace," 251. See also Spiller, *Cyber Reader*, 150–51.

112. Strate, "Hypermedia, Space, and Dimensionality," 275.

113. Foucault, "Of Other Spaces," 23.

114. Ibid., 24.

115. Nunes, "Virtual Topographies," esp. 65; cf. Tomas, "Old Rituals for New Space," esp. 36.

Epilogue: For All Practical Purposes

The epigraph is from Bush, "As We May Think," 101.

1. Bush, "As We May Think."

2. Cf. Machan, "Chaucer's Poetry, Versioning, and Hypertext."

3. Conner, "ANSAXNET." On the *Beowulf Workstation*, see Conner, "The *Beowulf* Workstation"; for SEAFARER, a hypertextual "mini-encyclopedia" of the early Middle Ages which began in 1992 as a Hypercard stack program and then was ported to HTML in 1998, see www.wheatonma.edu/kacc/LTLC/reports/Drout.html.

4. For an ongoing survey of electronic resources in Anglo-Saxon studies, see *Old English Newsletter*, "Circolwyrde."

5. P. Robinson, "Where We Are," par. 1. Cf. Prescott, "Electronic Beowulf."

6. Frantzen, "By the Numbers."

7. Howe, "The New Millennium," 501.

8. Bullough, Lusignan, and Ohlgren, "Computers and the Medievalist," 392n2.

9. Ibid., 392.

10. On the Domesday Project, see Finney, "Domesday"; O'Donnell, "Doomsday Machine."

11. McKie and Thorpe, "Digital Domesday Book Lasts 15 Years."

12. Montfort, "Time Frames," 711. See also P. Robinson, "Current Issues," §6–7.

13. O'Donnell, "Doomsday Machine"; "Domesday 1986."

14. Manovich, *Language of New Media*, 39–45; Raitt, "Digiral Library Initiatives."

15. See Text Encoding Initiative home page.

16. Renear, Mylonas, and Durand, "What Text Really Is."

17. Several initiatives to develop protocol for the encoded transcription and description of medieval manuscripts have already come and gone. TEI's most recent standard, P5, contains an extensive set of guidelines for providing "detailed descriptive information about handwritten primary sources," derived from an early set of guidelines specifically designed for medieval manuscripts: see Text Encoding Initiative, "Manuscript Description." For links to other current projects related to encoding manuscripts, see their wiki at "TEI Special Interest Group on Manuscripts (TEI MS SIG)." For a more flexible architecture, see Kevin Kiernan's *Electronic Production and Presentation Technology* (EPPT) project.

18. Tokunaga and Kishida, "Computer-Assisted Analysis of Caxton's Typography."

19. In the first draft of this chapter, I automatically wrote "that deserve an entire *book* in their own right," revealing my own typographic interiority.

20. For a developed discussion of a new typology for New Media texts, see Aarseth, "Nonlinearity and Literary Theory."

21. See Strickland, "Paradigm for Interaction."

22. Pilgrim, "What Is RSS?"; *Digital Medievalist Project*; Berry, "Video Game Technology."

23. Ulmer, *Applied Grammatology*, 58.

24. Landow, *Hypertext 2.0*, 33–34.

25. Clement, "Antique, Medieval, and Renaissance Book Production."

26. See JSTOR.

27. Google, "About Google Book Search" and "All the World's Books."

28. Biggs, "Hybrids, An Imaginary Ecology."

29. Aarseth, "Nonlinearity and Literary Theory," 82.

30. Laurel, *Computers as Theatre*, 115.

Bibliography

Aarseth, Espen J. "Nonlinearity and Literary Theory." In Landow, *Hyper/Text/Theory*, 51–86.

Abbott, Edwin A. *The Annotated Flatland: A Romance of Many Dimensions.* Edited by Ian Stewart. Cambridge, Mass.: Perseus, 2001.

Alexander, J.G.G. *The Decorated Letter.* New York: Braziller, 1978.

Allen, J. Romilly. "Pre-Norman Cross-Shaft at Nunburnholme, Yorkshire." *Reliquary* 7 (1901): 98–106.

Allen, Judson Boyce, and Theresa Anne Moritz. *A Distinction of Stories: The Medieval Unity of Chaucer's Fair Chain of Narratives for Canterbury.* Columbus: Ohio State University Press, 1981.

Andersen, Deborah Lines, ed. *Digital Scholarship in the Tenure, Promotion, and Review Process.* Armonk, N.Y.: M. E. Sharpe, 2003.

Andrews, Lew. *Story and Space in Renaissance Art: The Rebirth of Continuous Narrative.* Cambridge: Cambridge University Press, 1995.

Anselm of Canterbury. *Basic Writings.* Edited and translated by S. N. Deane. 2nd ed. LaSalle, Ill.: Open Court, 1962.

———. *Monologion.* In *Opera Omnia*, 1:5–87.

———. *Opera Omnia ad fidem codicum.* Edited by F. S. Schmitt. 6 vols. Edinburgh: Thomas Nelson, 1946–61.

———. *Orationes sive Meditationes.* In *Opera Omnia*, 3:1–91.

———. *Proslogion.* In *Opera Omnia*, 1:93–122.

Antiquariolus [pseud.]. "Tapestry of William the Conqueror's Queen." *Gentleman's Magazine*, 1st ser., 73 (1803): 1136–38, 1226–28; 74 (1804): 18–19.

Astill, Grenville, and John Langdon. *Medieval Farming and Technology.* Leiden: Brill, 1997.

Bachrach, Bernard S. "Some Observations on the Bayeux Tapestry." *Cithara* 27.1 (1987): 5–28.

Bailey, Richard N. "Innocent from the Great Offence." In Karkov and Orton, *Theorizing Anglo-Saxon Stone Sculpture*, 93–103.

———. *Viking Age Sculpture in Northern England.* London: Collins, 1980.

Barlow, Frank, ed. *The Carmen de Hastingae Proelio of Guy, Bishop of Amiens.* 2nd ed. Oxford: Clarendon, 1999.

———. *Edward the Confessor.* London: Eyre Metheun, 1979.

Barthes, Roland. *S/Z.* New York: Hill and Wang, 1974.

Bately, Colleen. "Aspects of Rural Settlement in Northern Britain." In Hooke and Burnell, *Landscape and Settlement*, 69–94.

Bately, Janet M., ed. *MS A.* Vol. 3 of *The Anglo-Saxon Chronicle: A Collaborative Edition.* Cambridge: D. S. Brewer, 1986.

————, ed. *The Old English Orosius*. EETS, s.s., 6. Oxford: Oxford University Press, 1980.

————. "The Relationship between Geographical Information in the Old English Orosius and Latin Texts Other than Orosius." *Anglo-Saxon England* 1 (1972): 45–62.

Baudrillard, Jean. *Simulacra and Simulation*. Translated by Sheila Faria Glaser. Ann Arbor: University of Michigan Press, 1994.

————. *Symbolic Exchange and Death*. Translated by Iain Hamilton Grant. London: Sage, 1993.

Beckett, Katharine Scarfe. "Old English References to the Saracens." In Roberts and Nelson, *Essays on Anglo-Saxon and Related Themes*, 482–509.

Bede. *A Biblical Miscellany*. Edited and translated by W. Trent Foley and Arthur G. Holder. Liverpool: Liverpool University Press, 1999.

————. *De temporum ratione de concordia maris et lunae*. In *Bedae Opera de temporibus*, edited by Charles W. Jones. Cambridge, Mass.: Mediaeval Academy of America, 1943.

Bell, Alexander, ed. *L'estoire des Engleis*, by Geffrei Gaimar. Oxford: Basil Blackwell, 1960.

Benedikt, Michael. *Cyberspace: First Steps*. Cambridge, Mass.: MIT Press, 1991.

————. "Cyberspace, Some Proposals." In *Cyberspace: First Steps*, 119–224.

Benjamin, Walter. *Illuminations*. Edited by Hannah Arendt. Translated by Harry Zohn. New York: Harcourt, Brace and World, 1968.

————. *Reflections*. Edited by Peter Demetz. Translated by Edmund Jephcott. New York: Harcourt Brace Jovanovich, 1978.

Bennett, Matthew. "Poetry as History? The 'Roman de Rou' of Wace as a Source for the Norman Conquest." *Anglo-Norman Studies* 5 (1982): 21–39.

Bernstein, David J. *The Mystery of the Bayeux Tapestry*. Chicago: University of Chicago Press, 1986.

Berry, Clayton. "Theologians Use Video Game Technology to Create Virtual Tour of 13th Century Buscilica." <www.slu.edu/x12540.xml>.

Bertrand, Simone. "The History of the Tapestry." In Stenton, *The Bayeux Tapestry*, 76–88.

————. "A Study of the Bayeux Tapestry." In Gameson, *Study*, 31–38.

————. *La tapisserie de Bayeux et la manière de vivre au onzième siècle*. La Pierre-qui-Vire, Yonne: Zodiaque, 1966.

Bestul, Thomas H. "The Collection of Anselm's Prayers in British Library Ms. Cotton Vespasian D.xxvi." *Medium Aevum* 47 (1978): 1–5.

————. "The Collection of Private Prayers in the *Portiforium* of Wulfstan of Worcester and the *Orationes Sive Meditationes* of St. Anselm." In *Les mutations socio-culturelles au tournant des XIe–XIIe siècles*, edited by Raymonde Foreville, 355–64. Paris: Centre National de la Recherche Scientifique, 1984.

————, ed. *A Durham Book of Devotions*. Toronto: Pontifical Institute of Mediaeval Studies, 1987.

————. "St. Anselm and the Continuity of Anglo-Saxon Devotional Traditions." *Annuale Medievale* 18 (1977): 20–41.

————. "St. Anselm, the Monastic Community at Canterbury, and Devotional Writing in Late Anglo-Saxon England." *Anselm Studies* 1 (1983): 185–98.

————. "St. Augustine and the *Orationes Sive Meditationes.*" *Anselm Studies* 2 (1988): 597–606.

————. "The Verdun Anselm, Ralph of Battle, and the Formation of the Anselmian Apocrypha." *Revue Bénédictine* 87 (1977): 383–89.

Bhabha, Homi K. "Of Mimicry and Man: The Ambivalence of Colonial Discourse." In *The Location of Culture*, 85–92. London: Routledge, 1994.

Biggs, Simon. "Hybrids, An Imaginary Ecology." <hosted.simonbiggs.easynet.co.uk/texts/hybrids.htm>.

Binns, A. L. *The Viking Century in East Yorkshire*. York: East Yorkshire Local Historical Society, 1963.

Birkerts, Sven. *The Gutenberg Elegies: The Fate of Reading in an Electronic Age*. New York: Fawcett Columbine, 1994.

Bishop, Morris. "1066." *Horizon* 8.4 (1966): 4–27.

Blake, N. F. "Manuscript to Print." In Griffiths and Pearsall, *Book Production and Publishing*, 403–32.

Bland, Mark. "The Appearance of the Text in Early Modern England." *Text* 11 (1998): 91–152.

Bolter, Jay David. "Topographic Writing: Hypertext and the Electronic Writing Space." In Delany and Landow, *Hypermedia and Literary Studies*, 105–18.

————. *Writing Space: The Computer, Hypertext, and the History of Writing*. Hillsdale, N.J.: Lawrence Erlbaum, 1991.

Bolter, Jay David, and Richard Grusin. *Remediation: Understanding New Media*. Cambridge, Mass.: MIT Press, 2000.

Bornstein, George, and Theresa Tinkle, eds. *The Iconic Page in Manuscript, Print, and Digital Culture*. Ann Arbor: University of Michigan Press, 1998.

Bosanquet, Geoffrey, ed. and trans. *Eadmer's History of Recent Events in England: Historia Novorum in Anglia*. London: Cresset, 1964.

Bouet, Pierre. "Is the Bayeux Tapestry Pro-English?" In Bouet, Levy, and Neveux, *The Bayeux Tapestry*, 197-215.

Bouet, Pierre, Brian Levy, and François Neveux, eds. *The Bayeux Tapestry: Embroidering the Facts of History; The Proceedings of the Cerisy Colloquium (1999)*. Caen: Presses Universitaires de Caen, 2004.

Bridges, Margaret. "Of Myths and Maps: The Anglo-Saxon Cosmographer's Europe." In *Writing and Culture*, edited by Balz Engler, 68–84. Tübingen: Günter Narr, 1992.

Brilliant, Richard. "The Bayeux Tapestry, a Stripped Narrative for Their Eyes and Ears." In Gameson, *Study*, 111–37.

Brody, Florian. "The Medium Is the Memory." In *The Digital Dialectic*, edited by Peter Lunenfeld, 130–49. Cambridge, Mass.: MIT Press, 1999.

Brooks, N. P., and H. E. Walker. "The Authority and Interpretation of the Bayeux Tapestry." *Proceedings of the Battle Conference* 1 (1978): 1–34.

Brooks, Peter. *Reading for the Plot: Design and Intention in Narrative*. New York: Knopf, 1984.

Brown, Cecil H. "Where Do Cardinal Direction Terms Come From?" *Anthropological Linguistics* 25.2 (1983): 121–61.

Brown, Cynthia J., and Barbara Valentine. "Networking in Medieval and Postmodern Cultures: Texts, Authorship, and Intellectual Property." *Journal of the Early Book Society* 2 (1999): 157–75.

Brown, Michelle P. *Anglo-Saxon Manuscripts*. Toronto: University of Toronto Press, 1991.

Brown, R. Allen. *The Normans and the Norman Conquest*. 2nd ed. Woodbridge, U.K.: Boydell, 1985.

Brown, Shirley Ann. *The Bayeux Tapestry: History and Bibliography*. Woodbridge, U.K.: Boydell, 1988.

———. "The Bayeux Tapestry: History or Propaganda?" In *The Anglo-Saxons: Synthesis and Achievement*, edited by J. Douglas Woods and David A. E. Pelteret. Waterloo, Ont.: Wilfrid Laurier University Press, 1985, 11-25.

———. "The Bayeux Tapestry: Why Eustace, Odo and William?" *Anglo-Norman Studies* 12 (1990): 7–28.

———. "Bibliography of Bayeux Tapestry Studies: 1985–1999." In Bouet, Levy, and Neveux, *The Bayeux Tapestry*, 411-18.

Brown, Shirley Ann, and Michael W. Herren. "The 'Adelae Comitissae' of Baudri of Bourgeuil and the Bayeux Tapestry." *Anglo-Norman Studies* 16 (1994): 55–73.

Bullough, Vern L., Serge Lusignan, and Thomas H. Ohlgren. "Computers and the Medievalist." *Speculum* 49 (1974): 392–402.

Burt, Richard. "Re-embroidering the Bayeux Tapestry in Film and Media: The Flip Side of History in Opening and End Title Sequences." *Exemplaria* 18.2 (2008): forthcoming.

Bush, Vannevar. "As We May Think." *Atlantic Monthly* 176 (July 1945): 101–8.

Camille, Michael. "Philological Iconoclasm: Edition and Image in the Vie De Saint Alexis." In *Medievalism and the Modernist Temper*, edited by R. Howard Bloch and Stephen G. Nichols, 371–401. Baltimore: Johns Hopkins University Press, 1996.

———. "Sensations of the Page: Imaging Technologies and Medieval Illuminated Manuscripts." In Bornstein and Tinkle, *Iconic Page*, 33–53.

———. "Signs of the City: Place, Power, and Public Fantasy in Medieval Paris." In Hanawalt and Kobialka, *Medieval Practices of Space*, 1–36.

Campbell, Eila. "Introduction to the History of Cartography." English text in *Introducció general a la història de la cartografia*. Barcelona: Institut Cartogràfic de Catalunya, 1990.

Campbell, Mary B. *The Witness and the Other World: Exotic European Travel Writing, 400–1600*. Ithaca: Cornell University Press, 1988.

Capella, Martianus. *De Nuptiis Philologiae et Mercurii*. Edited by James Willis in *Martianvs Capella*. Leipzig: BSB B.G. Teubner, 1983.

Carr, David. *Time, Narrative, and History.* Bloomington: Indiana University Press, 1986.

Cassidy, Brendan, ed. *The Ruthwell Cross: Papers from the Colloquium Sponsored by the Index of Christian Art, Princeton University, 8 December 1989.* Princeton, N.J.: Princeton University, 1992.

Certeau, Michel de. *The Practice of Everyday Life.* Translated by Steven Rendall. Berkeley and Los Angeles: University of California Press, 1984.

Cetto, Anna Maria. *The Bayeux Tapestry.* Translated by Britta M. Charleston. Orbus Pictus Series. Bern: Hallwag, 1970.

Chartier, Roger. *The Cultural Uses of Print in Early Modern France.* Translated by Lydia G. Cochrane. Princeton, N.J.: Princeton University Press, 1987.

———, ed. *The Culture of Print: Power and the Uses of Print in Early Modern Europe.* Translated by Lydia G. Cochrane. Princeton, N.J.: Princeton University Press, 1989.

Chibnall, Marjorie. *Anglo-Norman England, 1066–1166.* Oxford: Blackwell, 1986.

———, ed. and trans. *The Ecclesiastical History of Orderic Vitalis.* 6 vols. Oxford: Clarendon, 1969–80.

Christianson, C. Paul. "Evidence for the Study of London's Late Medieval Manuscript-Book Trade." In Griffiths and Pearsall, *Book Production and Publishing,* 87–108.

Christie, Edward. "The Image of the Letter: From the Anglo-Saxons to the *Electronic Beowulf.*" *Culture, Theory, and Critique* 44.2 (2003): 129–50.

———. Quid Est Littera? The Materiality of the Letter and the Presence of the Past from Alcuin of York to the Electronic Beowulf. Ph.D. diss. West Virginia University, 2003.

Clanchy, M. T. *From Memory to Written Record: England, 1066–1307.* Cambridge, Mass.: Harvard University Press, 1979.

———. "Looking Back from the Invention of Printing." In *Literacy in Historical Perspective,* edited by Daniel P. Resnick, 7–22. Washington, D.C.: Library of Congress, 1983.

Clegg, Cyndia Susan. "The History of the Book and a History of Two Books: How Print Culture Can Inform Literary Study." *Literature Compass* 1, 17C 050 (2004): 1–16.

Clement, Richard W. "The Beginnings of Printing in Anglo-Saxon, 1565–1630." *Papers of the Bibliographic Society of America* 91.2 (1997): 192–244.

———. "A Survey of Antique, Medieval, and Renaissance Book Production." In *Art Into Life: Collected Papers from the Kresge Art Museum Medieval Symposia,* edited by Carol Garrett Fisher and Kathleen L. Scott, 9–28. East Lansing: Michigan State University Press, 1995.

Colby, Fred Myron. "Bayeux and Its Marvels." *National Repository* 6 (1879): 33–38.

Colgrave, Bertram, and R.A.B. Mynors, eds. *Bede's Ecclesiastical History of the English People.* Oxford: Clarendon, 1969.

Colish, Marcia L. "St. Anselm's Philosophy of Language Reconsidered." *Anselm Studies* 1 (1983): 113–23.

Collingwood, W. G. "Anglian and Danish Sculpture in the East Riding, with Addenda to the North Riding." *Yorkshire Archaeological Journal* 21 (1910): 254–302.

Conner, Patrick W. "ANSAXNET: Telecommunications for Anglo-Saxonists." *Old English Newsletter* 20.2 (1987): 25.

———. "The *Beowulf* Workstation: One Model of Computer-Assisted Literary Pedagogy." *Literary and Linguistic Computing* 6 (1991): 50–58.

———. "Beyond the ASPR: Electronic Editions of Old English Poetry." In *New Approaches to Editing Old English Verse*, edited by Sarah Larratt Keefer and Katherine O'Brien O'Keeffe, 109–26. Cambridge: D. S. Brewer, 1998.

Cook, Albert S., ed. *The Dream of the Rood: An Old English Poem Attributed to Cynewulf*. Oxford: Clarendon, 1905.

Coover, Robert. "The End of Books." *New York Times Book Review*, June 21, 1992, 23–25.

Cowdrey, H.E.J. "Towards an Interpretation of the Bayeux Tapestry." In Gameson, *Study*, 93–110.

Cramp, Rosemary. *Studies in Anglo-Saxon Sculpture*. London: Pindar, 1992.

Crang, Mike, Phil Crang, and Jon May, eds. *Virtual Geographies: Bodies, Space, and Relations*. London: Routledge, 1999.

Crawford, O.G.S. "Some Medieval Theories About the Nile." *Geographical Journal* 114 (1949): 6–29.

Crick, Julia. "The Art of the Unprinted: Transcription and English Antiquity in the Age of Print." In *The Uses of Script and Print, 1300–1700*, edited by Julia Crick and Alexandra Walsham, 116–34. Cambridge: Cambridge University Press, 2003.

Crone, G. R. *Maps and Their Makers: An Introduction to the History of Cartography*. London: Hutchinson, 1953.

Crone, G. R., E.M.J. Campbell, and R. A. Skelton. "Landmarks of British Cartography." *Geographical Journal* 128.4 (1962): 406–26.

Crosby, Alfred W. *The Measure of Reality: Quantification and Western Society, 1250–1600*. Cambridge: Cambridge University Press, 1997.

Cubbin, G. P., ed. *MS D*. Vol. 6 of *The Anglo-Saxon Chronicle: A Collaborative Edition*. Cambridge: D. S. Brewer, 1996.

Cyan Productions. *Myst*. Novato, Calif.: Brøderbund, 1994.

———. *Riven: The Sequel to Myst*. Novato, Calif.: Brøderbund, 1997.

Daly, Lowrie J. *Benedictine Monasticism: Its Formation and Development through the 12th Century*. New York: Sheed and Ward, 1965.

Darlington, R. R., and P. McGurk, eds. *The Chronicle of John of Worcester*. Translated by Jennifer Bray and P. McGurk. Vol. 2. Oxford: Clarendon, 1995.

Davies, P.C.W. *Space and Time in the Modern Universe*. Cambridge: Cambridge University Press, 1977.

Davis, R.H.C., and Marjorie Chibnall, eds. *The Gesta Guillelmi of William of Poitiers*. Oxford: Clarendon, 1998.

Dawson, Charles. "The Bayeux Tapestry in the Hands of 'Restorers' and How It Has Fared." *Antiquary* 43 (1907): 253–58, 288–92.

Deane, S. N., ed. and trans. *St. Anselm: Basic Writings*. 2nd ed. LaSalle, Ill.: Open Court, 1962.

Deegan, Marilyn, and Peter Robinson. "The Electronic Edition." In Szarmach and Scragg, *Editing of Old English*, 27–37.

Deibert, Ronald J. *Parchment, Printing, and Hypermedia: Communication in World Order Transformation*. New York: Columbia University Press, 1997.

Dekker, Kees. "'That Most Elaborate One of Fr. Junius': An Investigation of Francis Junius's Manuscript Old English Dictionary." In Graham, *Recovery of Old English*, 301–43.

De Landa, Manuel. "Virtual Environments and the Emergence of Synthetic Reason." In *Flame Wars: The Discourse of Cyberculture*, edited by Mark Dery, 263–85. Durham, N.C.: Duke University Press, 1994.

Delany, Paul, and George P. Landow, eds. *Hypermedia and Literary Studies*. Cambridge, Mass.: MIT Press, 1991.

Deleuze, Gilles. "Nomad Art: Space." In *The Deleuze Reader*, edited by Constantin V. Boundas, 165–72. New York: Columbia University Press, 1993.

Deleuze, Gilles, and Félix Guattari. *A Thousand Plateaus: Capitalism and Schizophrenia*. Translated by Brian Massumi. Minneapolis: University of Minnesota Press, 1987.

Denny, Norman, and Josephine Filmer-Sankey. *The Bayeux Tapestry: The Story of the Norman Conquest, 1066*. London: Collins, 1966.

Despres, Denise L. "Ecstatic Reading and Missionary Mysticism: *The Orcherd of Syon*." In *Prophets Abroad: The Reception of Continental Holy Women in Late-Medieval England*, edited by Rosalynn Voaden, 141–60. Cambridge: D. S. Brewer, 1996.

Destombes, Marcel, ed. *Mappemondes A.D. 1200–1500*. Catalogue préparé par la Commission des Cartes Anciennes de l'Union Géographique Internationale. Amsterdam: N. Israel, 1964.

De Villiers, J.A.J. "Famous Maps in the British Museum." *Geographical Journal* 44.2 (1914): 168–84.

Dibdin, Thomas Frognall. *A Bibliographical, Antiquarian and Picturesque Tour in France and Germany*. 2nd ed. 3 vols. London: Robert Jennings and John Major, 1829.

Dickey, William. "Poem Descending a Staircase: Hypertext and the Simultaneity of Experience." In Delany and Landow, *Hypermedia and Literary Studies*, 143–52.

Digby, George Wingfield. "Technique and Production." In Stenton, *The Bayeux Tapestry*, 37–55.

Digital Medievalist Project. <www.digitalmedievalist.org>.

Digital Michelangelo Project. <www.graphics.stanford.edu/projects/mich/>.

Doane, A. N. "Editing Old English Oral/Written Texts: Problems of Method." In Szarmach and Scragg, *Editing of Old English*, 125–45.

Dodwell, C. R. *Anglo-Saxon Art: A New Perspective*. Ithaca, N.Y.: Cornell University Press, 1982.

———. "The Bayeux Tapestry and the French Secular Epic." *Burlington Magazine* 108.764 (1966): 549–60.

Doel, Marcus A., and David B. Clarke. "Virtual Worlds: Simulation, Suppletion, S(ed)uction and Simulacra." In Crang, Crang, and May, *Virtual Geographies*, 261–83.

"Domesday 1986." <www.domesday1986.com>.

Donato, Eugenio. "Ending/Closure: On Derrida's Edging of Heidegger." *Yale French Studies* 67 (1984): 3–22.

Doss, Phillip. "Traditional Theory and Innovative Practice: The Electronic Editor as Poststructuralist Editor." In Finneran, *Literary Text in the Digital Age*, 213–24.

Douglas, David C. *William the Conqueror: The Norman Impact upon England.* Berkeley and Los Angeles: University of California Press, 1964.

Douglas, J. Yellowlees. *The End of Books—or Books without End? Reading Interactive Narratives.* Ann Arbor: University of Michigan Press, 2000.

Douglas, J. Yellowees, and Andrew Hargadon. "The Pleasures of Immersion and Interaction: Schemas, Scripts, and the Fifth Business." In Wardrip-Fruin and Harrigan, *First Person*, 192–206.

Driver, Martha W. "Medieval Manuscripts and Electronic Media: Observations on Future Possibilities." In Pearsall, *New Directions*, 53–64.

Duggan, Hoyt N. "Some Unrevolutionary Aspects of Computer Editing." In Finneran, *Literary Text in the Digital Age*, 77–98.

Eadmer of Canterbury. *The Life of St. Anselm, Archbishop of Canterbury.* Edited and translated by R. W. Southern. London: Thomas Nelson, 1962.

Eco, Umberto. *Travels in Hyperreality.* Translated by William Weaver. San Diego: Harcourt Brace Jovanovich, 1986.

Edgerton, Samuel Y., Jr. *The Heritage of Giotto's Geometry: Art and Science on the Eve of the Scientific Revolution.* Ithaca, N.Y.: Cornell University Press, 1991.

Edson, Evelyn. *Mapping Time and Space: How Medieval Mapmakers Viewed Their World.* London: British Library, 1997.

———. "The Oldest World Maps: Classical Sources of Three VIIIth Century Mappaemundi." *Ancient World* 24 (1993): 169–84.

———. "World Maps and Easter Tables: Medieval Maps in Context." *Imago Mundi* 48 (1996): 25–42.

Edwards, A.S.G. "Representing the Middle English Manuscript." In Pearsall, *New Directions*, 65–80.

Edwards, Edward, ed. *Liber Monasterii de Hyda: Comprising a Chronicle of the Affairs of England, from the Settlement of the Saxons to the Reign of King Canute, and a Chartulary of the Abbey of Hyde, in Hampshire, A.D. 455–1023.* Rolls Series 45. London: Longmans, 1886.

Eisenstein, Elizabeth L. *The Printing Press as an Agent of Change.* 2 vols. Cambridge: Cambridge University Press, 1980.

———. *The Printing Revolution in Early Modern Europe.* Cambridge: Cambridge University Press, 1984.

Englisch, Brigitte. *Ordo Orbis Terrae*. Berlin: Akademie, 2002.

Evans, Gillian R. *Anselm and a New Generation*. Oxford: Clarendon, 1980.

———. *Anselm and Talking About God*. Oxford: Clarendon, 1978.

———. "Mens Devota: The Literary Community of the Devotional Works of John of Fécamp and St. Anselm." *Medium Aevum* 48 (1974): 105–11.

Febvre, Lucien, and Henri-Jean Martin. *The Coming of the Book: The Impact of Printing, 1450–1800*. Translated by David Gerard. London: New Left Books, 1976.

Feinstein, Sandy. "Hypertextuality and Chaucer, or Re-Ordering the *Canterbury Tales* and Other Reader Prerogatives." In Gibson and Oviedo, *The Emerging Cyberculture*, 45–60.

Ferguson, Eugene S. "Leupold's 'Theatrum Machinarum': A Need and an Opportunity." *Technology and Culture* 12.1 (1971): 64–68.

Finneran, Richard J., ed. *The Literary Text in the Digital Age*. Ann Arbor: University of Michigan Press, 1996.

Finney, Andy. "Domesday." <www.atsf.co.uk/dottext/domesday.html>.

Fish, Stanley. *Is There a Text in This Class? The Authority of Interpretive Communities*. Cambridge, Mass.: Harvard University Press, 1980.

Flegg, Graham. *Numbers: Their History and Meaning*. New York: Schocken Books, 1983.

———, ed. *Numbers Through the Ages*. London: Macmillan, 1989.

Flint, Valerie I. J. *The Imaginative Landscape of Christopher Columbus*. Princeton, N.J.: Princeton University Press, 1992.

Foot, Sarah. "The Making of *Angelcynn*: English Identity before the Norman Conquest." *Transactions of the Royal Historical Society*, 6th ser., 6 (1996): 25–50.

Foucault, Michel. "Of Other Spaces." *Diacritics* 16 (1986): 22–27.

———. "What Is an Author?" Translated by Josué V. Harari. In *Textual Strategies: Perspectives in Post-Structuralist Criticism*, edited by Josué V. Harari, 141–60. Ithaca, N.Y.: Cornell University Press, 1979.

Fowke, Frank Rede. *The Bayeux Tapestry: A History and Description*. 2nd ed. London: George Bell, 1898.

Foxe, John. *Actes and Monuments of Matters Most Speciall and Memorable*. Edited by David G. Newcombe with Michael Pidd. CD-ROM. Oxford University Press for the British Academy, 2001.

Foys, Martin K. "Above the Word, Beyond the Page: The Past and Present Dilemma of the Bayeux Tapestry." *Envoi* 8.3 (1999): 87–103.

———. *The Digital Edition of the Bayeux Tapestry*. Leicester, U.K.: SDE/Boydell and Brewer, 2003.

———. "Hypertextile Scholarship: Digitally Editing the Bayeux Tapestry." *Documentary Editing* 23 (2001): 34–43.

———. "New Media and the Nunburnholme Cross." *Papers from the* Halig Rod—Sanctus Crucis *Conferences*. Edited by Karen Jolly, Sarah Keefer, and Catherine Karkov. Morgantown: West Virginia University Press, forthcoming.

———. "The Virtual Reality of the Anglo-Saxon *Mappamundi.*" *Literature Compass* 1, ME 016 (2004): 1–14.

Frank, Joseph. *The Widening Gyre: Crisis and Mastery in Modern Literature.* 1963. Bloomington: Indiana University Press, 1968.

Frantzen, Allen J. "By the Numbers: Anglo-Saxon Scholarship at the Century's End." In Pulsiano and Treharne, *Companion,* 472–95.

———. *Desire for Origins: New Language, Old English, and Teaching the Tradition.* New Brunswick, N.J.: Rutgers University Press, 1990.

———. *King Alfred.* Boston: Twayne, 1986.

———. *Seafarer: A Hypermedia Model for the Study of Anglo-Saxon Culture.* <www. Anglo-Saxon.net> and <www.wheatonma.edu/kacc/LTLC/reports/Drout.html>.

Freeman, Edward A. *The History of the Norman Conquest of England.* 2nd ed. 6 vols. Oxford: Clarendon, 1867–79.

Friedman, John Block. *The Monstrous Races in Medieval Art and Thought.* Cambridge, Mass.: Harvard University Press, 1981.

Fry, Timothy, ed. *RB 1980: The Rule of St. Benedict in Latin and English with Notes.* Collegeville, Minn.: Liturgical Press, 1981.

Gaggi, Silvio. *From Text to Hypertext: Decentering the Subject in Fiction, Film, the Visual Arts, and Electronic Media.* Philadelphia: University of Pennsylvania Press, 1997.

Galbraith, V. H., ed. *The St. Alban's Chronicle, 1406–1420, Edited from Bodley MS 462.* Oxford: Clarendon, 1937.

Gameson, Richard. "The Origin, Art, and Message of the Bayeux Tapestry." In *Study,* 157–211.

———, ed. *The Study of the Bayeux Tapestry.* Rochester, N.Y.: Boydell, 1997.

Garnett, George. "Coronation and Propaganda: Some Implications of the Norman Claim to the Throne of England in 1066." *Transactions of the Royal Historical Society,* 5th ser., 36 (1986): 91–116.

Gellner, Ernest. *Nations and Nationalism.* Ithaca, N.Y.: Cornell University Press, 1983.

Gellrich, Jesse. *The Idea of the Book in the Middle Ages: Language Theory, Mythology, and Fiction.* Ithaca, N.Y.: Cornell University Press, 1985.

Gerlach, John. *Toward the End: Closure and Structure in the American Short Story.* Tuscaloosa: University of Alabama Press, 1985.

Gibbs-Smith, Charles H. *The Bayeux Tapestry.* London: Phaidon, 1973.

———. "Notes on the Plates." In Stenton, *The Bayeux Tapestry,* 162–76.

Gibson, Stephanie B. "Literacy, Paradigm, and Paradox: An Introduction." In Gibson and Oviedo, *The Emerging Cyberculture,* 1–20.

Gibson, Stephanie B., and Ollie O. Oviedo, eds. *The Emerging Cyberculture: Literacy, Paradigm, and Paradox.* Cresskill, N.J.: Hampton, 2000.

Gildas. *The Ruin of Britain and Other Works.* Edited and translated by Michael Winterbottom. London: Phillimore, 1978.

Gilles, Sealy. "Territorial Interpolations in the Old English Orosius." In Tomasch and Gilles, *Text and Territory,* 79–96.

Gillingham, John. "William the Bastard at War." *The Battle of Hastings: Sources and Interpretations*, edited by Stephen Morillo, 95–112. Woodbridge, U.K.: Boydell, 1996.

Godden, Malcolm. "Old English." In *Editing Medieval Texts: English, French, and Latin Written in England*, edited by A. G. Riggs, 9–33. Toronto: University of Toronto Press, 1977.

Goldschmidt, E. Ph. *Medieval Texts and Their First Appearance in Print.* London: Bibliographical Society at the University Press, Oxford, 1943.

Google. "About Google Book Search." <books.google.com/intl/en/googlebooks/about.html>. Accessed March 2006.

———. "All the World's Books at Your Fingertips." <books.google.com/googlebooks/vision.html>. Accessed March 2006.

Gordon, B. L. "Sacred Directions, Orientation and the Top of the Map." *History of Religions* 10 (1971): 211–27.

Graham, Timothy. "Anglo-Saxon Studies: Sixteenth to Eighteenth Centuries." In Pulsiano and Treharne, *Companion*, 415–33.

———. "John Joscelyn, Pioneer of Old English Lexicography." In *The Recovery of Old English*, 83–140.

———, ed. *The Recovery of Old English: Anglo-Saxon Studies in the Sixteenth and Seventeenth Centuries.* Kalamazoo, Mich.: Medieval Institute Publications, 2000.

Grape, Wolfgang. *The Bayeux Tapestry: Monument to a Norman Triumph.* Translated by David Britt. Munich: Prestel, 1994.

Green, D. H. "Orality and Reading: The State of Research in Medieval Studies." *Speculum* 65.2 (1990): 267–80.

Greenblatt, Stephen. "Towards a Poetics of Culture." In *The New Historicism*, edited by H. Aram Veeser, 1–14. New York: Routledge, 1989.

Griffiths, Jeremy, and Derek Pearsall, eds. *Book Production and Publishing in Britain, 1375–1475.* Cambridge: Cambridge University Press, 1989.

Gurney, Hudson. "Observations on the Bayeux Tapestry." *Archaeologia* 18 (1817): 359–70.

H. D. "Further Remarks on the Bayeux Tapestry." *Gentleman's Magazine*, 1st ser., 74 (1804): 313–15.

Hadley, D. M. "'And They Proceeded to Plough and to Support Themselves': The Scandinavian Settlement of England." *Anglo-Norman Studies* 19 (1997): 69–96.

———. "In Search of the Vikings: The Problems and the Possibilities of Interdisciplinary Approaches." In *Vikings and the Danelaw: Select Papers from the Proceedings of the Thirteenth Viking Congress, Nottingham and York, 21–30 August 1997*, edited by James Graham-Campbell et al., 13–30. Oxford: Oxbow, 2001.

Hall, J. R. "Anglo-Saxon Studies in the Nineteenth Century: England, Denmark, America." In Pulsiano and Treharne, *Companion*, 434–54.

Hall, Thomas N. "Prophetic Vision in *The Dream of the Rood*." In *Studies Presented in Honor of Helen Damico*, edited by Catherine Karkov. Kalamazoo, Mich.: Medieval Institute Publications, forthcoming.

Hammond, N.G.L., and H. H. Scullard, eds. *Oxford Classical Dictionary.* 2nd ed. Oxford: Clarendon, 1970.

Hanawalt, Barbara A., and Michal Kobialka, eds. *Medieval Practices of Space.* Minneapolis: University of Minnesota Press, 2000.

Härke, Heinrich. "Kings and Warriors: Population and Landscape from Post-Roman to Norman Britain." In *The Peopling of Britain: The Shaping of a Human Landscape,* edited by Paul Slack and Ryk Ward, 145–76. Oxford: Oxford University Press, 2002.

Harley, J. B. "The Iconology of Early Maps." In *Imago et Mensura Mundi,* edited by Carla Clivio Marzoli, 1:29–38. Rome: Instituto della Enciclopedia Italiana, 1985.

———. *The New Nature of Maps.* Baltimore: Johns Hopkins University Press, 2001.

Harley, J. B., and David Woodward. "Concluding Remarks." In *History of Cartography,* 1:502–10.

———, eds. *History of Cartography.* Vol. 1, *Cartography in Prehistoric, Ancient, and Medieval Europe and the Mediterranean.* Chicago: University of Chicago Press, 1987.

Harpold, Terence. "Conclusions." In Landow, *Hyper/Text/Theory,* 189–222.

Harris, Stephen J. "The Alfredian World History and Anglo-Saxon Identity." *Journal of English and Germanic Philology* 100 (2001): 482–510.

Harvey, P.D.A. *Mappa Mundi: The Hereford World Map.* London: British Library, 1996.

———. *Medieval Maps.* London: British Library, 1991.

———. "Medieval Maps: An Introduction." In Harley and Woodward, *History of Cartography,* 1:283–85.

Hawkes, Jane. "Reading Stone." In Karkov and Orton, *Theorizing Anglo-Saxon Stone Sculpture,* 5–30.

Heim, Michael. *Virtual Realism.* Oxford: Oxford University Press, 1998.

Henry, D. P. *The Logic of Saint Anselm.* Oxford: Clarendon, 1967.

———. "St. Anselm and the Linguistic Disciplines." *Anselm Studies* 2 (1988): 319–32.

Henry of Huntingdon. *Historia Anglorum: The History of the English People.* Edited and translated by Diana Greenway. Oxford: Clarendon, 1996.

Heron, Alasdair. "Anselm and the *Filioque*: A Responsio Pro Graecis." *Anselm Studies* 1 (1983): 159–64.

———. "'Who Proceedeth from the Father and the Son': The Problem of the *Filioque.*" *Scottish Journal of Theology* 24 (1971): 149–66.

Herren, Michael W. "The Transmission and Reception of Graeco-Roman Mythology in Anglo-Saxon England, 670–800." *Anglo-Saxon England* 27 (1998): 87–103.

Herz, J. C. *Joystick Nation: How Videogames Ate Our Quarters, Won Our Hearts, and Rewired Our Minds.* Boston: Little, Brown, 1997.

Higgins, Iain Macleod. "Defining the Earth's Center in a Medieval 'Multi-Text': Jerusalem in the *Book of John Mandeville.*" In Tomasch and Gilles, *Text and Territory,* 29–53.

Hill, David. *An Atlas of Anglo-Saxon England.* Oxford: Basil Blackwell, 1981.

———. "The Bayeux Tapestry: The Establishment of a Text." In Bouet, Levy, and Neveux, *The Bayeux Tapestry*, 383–99.

Hillis, Ken. *Digital Sensations: Space, Identity and Embodiment in Virtual Reality.* Minneapolis: University of Minnesota Press, 1999.

Hobart, Michael E., and Zachary S. Schiffman. *Information Ages: Literacy, Numeracy, and the Computer Revolution.* Baltimore: Johns Hopkins University Press, 1998.

Hodgkiss, Alan G. *Understanding Maps: A Systematic History of Their Use and Development.* Folkstone, U.K.: Dawson, 1981.

Hodgson, Phyllis. "The *Orcherd of Syon* and the English Mystical Tradition." *Proceedings of the British Academy* 50 (1964): 229–49.

Hodgson, Phyllis, and Gabriel M. Liegey, eds. *The Orcherd of Syon.* EETS, o.s., 258. London: Oxford University Press, 1966.

Holden, A. J., ed. *Le "Roman de Rou" de Wace.* 2 vols. Paris: A. & J. Picard, 1970.

Holmes, Martin R. Review of *The Bayeux Tapestry: A Comprehensive Survey*, edited by Frank Stenton. *Medieval Archaeology* 1 (1957): 178–82.

Hooke, Della. "The Mid-Late Anglo-Saxon Period: Settlement and Land Use." In Hooke and Burnell, *Landscape and Settlement*, 95–114.

Hooke, Della, and Simon Burnell, eds. *Landscape and Settlement in Britain, AD 400–1066.* Exeter: Exeter University Press, 1995.

Hopkins, Jasper. *A Companion to the Study of St. Anselm.* Minneapolis: University of Minnesota Press, 1972.

Howe, Nicholas. *An Angle on This Earth: Sense of Place in Anglo-Saxon England.* Toller Memorial Lecture. Manchester: Manchester Study for Anglo-Saxon Studies, 2000.

———. "The Landscape of Anglo-Saxon England." In *Inventing Medieval Landscapes: Senses of Place in Western Europe*, edited by John Howe and Michael Wolfe, 91–112. Gainesville: University Press of Florida, 2002.

———. *Migration and Mythmaking in Anglo-Saxon England.* New Haven, Conn.: Yale University Press, 1989.

———. "The New Millennium." In Pulsiano and Treharne, *Companion*, 496–505.

———. North Looking South: The Anglo-Saxon Construction of Geographical Identity. Paper presented at the International Society of Anglo-Saxonists conference, Helsinki, August 2001.

Hulme, T. E. *Speculations: Essays on Humanism and the Philosophy of Art.* Edited by Herbert Read. 2nd ed. London: Routledge and Kegan Paul, 1936.

Hulme, William H. "The Old English Gospel of Nicodemus." *Modern Philology* 1 (1903–4): 579–614.

Hult, David. "'Ci falt la geste': Scribal Closure in the Oxford Roland." *Modern Language Notes* 97 (1982): 890–905.

———, ed. *Concepts of Closure.* Yale French Studies 67. New Haven, Conn.: Yale University Press, 1984.

Hunter, Michael. "The Sense of the Past in Anglo-Saxon England." *Anglo-Saxon England* 3 (1974): 29–50.

Huppé, Bernard F. *The Web of Words: Structural Analyses of the Old English Poems Vainglory, the Wonder of Creation, the Dream of the Rood, and Judith*. Albany: State University of New York Press, 1970.

Ifrah, Georges. *From One to Zero: A Universal History of Numbers*. Translated by Lowell Bair. New York: Viking, 1985.

Imken, Otto. "The Convergence of Virtual and Actual in the Global Matrix: Artificial Life, Geo-Economics and Psychogeography." In Crang, Crang, and May, *Virtual Geographies*, 92–106.

Irvine, Martin. "Anglo-Saxon Literary Theory Exemplified in Old English Poems: Interpreting the Cross in *The Dream of the Rood* and *Elene*." In *Old English Shorter Poems: Basic Readings*, edited by Katherine O'Brien O'Keeffe, 31–64. New York: Garland, 1994.

Ivins, William Mills. *Prints and Visual Communication*. Cambridge, Mass.: Harvard University Press, 1953.

Jameson, Frederic. *Postmodernism, or, The Cultural Logic of Late Capitalism*. Durham, N.C.: Duke University Press, 1991.

Johnson, David F. "Digitizing the Middle Ages." *Literature Compass* 1, ME 041 (2004): 1–12.

———. "Old English Religious Poetry: *Christ and Satan* and *The Dream of the Rood*." In *Companion to Old English Poetry*, edited by Henk Aertsen and Rolf H. Bremmer Jr., 159–87. Amsterdam: Vrije Universiteit Press, 1994.

Joyce, Michael. *Afternoon: A Story*. 1987. CD. Watertown, Mass: Eastgate Systems, 2001.

———. "The Lingering Errantness of Place, or Library as Library." In Gibson and Oviedo, *The Emerging Cyberculture*, 151–64.

JSTOR. <www.jstor.org>.

Karkov, Catherine E. "Naming and Renaming: The Inscription of Gender in Anglo-Saxon Sculpture." In Karkov and Orton, *Theorizing Anglo-Saxon Stone Sculpture*, 31–64.

Karkov, Catherine E., and Fred Orton, eds. *Theorizing Anglo-Saxon Stone Sculpture*. Morgantown: West Virginia University Press, 2003.

Keats-Rohan, K.S.B. "William I and the Breton Contingent in the Non-Norman Conquest, 1060–1087." *Anglo-Norman Studies* 13 (1991): 157–72.

Kemble, John M., ed. *The Anglo-Saxon Poems of Beowulf, The Travellers Song, and the Battle of Finnes-Burh*. 2 vols. London: Pickering, 1833.

Ker, N. R. *Catalogue of Manuscripts Containing Anglo-Saxon*. Oxford: Clarendon, 1957.

Kermode, Frank. *The Sense of an Ending*. New York: Oxford University Press, 1967.

Kern, Stephen. *The Culture of Time and Space, 1880–1918*. Cambridge, Mass.: Harvard University Press, 1983.

Kienzler, Klaus. *International Bibliography, Anselm of Canterbury*. Lewiston, N.Y.: Edwin Mellen, 1999.

Kiernan, Kevin. "Alfred the Great's Burnt Boethius." In Bornstein and Tinkle, *Iconic Page*, 7–32.

———, ed. *Electronic Beowulf*. Ann Arbor: University of Michigan Press, 1999.

———. *Electronic Production and Presentation Technology* (EPPT). <http://beowulf. engl.uky.edu/~eft/eppt-trial/EPPT-TrialProjects.htm>.

Kimble, George H. T. *Geography in the Middle Ages*. 1938. New York: Russell and Russell, 1968.

King, Geoff. *Mapping Reality: An Exploration of Cultural Cartographies*. London: Macmillan, 1996.

Kleinman, Neil. "The Gutenberg Promise: Stones, Mirrors or a Printing Press." In Gibson and Oviedo, *The Emerging Cyberculture*, 61–98.

Kleinschmidt, Harald. *Understanding the Middle Ages: The Transformation of Ideas and Attitudes in the Middle Age*. Woodbridge, U.K.: Boydell, 2000.

Kline, Naomi Reed. *Maps of Medieval Thought: The Hereford Paradigm*. Woodbridge, U.K.: Boydell, 2001.

Kobialka, Michal. "Staging Place/Space in the Eleventh-Century Monastic Practices." In Hanawalt and Kobialka, *Medieval Practices of Space*, 128–48.

Kolodny, Annette. "Dancing through the Minefield: Some Observations on the Theory, Practice, and Politics of a Feminist Literary Criticism." In *The New Feminist Criticism: Essays on Women, Literature, and Theory*, edited by Elaine Showalter, 144–67. New York: Pantheon, 1985.

Koslin, Desirée. "Turning Time in the Bayeux Embroidery." *Textile and Text* 13.1 (1990): 28–45.

Krapp, George Philip, ed. *The Vercelli Book*. New York: Columbia University Press, 1932.

Krapp, George Philip, and Elliott Van Kirk Dobbie, eds. *The Exeter Book*. New York: Columbia University Press, 1936.

Kupfer, Marcia. "Medieval World Maps: Embedded Images, Interpretative Frames." *Word and Image* 10 (1994): 262–88.

Landow, George P., ed. *Hyper/Text/Theory*. Baltimore: Johns Hopkins University Press, 1994.

———. *Hypertext 2.0*. Rev. ed. Baltimore: Johns Hopkins University Press, 1997.

———. *Hypertext 3.0: Critical Theory and New Media in an Era of Globalization*. Baltimore: Johns Hopkins University Press, 2006.

———. "The Rhetoric of Hypermedia: Some Rules for Authors." In Delany and Landow, *Hypermedia and Literary Studies*, 81–103.

———. "What's a Critic to Do? Critical Theory in the Age of Hypertext." In *Hyper/Text/Theory*, 1–48.

Lang, James T. "Anglo-Scandinavian Sculpture in Yorkshire." In *Viking Age York and the North*, edited by R. A. Hall, 11–20. London: Council for British Archaeology, 1978.

———. *Corpus of Anglo-Saxon Stone Sculpture*. Vol. 3, *York and Eastern Yorkshire*. Oxford: Oxford University Press, 1991.

———. "Pre-Conquest Sculpture in Eastern Yorkshire." In *Medieval Art and Architecture in the East Riding of Yorkshire*, edited by Christopher Wilson, 1–8. Conference Transactions 9 (1983). London: British Archaeological Association, 1989.

———. "The Sculptors of the Nunburnholme Cross." *Archaeological Journal* 133 (1976): 75–94.

———. "Sigurd and Weland in Pre-Conquest Carving from Northern England." *Yorkshire Archaeological Journal* 48 (1976): 83–94.

Langer, Susanne K. *Feeling and Form: A Theory of Art*. New York: Scribners, 1953.

———. *Philosophy in a New Key: A Study in the Symbolism of Reason, Rite, and Art*. Cambridge, Mass.: Harvard University Press, 1942.

Lanham, Richard. *The Electronic Word: Democracy, Technology and the Arts*. Chicago: University of Chicago Press, 1993.

Lapidge, Michael. "On the Emendation of Texts." In Szarmach and Scragg, *Editing of Old English*, 53–67.

Laurel, Brenda. *Computers as Theatre*. Reading, Mass.: Addison-Wesley, 1993.

Lawton, David. "The Surveying Subject and the 'Whole World' of Belief: Three Case Studies." *New Medieval Literatures* 4 (2001): 9–38.

Lee, Stuart. "Oxford, Bodleian Library, MS Laud Misc. 381: William L'Isle, Ælfric, and the *Ancrene Wisse*." In Graham, *Recovery of Old English*, 207–42.

Lees, Claire. "Whose Text Is It Anyway? Contexts for Editing Old English Prose." In Szarmach and Scragg, *Editing of Old English*, 97–123.

Lefebvre, Henri. *The Production of Space*. Translated by Donald Nicholson-Smith. Oxford: Blackwell, 1991.

Lefèvre, P. "Un reliquaire du XIe siècle conservé à la cathédrale Saint-Michel à Bruxelles." *Bulletin de la Classe des Beaux-Arts, Académie Royale de Belgique, Cl. Des Beaux Arts* 49 (1969–70), 224–45.

Le Goff, Jacques. *The Birth of Purgatory*. Translated by Arthur Goldhammer. Chicago: University of Chicago Press, 1984.

Lejard, André. *The Bayeux Tapestry*. Paris: Vendôme, 1947.

Lerer, Seth. "The Anglo-Saxon Pindar: Old English Scholarship and Augustan Criticism in George Hickes's *Thesaurus*." *Modern Philology* 99.1 (2001): 26–65.

———. "Medieval Literature and Early Modern Readers: Cambridge University Library Sel. 5.51–5.63." *Papers of the Bibliographical Society of America* 97.3 (2003): 311–32.

Lesieur, Thierry. "Lisible et visible dans la tapisserie de Bayeux ou la stratégie de l'ambiguïté." *Licorne* 23 (1992): 173–82.

Lethaby, William Richard. "The Perjury at Bayeux." *Archaeological Journal* 74 (1917): 136–38.

Leupold, Jacob. *Theatrum arithmetico-geometricum*. Leipzig, 1727.

Lévy, Pierre. *Becoming Virtual: Reality in the Digital Age*. Translated by Robert Bononno. New York: Plenum Trade, 1998.

Lewis, Suzanne. *The Rhetoric of Power in the Bayeux Tapestry*. Cambridge: Cambridge University Press, 1999.

Light, Jennifer. "From City Space to Cyberspace." In Crang, Crang, and May, *Virtual Geographies*, 109–30.

Linderski, Jerzy. "Alfred the Great and the Tradition of Ancient Geography." *Speculum* 39 (1964): 434–39.

Lindsay, W. M., ed. *Isidori Hispalensis Episcopi Etymologiarum Sive Originum*. Vol. 2. Oxford: Clarendon, 1911.

L'Isle, William, ed. *A Saxon Treatise Concerning the Old and New Testament*, by Ælfric, abbot of Eynsham. London, 1623.

Lockett, W. G. Jacob Leupold as Hydraulic Engineer: A Study of His Theatrum Machinarum. Ph.D diss., University of Toronto, 1994.

Lowe, Kathryn A. "'The Oracle of His Countrey'? William Somner, *Gavelkind*, and Lexicography in the Seventeenth and Eighteenth Centuries." In Graham, *Recovery of Old English*, 281–300.

Lowell, Edward J. "The Bayeux Tapestry." *Scribner's Magazine* 1 (1887): 333–47.

Loyn, H. R. *The Governance of Anglo-Saxon England, 500–1087*. Stanford, Calif.: Stanford University Press, 1984.

Lucas, Peter J. "From Politics to Practicalities: Printing Anglo-Saxon in the Context of Seventeenth-Century Scholarship." *Library*, 7th ser., 4.1 (2003): 28–48.

———. "A Testimonye of Verye Ancient Tyme? Some Manuscript Models for the Parkerian Anglo-Saxon Type-Designs." In *Of the Making of Books: Medieval Manuscripts, Their Scribes and Readers; Essays Presented to M. B. Parkes*, edited by P. R. Robinson and Rivkah Zim, 147–90. Aldershot, U.K.: Ashgate, 1997.

Lund, Niels, ed. *Two Voyagers at the Court of King Alfred*. Translated by Christine E. Fell. York: William Sessions, 1984.

Lutz, Angelika. "The Study of the Anglo-Saxon Chronicle in the Seventeenth Century and the Establishment of Old English Studies in the Universities." In Graham, *Recovery of Old English*, 1–82.

Machan, Tim William. "Chaucer's Poetry, Versioning, and Hypertext." *Philological Quarterly* 73 (1994): 299–316.

Maclagan, Eric. *The Bayeux Tapestry*. Rev. ed. London: Penguin, 1949.

MacLean, Douglas. "The Date of the Ruthwell Cross." In Cassidy, *The Ruthwell Cross*, 49–70.

Malone, Kemp. "King Alfred's North: A Study in Mediaeval Geography." *Speculum* 5 (1930): 139–67.

Manovich, Lev. *The Language of New Media*. Cambridge, Mass.: MIT Press, 2001.

———. "New Media from Borges to HTML." In Wardrip-Fruin and Montfort, *The New Media Reader*, 13–25.

Martin, Ernst. *The Calculating Machines (Die Rechnenmaschinen): Their History and Development*. Translated and edited by Peggy Aldrich Kidwell and Michael R. Williams. Charles Babbage Institute Reprint Series for the History of Computing, 16. Cambridge, Mass.: MIT Press, 1992.

McArthur, Tom. *Worlds of Reference: Lexicography, Learning and Language from the Clay Tablet to the Computer*. Cambridge: Cambridge University Press, 1986.

McCloud, Scott. *Understanding Comics*. Northhampton, Mass.: Kitchen Sink Press, 1993.

McGann, Jerome J. "The Rationale of Hypertext." In Sutherland, *Electronic Text*, 19–46.

———. *The Textual Condition*. Princeton, N.J.: Princeton University Press, 1991.

———. "What Is Critical Editing?" *Text* 5 (1991): 15–29.

McGerr, Rosemarie P. "Medieval Concepts of Literary Closure: Theory and Practice." *Exemplaria* 1.1 (1989): 149–79.

McGillivray, Murray. "Towards a Post-Critical Edition: Theory, Hypertext, and the Presentation of Middle English Works." *Text* 7 (1994): 175–99.

McGurk, Patrick, D. N. Dumville, Malcolm R. Godden, and Ann Knock, eds. *An Eleventh-Century Anglo-Saxon Illustrated Miscellany: British Library Cotton Tiberius B.V, Part 1*. Copenhagen: Rosenkilde and Bagger, 1983.

McKie, Robin, and Vanessa Thorpe. "Digital Domesday Book Lasts 15 Years Not 1000." *Observer*, March 3, 2002.

McKitterick, David. *Print, Manuscript, and the Search for Order, 1450–1830*. Cambridge: Cambridge University Press, 2003.

McLuhan, Marshall. *The Gutenberg Galaxy: The Making of Typographic Man*. Toronto: University of Toronto Press, 1962.

———. *Understanding Media: The Extensions of Man*. New York: McGraw-Hill, 1964.

Messent, Jan. *The Bayeux Tapestry Embroiderers' Story*. Thirsk: Madeira Threads, 1997.

Migne, Jacques-Paul. *Patrologia Latina Database*. <pld.chadwyck.com> and/or CD-ROM.

Miller, D. A. *Narrative and Its Discontents: Problems of Closure in the Traditional Novel*. Princeton, N.J.: Princeton University Press, 1981.

Miller, J. Hillis. "The Problematic of Ending in Narrative." *Nineteenth-Century Fiction* 33 (1978) 3–7.

Miller, Konrad. *Mappaemundi: Die ältesten Weltkarten*. 6 vols. Stuttgart: J. Roth, 1895–98.

Mitchell, Bruce. "The Dangers of Disguise: Old English Texts in Modern Punctuation." *Review of English Studies*, n.s., 31 (1980): 385–413.

———. *An Invitation to Old English and Anglo-Saxon England*. Oxford: Blackwell, 1995.

Mitchell, Stephen. *Anatolia: Land, Men, and Gods in Asia Minor*. 2 vols. Oxford: Clarendon, 1993.

Mitchell, W.J.T. "Spatial Form in Literature: Toward a General Theory." *Critical Inquiry* 6 (1980): 539–67.

Montfaucon, Bernard de. "La conquête de l'Angleterre par Guillaume le Bâtard, duc de Normandie, dit le Conquérant." In *Les monumens de la monarchie françoise*, vol. 2, plates I–IX. Paris: Gandouin et Giffart, 1730.

Montfort, Nick. "Time Frames." In Wardrip-Fruin and Montfort, *The New Media Reader*, 711.

Moretti, Franco. *Atlas of the European Novel: 1800–1900*. London: Verso, 1998.

Morris, C. D. "Northumbria and the Viking Settlement: The Evidence for Land-Holding." *Archaeologia Aeliana* 5 (1977): 81–103.

Morris, M.C.F. *Nunburnholme: Its History and Antiquities*. London: Henry Frowde, 1907.

Moulthrop, Stuart. "Reading from the Map: Metonymy and Metaphor in the Fiction of Forking Paths." In Delany and Landow, *Hypermedia and Literary Studies*, 119–32.

———. "You Say You Want a Revolution? Hypertext and the Laws of Media." In *Essays in Postmodern Culture*, edited by Eyal Amiran and John Unsworth, 69–97. Oxford: Oxford University Press, 1993.

Musset, Lucien. *The Bayeux Tapestry*. Translated by Richard Rex. Woodbridge: Boydell, 2005.

Mynors, R.A.B., ed. and trans. *Gesta Regum Anglorum: The History of the English Kings*, by William of Malmesbury. 2 vols. Completed by R. M. Thomson and M. Winterbottom. Oxford: Clarendon, 1998–99.

Naimark, Michael. "Aspen Movie Map." <www.naimark.net/projects/aspen.html>.

Napier, Arthur, ed. *Wulfstan: Sammlung der ihm zugeschriebenen Homilien nebst Untersuchungen über ihre Echtheit*. Vol. 1, *Text und Varianten*. Berlin: Weidmann, 1883.

National Endowment for the Humanities. "Summer Stipends Awards Program Guidelines." <www.neh.gov/grants/guidelines/stipends.html>.

Negroponte, Nicholas. *Being Digital*. New York: Vintage, 1995.

Nelson, Janet L. "The Rites of the Conqueror." In *Politics and Ritual in Early Medieval Europe*, 375–401. London: Hambledon, 1986.

Nelson, Theodore. *Literary Machines 93.1*. Sausalito, Calif.: Mindeful Press, 1993.

Neveux, François. *The Bayeux Tapestry*. Translated by Angela Moyon. Paris: Jean-Paul Gisserot, 1995.

Newton, A. P. "The Conception of the World in the Middle Ages." In *Travel and Travellers of the Middle Ages*, 1–18. London: K. Paul, Trench, Trubner, 1926.

Nichols, Stephen J. "Philology and Its Discontents." In *The Future of the Middle Ages: Medieval Literature in the 1990s*, edited by William D. Paden, 113–41. Gainesville: University Press of Florida, 1994.

———. "Philology in a Manuscript Culture." *Speculum* 65 (1990): 1–10.

Novak, Marcos. "Liquid Architectures in Cyberspace." In Benedikt, *Cyberspace*, 225–54.

Noxon, Gerald. "The Bayeux Tapestry." *Journal of the Society of Cinematologists* 7 (1967): 29–35.

Nunes, Mark. "Virtual Topographies: Smooth and Striated Cyberspace." In *Cyberspace Textuality: Computer Technology and Literary Theory*, edited by Marie-Laure Ryan, 61–77. Bloomington: Indiana University Press, 1999.

Ó Carragáin, Éamonn. *Ritual and the Rood: Liturgical Images and the Old English poems of the Dream of the Rood Tradition*. London and Toronto: British Library and University of Toronto Press, 2005.

———. "The Ruthwell Crucifixion Poem in Its Iconographic and Liturgical Contexts." *Peritia* 6–7 (1987–88): 1–71.

O'Donnell, Daniel Paul. "The Doomsday Machine, or, 'If you build it, will they still come ten years from now?': What medievalists working in digital media can do to ensure the longevity of their research." *Heroic Age* 7 (2004). <www.mun.ca/mst/heroicage/issues/7/ecolumn.html>.

Oger, Brigitte. "The Bayeux Tapestry: Results of the Scientific Tests (1982–1983)." In Bouet, Levy, and Neveux, *The Bayeux Tapestry*, 117–23.

O'Keeffe, Katherine O'Brien. "Editing and the Material Text." In Szarmach and Scragg, *Editing of Old English*, 147–54.

———. "The Geographic List of *Solomon and Saturn II*." *Anglo-Saxon England* 20 (1991): 123–41.

———. *Visible Song: Transitional Literacy in Old English Verse*. Cambridge: Cambridge University Press, 1990.

Old English Newsletter. "*Circolwyrde*: Electronic Resources for Anglo-Saxon Studies." Annual. <www.oenewsletter.org/OEN/links.php>.

Ong, Walter J. *Orality and Literacy: The Technologizing of the Word*. London: Methuen, 1982.

Orosius, Paulus. *Pauli Orosii Historiarum Adversum Paganos Libri VII*. Edited by Karl Zangemeister. 1882. New York: Johnson Reprint, 1966.

———. *Seven Books of History against the Pagans: The Apology of Paulus Orosius*. Translated by Irving Woodworth Raymond. New York: Columbia University Press, 1936.

Ortenberg, Veronica. "Archbishop Sigeric's Journey to Rome in 990." *Anglo-Saxon England* 19 (1990): 197–246.

Orton, Fred. "Northumbrian Identity in the Eighth Century: The Ruthwell and Bewcastle Monuments; Style, Classification, Class, and the Form of Ideology." *Journal of Medieval and Early Modern Studies* 34.1 (2004): 95–145.

———. "Rethinking the Ruthwell and Bewcastle Monuments: Some Strictures on Similarity; Some Questions of History." In Karkov and Orton, *Theorizing Anglo-Saxon Stone Sculpture*, 65–92.

———. Rethinking the Ruthwell Monument: Interpretation and Overinterpretation; Fragments and Critique; Tradition and History; Tongues and Sockets . . . Again. Lecture, University of London, March 2002.

Owen-Crocker, Gale. "Telling a Tale: Narrative Techniques in the Bayeux Tapestry and the Old English Epic Beowulf." In *Medieval Art: Recent Perspectives; A Memorial Tribute to C. R. Dodwell*, edited by Gale R. Owen-Crocker and Timothy Graham, 40–60. Manchester: Manchester University Press, 1998.

Pächt, Otto. "The Illustrations of St. Anselm's Prayers and Meditations." *Journal of the Warburg and Courtauld Institutes* 19 (1956): 68–83.

Parisse, Michel. *The Bayeux Tapestry*. English edition translated by William Courtney. Paris: Denoël, 1983.

Parkes, M. B. *Pause and Effect: An Introduction to the History of Punctuation in the West.* Berkeley and Los Angeles: University of California Press, 1993.

Pasternack, Carol Braun. "Stylistic Disjunctions in *The Dream of the Rood*." *Anglo-Saxon England* 13 (1984): 167–86.

———. *The Textuality of Old English Poetry.* Cambridge: Cambridge University Press, 1995.

Patterson, Lee. *Negotiating the Past.* Madison: University of Wisconsin Press, 1987.

Pattison, I. R. "The Nunburnholme Cross and Anglo-Danish Sculpture in York." *Archaeologia* 104 (1973): 209–34.

Pearsall, Derek, ed. *New Directions in Later Medieval Manuscript Studies.* Woodbridge, U.K.: Boydell Press, York Medieval Press, 2000.

———, ed. *Studies in the Vernon Manuscript.* Cambridge: D. S. Brewer, 1990.

Pilgrim, Mark. "What Is RSS?" <www.xml.com/pub/a/2002/12/18/dive-into-xml.html>.

Piper, Karen. *Cartographic Fictions: Maps, Race, and Identity.* New Brunswick, N.J.: Rutgers University Press, 2002.

Plumer, Danielle Cunniff. "The Construction of Structure in the Earliest Editions of Old English Poetry." In Graham, *Recovery of Old English*, 243–79.

Poole, Steven. *Trigger Happy: Videogames and the Entertainment Revolution.* New York: Arcade, 2000.

Pope, John C., ed. *Eight Old English Poems.* 3rd ed. Prepared by R. D. Fulk. New York: W. W. Norton, 2001.

Powell, Kathryn. "XML and Early English Manuscripts: Extensible Medieval Literature." *Literature Compass* 1, ME 061 (2004): 1–5.

Prescott, Andrew. "The Electronic Beowulf and Digital Restoration." *Literary and Linguistic Computing* 12.3 (1997): 185–95.

The Princeton Encyclopedia of Classical Sites. Edited by Richard Stillwell et al. Princeton, N.J.: Princeton University Press, 1976.

Provenzo, Eugene F., Jr. *Beyond the Gutenberg Galaxy: Microcomputers and the Emergence of Post-Typographic Culture.* New York: Teachers College Press, 1986.

Pulsiano, Phillip. "William L'Isle and the Editing of Old English." In Graham, *Recovery of Old English*, 173–206.

Pulsiano, Phillip, and Elaine Treharne, eds. *A Companion to Anglo-Saxon Literature.* Oxford: Blackwell, 2001.

Raitt, David. "Digital Library Initiatives Across Europe." *Computers in Libraries* 20.10: (2000), 26–35. <http://www.infotoday.com/cilmag/novoo/raitt.htm>.

Renear, Allen H., Elli Mylonas, and David G. Durand. "Refining Our Notion of What Text Really Is: The Problem of Overlapping Hierarchies." In *Research in Humanities Computing 4: Selected Papers from the ALLC/ACH Conference, Christ Church Oxford, April 1992*, edited by Susan Hockey and Nancy Ide, 263–80. Oxford: Clarendon, 1996.

Rider, Robin. "Shaping Information: Mathematics, Computing, and Typography." In

Inscribing Science: Scientific Texts and the Materiality of Communication, edited by Timothy Lenoir, 39–54. Stanford, Calif.: Stanford University Press, 1998.

Roberts, Jane, and Janet Nelson, eds. *Essays on Anglo-Saxon and Related Themes in Memory of Lynne Grundy*. London: King's College London, Centre for Late Antique and Medieval Studies, 2000.

Robertson, Douglas S. *The New Renaissance: Computers and the Next Level of Civilization*. Oxford: Oxford University Press, 1998.

Robinson, Benedict Scott. "'Dark Speech': Matthew Parker and the Reforming of History." *Sixteenth Century Journal* 29.4 (1998): 1061–83.

Robinson, Fred C. *The Editing of Old English*. Oxford: Blackwell, 1994.

Robinson, Peter. "Current Issues in Making Digital Editions of Medieval Texts—or, Do Electronic Scholarly Editions Have a Future?" *Digital Medievalist* 1.1 (2005). <www.digitalmedievalist.org/journal.cfm>.

———. "Is There a Text in These Variants?" In Finneran, *Literary Text in the Digital Age*, 99–115.

———. "Where We Are with Electronic Scholarly Editions, and Where We Want to Be." <computerphilologie.uni-muenchen.de/jg03/robinson.html>.

Roques, René. "Structure et caractères de la prière anselmienne." In *Sola Ratione: Anselm-Studien für Pater Dr. h.c. Franciscus Salesius Schmitt OSB*, edited by Helmut Kohlenberger, 119–88. Stuttgart: Friedrich Frommann, 1970.

Rothenberg, David. *Hand's End: Technology and the Limits of Nature*. Berkeley and Los Angeles: University of California Press, 1993.

Round, J. Horace. "The Bayeux Tapestry." *Monthly Review* 17.3 (1904): 109–26.

Roy, Gopa. "The Anglo-Saxons and the Shape of the World." In Roberts and Nelson, *Essays on Anglo-Saxon and Related Themes*, 455–81.

Rumble, Alexander. "Paleography and the Editing of Old English Texts." In Szarmach and Scragg, *Editing of Old English*, 39–43.

Ryan, Marie-Laure. *Narrative as Virtual Reality*. Baltimore: Johns Hopkins University Press, 2001.

Said, Edward. *The Question of Palestine*. New York: Times Books, 1979.

Salem, Hamed. "The Archaeology of the Text." In *Discourse and Palestine: Power, Text and Context*, edited by Annelies Moors et al., 27–40. Amsterdam: Het Spinhuis, 1995.

Sawyer, P. H. "Conquest and Colonization: Scandinavians in the Danelaw and in Normandy." In *Proceedings of the Eighth Viking Congress, Århus, 24–31 August 1977*, edited by Hans Bekker-Nielsen et al., 123–31. Odense: Odense University Press, 1981.

Scafi, Alessandro. "Mapping Eden: Cartographies of the Earthly Paradise." In *Mappings*, edited by Denis Cosgrove, 50–70. London: Reaktion, 1999.

Schillingsburg, Peter. "Principles for Electronic Archives, Scholarly Editions, and Tutorials." In Finneran, *Literary Text in the Digital Age*, 23–36.

Schufreider, Gregory. *Confessions of a Rational Mystic: Anselm's Early Writings*. West Lafayette, Ind.: Purdue University Press, 1994.

Scragg, D. G. "Postscript: Quo Vadis, Editio?" In Szarmach and Scragg, *Editing of Old English*, 299–309.

———, ed. *The Vercelli Homilies and Related Texts*. EETS, o.s., 300. Oxford: Oxford University Press, 1992.

Searle, Eleanor, ed. and trans. *The Chronicle of Battle Abbey*. Oxford: Clarendon, 1980.

Setton, Kenneth M. "900 Years Ago: The Norman Conquest." *National Geographic*, August 1966, 206–51.

Silberman, A., ed. and trans. *Pomponius Méla: Chorographie*. Paris: Belles Lettres, 1988.

Sklute, Larry. *Virtue of Necessity: Inconclusiveness and Narrative Form in Chaucer's Poetry*. Columbus: Ohio State University Press, 1984.

Slatin, John. "Reading Hypertext: Order and Coherence in a New Medium." In Delany and Landow, *Hypermedia and Literary Studies*, 153–69.

Smith, Barbara Herrnstein. *Poetic Closure: A Study of How Poems End*. Chicago: University of Chicago Press, 1968.

Smith, Catherine Delano. "Geography or Christianity? Maps of the Holy Land before AD 1000." *Journal of Theological Studies* 42 (1991): 143–52.

Smith, Mary Frances. "Archbishop Stigand and the Eye of the Needle." *Anglo-Norman Studies* 16 (1993): 199–219.

Smitten, Jeffrey. "Space and Spatial Form in Narrative: A Selected Bibliography of Modern Studies." In *Spatial Form in Narrative*, edited by Jeffrey R. Smitten and Ann Daghistany, 245–63. Ithaca, N.Y.: Cornell University Press, 1981.

Southern, R. W., ed. and trans. *The Life of St. Anselm, Archbishop of Canterbury*, by Eadmer. London: Thomas Nelson, 1962.

———. *The Making of the Middle Ages*. New Haven, Conn.: Yale University Press, 1953.

———. *Saint Anselm: A Portrait in a Landscape*. Cambridge: Cambridge University Press, 1990.

———. *Saint Anselm and His Biographer*. Cambridge: Cambridge University Press, 1963.

Sperberg-McQueen, C. M. "Text in the Electronic Age: Textual Study and Text Encoding, with Examples from Medieval Texts." *Literary and Linguistic Computing* 6.1 (1991): 34–46.

Spiller, Neil, ed. *Cyber Reader: Critical Writings for the Digital Era*. London: Phaidon, 2002.

Stahl, William Harris, ed. *Martianus Capella and the Seven Liberal Arts*. 2 vols. New York: Columbia University Press, 1971–77.

Stanley, E. G. "Some Observations on the A3 Lines in *Beowulf*." *Old English Studies in Honour of John C. Pope*, edited by Robert B. Burlin, Edward B. Irving Jr., and Marie Borroff, 139–64. Toronto: University of Toronto Press, 1974.

Stanzel, Franz K. "Consonant and Dissonant Closure in *Death in Venice* and 'The Dead.'" In *Neverending Stories: Toward a Critical Narratology*, edited by Ann Fehn,

Ingeborg Hoesterey, and Maria Tatar, 112–23. Princeton, N.J.: Princeton University Press, 1992.

Starrs, Paul F. "The Sacred, the Regional, and the Digital." *Geographical Review* 87.2 (1997): 193–218.

Steinberg, S. H. *Five Hundred Years of Printing*. Revised by John Trevitt. London: British Library, 1996.

Stenton, Frank, ed. *The Bayeux Tapestry: A Comprehensive Survey*. New York: Phaidon, 1957.

———. "The Historical Background." In Stenton, *The Bayeux Tapestry*, 9–24.

Stock, Brian. *The Implications of Literacy: Written Language and Models of Interpretation in the Eleventh and Twelfth Centuries*. Princeton, N.J.: Princeton University Press, 1983.

Stocker, David. "Monuments and Merchants: Irregularities in the Distribution of Stone Sculpture in Lincolnshire and Yorkshire in the Tenth Century." In *Cultures in Contact: Scandinavian Settlement in England in the Ninth and Tenth Centuries*, edited by Dawn M. Hadley and Julian D. Richards, 179–212. Turnhout: Brepols, 2000.

Stoppard, Tom. *Rosencrantz and Guildenstern Are Dead*. 1967. New York: Samuel French, 1995.

Stothard, Charles. "The Bayeux Tapestry." In *Vetusta Monumenta*, vol. 6, plates I–XVII. London: Society of Antiquaries, 1885.

———. "Some Observations on the Bayeux Tapestry." In Gameson, *Study*, 1-6.

Stothard, Mrs. Charles (later Anna Eliza Bray). *Letters Written during a Tour through Normandy, Britanny and Other Parts of France, in 1818*. London: Longman, Hurst, Rees, Orme, and Brown, 1820.

Strate, Lance. "Hypermedia, Space, and Dimensionality." In Gibson and Oviedo, *The Emerging Cyberculture*, 267–86.

Strickland, Stephanie. "Moving Through Me as I Move: A Paradigm for Interaction." In Wardrip-Fruin and Harrigan, *First Person*, 183–91.

Strohm, Paul. *Theory and the Premodern Text*. Minneapolis: University of Minnesota Press, 2000.

Sutherland, Kathryn. "Editing for a New Century: Elizabeth Elbstob's Anglo-Saxon Manifesto and Ælfric's St. Gregory Homily." In Szarmach and Scragg, *Editing of Old English*, 213–37.

———, ed. *Electronic Text: Investigations in Method and Theory*. Oxford: Clarendon, 1997.

Swan, Mary, and Elaine M. Treharne, eds. *Rewriting Old English in the Twelfth Century*. Cambridge, Cambridge University Press, 2000.

Swanton, Michael, ed. *The Anglo-Saxon Chronicle*. London: J. M. Dent, 1996.

———. "The Bayeux Tapestry: Epic Narrative, Not Stichic, but Stitched." In *The Formation of Culture in Medieval Britain: Celtic, Latin, and Norman Influences on English Music, Literature, History, and Art*, edited by Françoise H. M. Le Saux, 149–70. Lewiston, N.Y.: Edwin Mellen, 1995.

———, ed. *The Dream of the Rood*. Rev. ed. Exeter: University of Exeter Press, 1987.

Szarmach, Paul E., and D. G. Scragg, eds. *The Editing of Old English*. Cambridge: D. S. Brewer, 1994.

Taylor, Edgar, ed. *Master Wace, His Chronicle of the Norman Conquest from the "Roman de Rou."* London: Pickering, 1837.

Taylor, Jonathan. "The Emerging Geographies of Virtual Worlds." *Geographical Review* 87.2 (1997): 172–92.

Text Encoding Initiative. Home page: <www.tei-c.org>.

———. "Manuscript Description." <www.tei-c.org/release/doc/tei-p5-doc/html/MS.html>.

———. "TEI Special Interest Group on Manuscripts (TEI MS SIG)." <www.tei-c.org.uk/wiki/index.php/SIG:MSS>.

Thompson, Victoria. "Kingship-in-Death in the Bayeux Tapestry." *Reading Medieval Studies* 25 (1999): 107–21.

Thorpe, B. "Alfred's Anglo-Saxon Version of Orosius." In *The Life of Alfred the Great*. London: Henry G. Bohn, 1853.

Tokunaga, Satoko, and Tomohiro Kishida. Computer-Assisted Analysis of Caxton's Typography. Paper/demonstration given at De Montfort University, *New Technologies/Old Texts* Conference, July 2003.

Tomas, David. "Old Rituals for New Space: Rites de Passage and William Gibson's Cultural Model of Cyberspace." In Benedikt, *Cyberspace*, 31–48.

Tomasch, Sylvia. "Introduction: Medieval Geographical Desire." In Tomasch and Gilles, *Text and Territory*, 1–14.

Tomasch, Sylvia, and Sealy Gilles, eds. *Text and Territory: Geographical Imagination in the European Middle Ages*. Philadelphia: University of Pennsylvania Press, 1998.

Tooley, Marian J. "Bodin and the Medieval Theory of Climate." *Speculum* 28. (1953): 64–83.

Tufte, Edward R. *The Visual Display of Quantitative Information*. Cheshire, Conn.: Graphics, 1983.

Turner, Dawson. *Account of a Tour in Normandy*. 2 vols. London: John and Arthur Arch, 1820.

Ulmer, Gregory. *Applied Grammatology: Post(e)-Pedagogy from Jacques Derrida to Joseph Beuys*. Baltimore: Johns Hopkins University Press, 1985.

van Houts, Elisabeth M. C. "The Brevis Relatio de Guillelmo nobilissmo comite Normannorum, Written by a Monk of Battle Abbey." In *Chronology, Conquest and Conflict in Medieval England*, 1–48. Camden Miscellany 34. Cambridge: Cambridge University Press, 1997.

———, ed. and trans. *The "Gesta Normannorum Ducum" of William of Jumièges, Orderic Vitalis, and Robert of Torigni*. 2 vols. Oxford: Clarendon, 1992–95.

Verrier, Jean. *La broderie de Bayeux dite Tapisserie de la reine Mathilde/The Bayeux Embroidery Known as Queen Matilda's Tapestry*. English text translated by R. Schödelin. Paris: Éditions "Tel," 1946.

Voights, Linda Ehrsam. "Scientific and Medical Books." In Griffiths and Pearsall, *Book Production and Publishing*, 345–402.

Walker, Ian W. *Harold, the Last Anglo-Saxon King*. Stroud, U.K.: Sutton, 1997.

Walker, Jill. "How I Was Played by *Online Caroline*." In Wardrip-Fruin and Harrigan, *First Person*, 302–9.

Wallis, Faith, ed. *Bede: The Reckoning of Time*. Liverpool: Liverpool University Press, 1999.

Ward, Benedicta. "'Inward Feeling and Deep Thinking': The Prayers and Meditations of St. Anselm Revisited." *Anselm Studies* 1 (1983): 177–84.

———, trans. *The Prayers and Meditations of Saint Anselm*. Harmondsworth, U.K.: Penguin, 1973.

Wardrip-Fruin, Noah, and Pat Harrigan, eds. *First Person: New Media as Story, Performance, and Game*. Cambridge, Mass.: MIT Press, 2004.

Wardrip-Fruin, Noah, and Nick Montfort, eds. *The New Media Reader*. Cambridge, Mass.: MIT Press, 2003.

Weitzmann, Kurt. *Illustrations in Roll and Codex: A Study of the Origin and Method of Text Illustration*. 1947. Reprinted with addenda. Princeton, N.J.: Princeton University Press, 1970.

Werckmeister, O. K. "The Political Ideology of the Bayeux Tapestry." *Studi Medievali* 17.2 (1976): 535–95.

Wertheim, Margaret. *The Pearly Gates of Cyberspace: A History of Space from Dante to the Internet*. New York: W. W. Norton, 1999.

Westra, Maria Salvina, ed. *A Talkyng of þe loue of God*. The Hague: Nijhoff, 1950.

Westrem, Scott D. "Against Gog and Magog." In Tomasch and Gilles, *Text and Territory*, 54–78.

———. *The Hereford Map: A Transcription and Translation of the Legends with Commentary*. Turnhout: Brepols, 2001.

White, Hayden. *The Content of the Form: Narrative Discourse and Historical Representation*. Baltimore: Johns Hopkins University Press, 1987.

Whitelock, Dorothy, ed. *The Anglo-Saxon Chronicle: A Revised Translation*. With David C. Douglas and Susie I. Tucker. New Brunswick, N.J.: Rutgers University Press, 1962.

Williams, Ann. *The English and the Norman Conquest*. Woodbridge, U.K.: Boydell, 1995.

Williams, Burma P., and Richard S. Williams. "Finger Numbers in the Greco-Roman World and the Early Middle Ages." *Isis* 86.4 (1995): 587–608.

Wilmart, André. *Auteurs spirituels et textes dévots du moyen âge latin*. Paris: Bloud et Gay, 1932.

———. "Les prières envoyées par S. Anselme à la comtesse Mathilde en 1104." *Revue Bénédictine* 41 (1929): 368–415.

———. "Le recueil des prierés de S. Anselme." In *Méditations et priéres de Saint Anselme*, edited by D. A. Castel, xix–lxi. Paris: P. Lethielleux, 1923.

———. "La tradition des prières de Saint Anselme." *Revue Bénédictine* 36 (1924): 52–71.

Wilson, David M. *The Bayeux Tapestry*. New York: Knopf, 1985.

Wilson, David M., and Ole Klindt-Jensen. *Viking Art*. Ithaca, N.Y.: Cornell University Press, 1966.

Winterson, Jeanette. *Sexing the Cherry*. New York: Grove Press, Atlantic Monthly Press, 1989.

Wissolik, Richard David. "Code in the Bayeux Tapestry." *Annuale Medievale* 19 (1979): 69–97.

Withers, Benjamin C. "A Sense of Englishness: Claudius B.iv, Colonialism, and the History of Anglo-Saxon Art in the Mid-Twentieth Century." In *The Old English Hexateuch: Aspects and Approaches*, edited by Rebecca Barnhouse and Benjamin C. Withers, 317–50. Kalamazoo, Mich.: Medieval Institute Publications, 2000.

Wogan-Browne, Jocelyn, et al., eds. *The Idea of the Vernacular: An Anthology of Middle English Literary Theory, 1280–1520*. University Park: Pennsylvania State University Press, 1999.

Wood, Ian. "Ruthwell: Contextual Searches." In Karkov and Orton, *Theorizing Anglo-Saxon Stone Sculpture*, 104–30.

Woodward, David. "Medieval *Mappaemundi*." In Harley and Woodward, *History of Cartography*, 1:286–370.

Wormald, Francis. "Style and Design." In Stenton, *The Bayeux Tapestry*, 25–36.

Wormald, Patrick. *The Making of English Law: King Alfred to the Twelfth Century*. Vol. 1, *Legislation and Its Limits*. Oxford: Blackwell, 1999.

Worringer, Wilhelm. *Form in Gothic*. Translated by Herbert Read. London: Alec Tiranti, 1957.

Yankelovich, Nicole, Norman Meyerowitz, and Andries van Dam. "Reading and Writing the Electronic Book." In Delany and Landow, *Hypermedia and Literary Studies*, 53–79.

Zumthor, Paul. "The Impossible Closure of the Oral Text." *Yale French Studies* 67 (1984): 25–42.

Index

Martin Foys is an associate professor of English at Hood College in Frederick, Maryland. His *Bayeux Tapestry Digital Edition* (Boydell/SDE, 2003, on CD-ROM) was a 2004 *Choice* Outstanding Academic Title and won the 2005 International Society of Anglo-Saxonists (ISAS) Publication Prize for Best Edition. He is currently at work on Anglo-Saxon maps of the world, including a digital edition of the Anglo-Saxon Cotton Map for the British Library, and on developing a networked architecture for the digital study of early medieval maps and their sources and analogues.